WHAT THE GOOD BOOK DIDN'T SAY

Other books by J. Stephen Lang

The Complete Book of Bible Trivia

Secrets from The Book

The Ultimate Book of Bible Trivia

The Complete Book of Bible Promises

The Bible: What's in It for Me?

Biblical Quotations for All Occasions

1,001 Things You Always Wanted to Know About the Bible

1,001 Things You Always Wanted to Know About Angels, Demons, and the Afterlife

1,001 More Things You Always Wanted to Know About the Bible

The 100 Most Important Events in Christian History

The Big Book of American Trivia

The Complete Book of Confederate Trivia

Drawn to the Civil War

The Complete Book of Presidential Trivia

The Complete Idiot's Guide to the Confederacy

WHAT THE GOOD BOOK DIDN'T SAY

Popular Myths and Misconceptions About the Bible

J. STEPHEN LANG

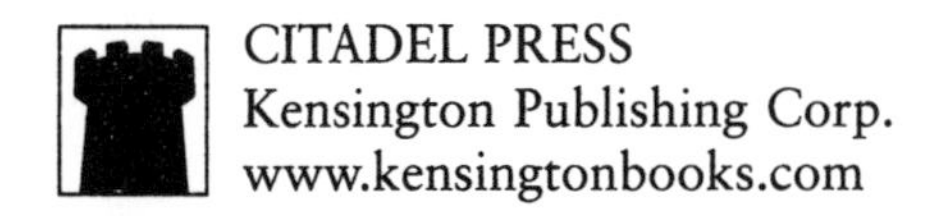
CITADEL PRESS
Kensington Publishing Corp.
www.kensingtonbooks.com

CITADEL PRESS BOOKS are published by

Kensington Publishing Corp.
850 Third Avenue
New York, NY 10022

Illustrations by Gustav Doré, reprinted from *The Doré Bible Illustrations* (1974, Dover Publications Inc.) and *Doré's Illustrations from "Paradise Lost"* (1993, Dover Publications Inc.)

First printing: April 2003

10 9 8 7 6 5 4 3 2 1

Printed in the United States of America

Library of Congress Control Number: 2002113466

ISBN 0-8065-2460-X

CONTENTS

INTRODUCTION

The Word—Misread, Twisted, and Lied About

Is the Bible the most read book in the world? Probably. Is it the most misunderstood, misconstrued, and misused book in the world? Definitely.

How it could it be otherwise? It has been around for centuries (well, *millennia,* actually) and was written in ancient languages. Words change, meanings change, cultures change. The wonder is not that people misconstrue the Bible, but that so much of it is actually very understandable. Maybe that is because human nature does not change. We may be "modern" or "contemporary," but there is something in us that still connects to Adam and Eve, Noah, Moses, Samson, David, Peter—long-dead people whose names still bring a flicker of recognition when they are mentioned.

But if people recognize the names, the details are vague—or just plain wrong. Everyone *knows* Adam and Eve ate an apple—though the Bible doesn't say so. Everyone *knows* there were three wise men who visited the baby Jesus—even though the Bible doesn't say how many wise men there were. Everyone *knows* Delilah gave Samson a haircut—but she didn't. These are "little white lies" about the Bible, not terribly important, but things this book was designed to correct. (If people bothered to read the Bible itself, these little white lies wouldn't be repeated so often.)

Some other "little white lies" are what I call the "King James difficulties." As beautiful a translation as the King James Version was, its language is dated and sometimes misleading to people today.

Also, its translators were sometimes just plain wrong—as when they included such nonexistent creatures as unicorms and satyrs in the Old Testament. Another example: the King James Version said that God parted the Red Sea. He didn't, as you will read on page 15. (A preview: God parted a large body of water, but not the Red Sea.) Most of these "King James difficulties" are rather amusing, as you will see.

There are also some "big dark lies" about the Bible. It has been accused, especially in the last few years, of being anti-woman, anti-sex, anti-environment, anti-you-name-it. Find an anti-, and someone has applied it to the Bible. Some brilliant books have been written to respond to such accusations, but they are not always easy reading. I've attempted to do here what the brilliant scholars do, but more pleasantly. (As with the "little lies," these big lies wouldn't get repeated if the critics actually bothered to read the Bible itself.)

Skeptics have been spouting off untruths and half-truths about the Bible for centuries. Until the late 1800s, for example, no one ever found evidence that the Hittite people of the Bible ever existed. So the skeptics assumed the Hittites were fictional—meaning the whole Bible was probably full of lies. But then archaeologists started digging up lots and lots of Hittites. In that same skeptical century, intellectuals claimed the Gospels were written centuries after Jesus lived, so they weren't reliable. Now the pendulum has swung the other way and we feel pretty certain the Gospels were written down very early. Then there is that tired old science-versus-the-Bible debate, as seen in the famous case of Galileo. Skeptics think this was a simple case of scientific truth bumping up against the outmoded Bible. The case was nothing of the kind, as you will see on page 91. As one of the Bible's defenders said five centuries ago, it is "an anvil that has worn out many hammers."

But the skeptics aren't the only ones who misconstrue the Bible. True people of faith do, too. Sometimes they find in the Bible commands that aren't there—for instance, commands against capital punishment, drinking, gambling, or eating meat. And there are some beliefs that have divided believers for centuries—such as the belief that Peter was the first pope, that Christians should (or definitely should not) speak in tongues, that worship should be on Saturday instead of Sunday. I took on these topics knowing I was walking on eggs. The goal here is not to set one group of believers against another but to clarify what the Bible does—and does not—say about certain issues. I am not anti-anyone, just pro-truth.

The book you are reading was written for people who do not believe the Bible is the inspired word of God—*and* for those who do. I make no attempt here to convince anyone that miracles are real, or that the Bible is a gift from God. The only goal is to correct various lies and misconceptions about the Bible—lies and misconceptions that have been repeated by both believers and skeptics. I hope that you all, like me, find some pleasure in the truth.

PART I

THE TOP TEN LIES AND MISCONCEPTIONS

THE REPENTANT MARY MAGDALENE
Mary Magdalene, Jesus' devoted follower, was a former prostitute . . . or was she?

1

Adam, Eve, and the Snake—But Not the Apple

"The forbidden fruit in the garden of Eden was an apple."

The expression *Adam's apple* has been used at least since the 1700s to refer to the "lump in the throat." Legend has it that when Adam disobeyed God and ate the forbidden fruit, a piece of it lodged in his throat, an eternal reminder that had man sinned against and disobeyed God.

To this day, the popular imagination associates Adam and Eve and their disobedience with apples. And why not? Apples are a sort of "generic fruit," known and loved in many parts of the world, making their way into an all-American pie, grown in literally hundreds of colors, shapes, textures, and flavors—all of them appealing, because most people familiar with apples like them and think of them as tasty and nutritious. What the scientists call *Malus pumila* was eaten as far back as the Roman Empire, and probably much earlier. The Pilgrims who settled Massachusetts planted extensive orchards, and traders among the Indians helped spread apples (and, more importantly, apple seeds) across the continent.

But were there apples in Eden? In the first place, the Book of Genesis says nothing whatever about the species that was "the tree of the knowledge of good and evil" (Genesis 2:6). We are told that

God had planted in Eden all kinds of trees, "trees that were pleasing to the eye and good for food." That suggests a variety of fruits (perhaps nuts as well), but whether the "tree of knowledge of good and evil" looked any different from the other trees is not related. It was in "the middle of the garden," so it might have been its location, not its particular fruit, that made it easier for Adam and Eve to remember that this one tree, and its fruit, was off-limits.

A botanically minded person would ask an obvious question: Where was the garden of Eden? If we knew where it was, that would tell us whether apples might have grown there, because apples won't thrive just anywhere. Apples are deciduous trees, shedding their leaves in autumn and requiring several months of dormancy (translation: cold weather, but not arctically cold). They are neither tropical nor subtropical, and they won't bear fruit in extremely hot and/or dry regions. That rules out Israel, which today produces 90 percent of the citrus fruit eaten in Europe, but does not grow apples. It also rules out the region we call Mesopotamia—today, roughly, the nation of Iraq. Genesis 2:14 refers to the garden being near the Tigris and Euphrates Rivers—that is, Mesopotamia, a region that will not produce apples.

Of course, for a sizable group of Bible readers, the question "Where was Eden?" is answered with "In the mind of the storyteller." Many people, including many Christians, take the story of Adam and Eve and their disobedience to be symbolic, a myth to explain how sin entered the world. We are all, according to this view of the story, Adam and Eve, choosing to disobey God and suffering the consequences. In this view, Eden existed in the mind, the imagination, the incredibly vast and awesome World of Myth and Legend.

Whether Eden really existed can't be settled here. As already mentioned, if it was a real place near the Tigris and Euphrates Rivers, it almost certainly wouldn't have been home to apple trees. Any region that was favorable to walking around naked all year would not have been a region suited for apple growing. On the other hand, if Eden existed only in the realm of story, then of course Eden could have been home to any kind of fruit—and maybe even some imaginary ones that never existed.

So what fruit might the First Parents have eaten? Artists through the centuries have had fun with this. Since most artists in Europe and America lived in apple-growing regions, they have often depicted Adam and Eve with a fruit that is, or at least resembles, the apple (although apples vary a lot on the outside—their color and shape—they are all fairly similar inside, being pretty uniformly white and smooth, with dark seeds in the core). Some artists have let their imaginations run wild, assuming that since there was only one "tree of the knowledge of good and evil," which no one has ever seen, they could paint whatever sort of fruit their clever minds could conceive. Thus the world's art museums have paintings in which the forbidden fruit appears to be enormous and purple, or star-shaped, or some other unworldly shape and size. Some artists, more aware of what sort of fruits actually grow in the Mesopotamian region, have shown the forbidden fruit as a pomegranate—a fruit widely grown in that region, pretty on the outside and even more so on the inside, with its bright red juicy seeds. (It's common in paintings of the garden of Eden to show the fruit with a bite taken out of it, giving the artist a chance to show the inside as well as the outside.)

It's worth mentioning here that while Genesis does *not* mention apples, other parts of the Bible do. So were the translators wrong? In all likelihood, yes. Bible scholars are painfully aware that some of the most difficult Bible passages to translate are those that refer to plants and animals. They simply are not always sure just what is being referred to, with the result that in the old and much-loved King James Version of 1611, we see references to "unicorns," which modern translators have more correctly identified as "rhinoceroses" or "wild oxen." (See page 101.) Likewise, the King James Version refers in several places to "apples," even though modern translators know that the Hebrew words are definitely not referring to apples. In fact, the Hebrew word translated as "apples" most likely refers to "apricots," which grow well in that region and were known and valued in biblical times. But here is an example of Bible translators bowing to tradition: almost all Bible translations continue to use *apple* in the places where the fruit is mentioned—mostly in the Song of Solomon (see 2:3, 2:5, 7:8, 8:5, and also Joel 1:12). The Hebrew authors may have had apricots in mind, but the translators are aware that "comfort me with apricots" just doesn't have the appeal of "comfort me with apples." (And imagine the line in the Bruce Springsteen song "Pink Cadillac": "Eve tempted Adam with an apple." Somehow "Eve tempted Adam with an apricot" doesn't trip off the tongue.)

One other interesting, and appealing, possibility: it may be that the fruit mentioned several times in the Song of Solomon was the orange.

2

Just How Many Evils Are Rooted in Money?

"Money is the root of all evil."

Money is the root of all evil rolls off the tongue easily, and the phrase has made its way into our language. In times past, when wise sayings from the Bible were often hung (in the form of crewel or needlepoint) on the walls of homes, this one was a favorite. (We can assume it was not often displayed in the homes of the wealthy.)

In fact, the Bible never says that "money is the root of all evil"—though it *almost* does. The Bible has a lot to say about money—and, more importantly, quite a lot about how human beings feel about it.

In John Milton's famous poem *Paradise Lost,* he depicts many angels and demons mentioned in the Bible. Among the demons is one named Mammon, who symbolizes the lust for money. Mammon, like the other demons, is actually a fallen angel, an angel who rebelled against God and was cast out of heaven. Milton mentions that even in his days as an angel, Mammon was fascinated by the golden streets of heaven.

Milton got the name (and concept) of Mammon from the Bible. Jesus, who had a lot to say about money, told his listeners that they could not serve two masters, that they could not "serve God and Mammon." Some readers have assumed Mammon was a god—a sort of a god of money. What Jesus actually meant by Mammon was money itself—or, more particularly, the love of it. In other words, Mammon is the idol that we make of money and the things it will buy. According to Jesus, no one can worship the true God and also worship money.

Meaning what? That true believers can't use money, that they must become so extremely spiritual that they totally withdraw from a society that operates on the basis of money? In the past, some Christians have tried to do just that, leaving society behind and seeking out desert places in order to get away from the corrupting influences of materialism. The many communities of monks and nuns that have existed for centuries tried to avoid—so far as possible—the taint of material goods, which explains why monks and nuns have taken vows of poverty. Even today, people living in these communities are discouraged from any individual ownership of goods or money.

Despite Jesus' warning about Mammon, is the Bible really anti-money? Not quite. Certainly the Old Testament isn't. The Book of Job presents us with an admirable character who is both wealthy *and* saintly—one who continues to praise God even when his wealth and health are gone. In the end, Job has all his wealth restored by God, which assures us that God is not completely anti-wealth. Likewise, the Old Testament speaks approvingly of King Solomon's wisdom and wealth, and the Book of Proverbs is pretty blunt in linking the two. Abraham, the righteous ancestor of all the Hebrews, is described as a wealthy man. In the New Testament, we meet with righteous, and wealthy, characters like Joseph of Arimathea.

Still, the Bible is, all in all, negative toward money—or, more correctly, is realistic about how it affects people. The Hebrew prophets condemned the rich people who reclined on their ivory couches while they exploited the poor. While it was possible to be both godly and rich, it was also rare. Jesus claimed it was easier for a camel to go through the eye of a needle than for a rich person to enter the kingdom of God. The nameless man known as the "rich young ruler" claimed he wanted to be righteous, but he would not accept Jesus' command to give all he had to the poor. His reaction was typical: most people value their money, and what it buys, more than they value a life of faith.

But is money itself corrupt? Of course not. Money can do a great deal of good, as we see in any disaster, when people donate money to help those in dire straits. Money, as John Wesley observed more than two centuries ago, is like manure—"useless if not spread around." But of course, human nature ensures that it doesn't get spread adequately. We want to hoard it, keep it to ourselves, because we *love* it. This isn't true of only the rich: we can be middle class or even lower class and still be obsessed with money.

And that obsession is precisely what the Bible addresses. It does not say, "Money is the root of all evil" but rather, "The love of money is the root of all evil" (1 Timothy 6:10). The apostle Paul, writing to his protégé Timothy, was voicing the same idea Jesus did: we should not love, or worship, money.

This verse gets misconstrued in another way: according to the King James Version, "The love of money is the root of all evil." Anyone who paused for a moment to think this through would have to ask, "You mean *all* evil? Really?" And the obvious answer is, no, for there is plenty of evil in the world that has no material or economic cause. Does love of money cause a man to cheat on his wife, or a rebellious teen to mouth off to a parent, or vandals to deface a building? No. And while we could come up with a huge list of evils that are rooted in the love of money, there is another huge list of sins that have no connection with money at all.

Consider a more recent, and more accurate, version of this Bible passage: "The love of money is a root of all kinds of evil." Not *the* root, but *a* root (which it definitely is), and not "all evil" but "all kinds of evil" (and who would disagree with that?). Paul continued by saying that "Some people, eager for money, have wandered away from the faith and pierced themselves with many griefs."

So for the record: money is *not* the root of all evil. But love of it does lead to all kinds of evil.

3

Charlton Heston, Yes—But Where?

"Moses led the people of Israel across the Red Sea."

Sometimes pop culture, particularly movies, can be a powerful force. Take the story of Moses and the exodus from Egypt. While many, many people have read the story in the Bible's Book of Exodus, a lot of people have also seen the Hollywood extravaganza *The Ten Commandments*. For quite a few people in the world, Charlton Heston *is* Moses, and the famous parting of the Red Sea, one of the highlights of the movie, is the way it actually happened.

Let's get one piece of business out of the way: we are not here to decide whether miracles are possible. If you believe that a personal God does intervene in awesome ways at times, then you will have no trouble believing God could have parted the Red Sea so the Israelites could pass through. You would likewise have no trouble believing that the same God could then release those waters to drown the Egyptian troops who were set on killing the Israelites. (God could, in theory, part the Pacific Ocean if he chose to.) On the other hand, if you do not believe such a God exists, or don't believe he could act in such a way, the whole matter of the Red Sea is pretty pointless.

But the point of this chapter is simply this: the Book of Exodus in the Old Testament *does not* say that God parted the Red Sea. To be more specific, the original Hebrew form of Exodus does not say so. What has influenced generations of Bible readers is that English versions of Exodus *do* refer to the Red Sea.

Where exactly is the Red Sea, anyway? Basically it's a skinny arm of the Indian Ocean, with Arabia on its east side and the continent of Africa on its west side. Its north end is the Sinai Peninsula, where the nations of Egypt and Jordan meet today. While is isn't one of the world's hugest seas, it is in fact about twelve hundred miles long. Its width varies from about 250 to 150 miles—not exactly tiny. At its north end, the Sinai Peninsula does split the Red Sea into two skinnier bodies, the Gulf of Suez on the Egyptian side, the Gulf of Aqaba on the Arabian side.

A little scientific tidbit: The Red Sea gets its name from a type of algae that at certain times makes the waters appear reddish.

Looking at Exodus 13, we learn that "God led the people around by the way of the wilderness toward the Red Sea." Looking at any atlas, we see that the Israelite slaves leaving Egypt would undoubtedly have crossed the Red Sea at the northern end, perhaps the skinny Gulf of Suez.

Exodus 14 presents us with one of the world's most dramatic stories, one that director Cecil B. DeMille tried to do justice to in *The Ten Commandments*. Moses, the son of Hebrew slaves in Egypt, was adopted by the Egyptian pharaoh's daughter and brought up in the royal court. But later, he learned of his Hebrew origins, fled Egypt, and had his life-changing confrontation in the wilderness, where God spoke to him from a burning bush. He returned to the pharaoh's court not as a royal brother but as God's prophet, informing the pharaoh that God wanted the Hebrews set free. The pharaoh wasn't about to be bullied by a spokesman for slaves, so God turned his power loose on the Egyptians, turning the sacred River Nile blood-red and plaguing the Egyptians with flies, frogs, hail, and the other pestilences described in Exodus. The pharaoh, who is often referred to as "hardhearted," finally agrees to let the Hebrews leave after the most horrible plague of all, the death of all the Egyptians' firstborn children. So the Hebrew horde left Egypt for their ancestral homeland, the land of Canaan.

But according to Exodus 14:5, "The mind of Pharaoh and his servants was changed toward the people, and they said, 'What is this we have done, that we have let Israel go from serving us?' " So the pharaoh and an army of charioteers headed off to reclaim—or kill—their former slaves.

As the movie shows, the Israelites were in a tight spot, with the water on one side trapping them when the Egyptians arrived in force. Moses comforted the terrified people: "Fear not, stand firm, and see the salvation of the LORD, which he will work for you today. For the Egyptians whom you see today you shall never see again" (Exodus 14:13).

Where did this take place? Definitely *not* the Red Sea. Exodus 13 and 14 use the Hebrew words *yam suph*—meaning, probably, "Reed Sea" or "Marshy Sea." There are no reeds in the Red Sea. Not far from Goshen, the section of Egypt where the Israelite slaves had lived, was a body of water that the Egyptians themselves referred to as Suph, the "papyrus marsh." Today it is referred to as Lake Timsah. It is certainly not a sea in the usual sense—that is, it's fresh water, not salt water, and it isn't an arm of any ocean. While it is large, it's nowhere near the size of the Red Sea. Though scholars aren't 100 percent certain that Lake Timsah, the "Reed Sea," is the body that God parted in Exodus, we are pretty certain. It's much more likely that the Israelites crossed Lake Timsah than the actual Red Sea.

Was it any less of a miracle? No. In all likelihood it was less dramatic—less "Hollywood"—than the scene in the movie. The Reed Sea was certainly not as deep or as wide as the sea parted so awesomely in the film. Exodus 14:21 tells us that "the LORD drove the sea back by a strong east wind all night and made the sea dry land, and the waters were divided. And the people of Israel went into the midst of the sea on dry ground." The Israelites crossed, and when the Egyptians tried to the same, "the waters returned and covered the chariots and the horsemen . . . not one of them remained."

Anyone who has ever seen a river or even a large stream flooded knows the power of a "wall of water." While Lake Timsah, the "Reed Sea," is nowhere as huge as the Red Sea, it is certainly large enough to drown in if the waters were stirred up enough.

It does sound pretty darn dramatic, and perhaps we can forgive Hollywood for overdoing it a little.

4

The Men Legends Are Made Of

"Three wise men, who were kings, brought gifts to the baby Jesus."

Despite the annual legal battles over Nativity scenes in public spaces, individuals still enjoy placing them in their homes. Inevitably, part of the familiar scene are the three wise men, usually in splendid robes, in striking contrast to the stable and to the plainly dressed Joseph and Mary.

Where would Christmas be without the three wise men? We would have to give up beloved songs like "We Three Kings of Orient Are." We would have to give up centuries of beautiful Christmas images, even the camels in live Nativity scenes, since camels are part of the wise men's caravan.

Well, in fact, we do not have to give up any of those things. It is possible that there were three wise men. But the purpose of this book is to set the record straight about the Bible. And the simple truth is, the Bible does *not* say that three wise men—much less three *kings*—came to visit the newborn Jesus.

Let's go right to the one source, the Gospel of Matthew. "Now after Jesus was born in Bethlehem of Judea in the days of Herod the king, behold, wise men from the east came. . . ." When they did find the baby they were seeking, "they offered him gifts, gold and frankincense and myrrh." Here is the one connection the Bible makes between the wise men and the number three. They brought three gifts, and somehow, in people's imaginations, it seemed logical that there were three wise men, one wise man per gift.

Most English Bibles refer to them as "wise men." The actual Greek word in Matthew's Gospel is *magoi,* plural of *magos.* Frankly, "wise man" does not really communicate just what a *magos* was. (The New English Bible used *astrologers,* which is more correct.) In the regions of Persia (today Iran) and Arabia, these men were a sort of combination of astrologers and sorcerers. They dabbled in dream interpretation, reading the stars, and other forms of divination. They were "wise" only in the sense that they could (supposedly) foretell the future. Some of them found their way into royal courts, where by luck or cleverness they convinced rulers that their services were badly needed in governing. (This isn't true only of ancient times. European courts had astrologers until fairly recently, and it is worth recalling that Nancy Reagan had an astrologer on call.) Some of them were just plain fakes, but there were probably many who were convinced that their magic arts were real.

What about the ones in Matthew's Gospel? We are only told that they were *magoi* "from the east." Matthew may not have known exactly where they came from (and it didn't matter) but simply assumed that, like all such people, they came from the eastern lands of Arabia and Persia. As early as the second century, Christian art depicted the wise men in Persian dress.

Why were they there in Bethlehem? Some Bible critics believe Matthew invented the story as a way of proving that Jesus was significant even as a baby. (No other part of the New Testament mentions the wise men, though that by itself doesn't prove the story isn't true.) It is likely that *magoi* in some places knew of the Jews' expectation of a Messiah, and the ones in the Gospel somehow connected this with the mysterious star of Bethlehem. In fact, Matthew's Gospel tells us that the wise men upset the Jewish king Herod greatly by telling him they were seeking the newborn "king of the Jews." The Gospel notes that this led the paranoid Herod to massacre all the male children in Bethlehem, an act commemorated in Christian tradition as the Slaughter of the Holy Innocents.

Back to Christmas: it is likely that, if the wise men journeyed from far in the east bearing expensive gifts, they were not poor folk. They may well have been, as in Nativity scenes, splendidly dressed, particularly if they were attached to some royal court. But were they *kings?*

Almost certainly not. While some eastern kings did dabble in magic and fortune-telling, most rulers would have considered this to be beneath them. Still, very early in Christian history, the Christian imagination went to work on the wise men. As early as the sixth century, stories gave them names: Gaspar, Melchior, and Balthasar. These are definitely not Jewish names, but names of eastern origin. Obviously by this time many people had decided that there were *three* wise men, although some stories claimed there were twelve.

But what about being kings? One idea prominent in the New Testament is that Jesus, when he returns to earth again, will be "King of Kings, and Lord of Lords." Unlike earthly kings, he is pure, just, and righteous. The Book of Revelation and other parts of the New Testament speak of everyone bowing to him. Since the Gospel of Matthew spoke of the wise men as seeking out Jesus to "worship" him, early Christians took a leap of the imagination and assumed that these eastern men with their expensive gifts were kings—the first earthly kings to pay their respects to the King of Kings. There was also a wonderful prophecy in the Old Testament: "And nations shall come to your light, and kings to the brightness of your rising" (Isaiah 60:3). Some Christians took this to be a prophecy that was fulfilled when the wise men—kings—visited baby Jesus.

The relics (bodily remains) of the "three kings" are supposedly housed at the cathedral of Cologne in Germany.

All of this is harmless stuff. Whether the wise men were kings or not is not particularly important to Christianity. Certainly it adds a pleasant dash of color to Christmas.

5

The Infamous Tale o' de Whale

"The Bible says Jonah was swallowed by a whale, which is impossible."

For such a brief book, Jonah has generated a lot of controversy. You will find it in the Bible near the end of the Old Testament, grouped with the other books known as the Prophets. It's pretty obvious that this book and those of the other prophets are radically different. The Book of Jonah is a *story,* while the rest of the Prophets is more like a collection of *sermons,* in which the prophets urge the wayward people to repent for their sins before something dreadful happens. In the Book of Jonah, the reluctant prophet attempts to run away from his task, because he does not want the sinful people of Nineveh to repent. And when they do repent, instead of being glad, he pouts. This is, to put it mildly, one of the odder books of the Bible.

Of course, the main point of the book is a valid one: God loves everybody, not just the people of Israel. He wants everyone, even the heathen inhabitants of Nineveh, to repent and to live a moral life. The Book of Jonah is a pleasant reminder that the people of Israel had learned that God wasn't just their own tribal God. He was the God of the whole earth, and he wanted to save people everywhere.

But this wonderful message is usually forgotten. People get caught up in the details of the story. And the most famous detail in the story is that Jonah, thrown overboard from a ship, was swallowed by a whale. "And the LORD appointed a great fish to swallow up Jonah. And Jonah was in the belly of the fish three days and three nights" (1:17). Jonah was, clearly, in a position where he felt he had to pray. "And the LORD spoke to the fish, and it vomited Jonah out upon the dry land" (2:10).

Now, let's admit that there are lots of people—including lots of Christians—who simply cannot swallow this story. A man inside a whale? And he survives it after three days? We think it's cute in Walt Disney's *Pinocchio* when the title character rescues his papa Gepetto from the innards of the whale Monstro. Cute, yes, and exciting—but not real.

And frankly, there are other touches in Jonah's story that seem more fictional than historical. For example, Chapter 3 tells us that after Jonah threatened Nineveh with divine punishment, everyone there repented, including the king—who is not named. If you read the books of 1 and 2 Kings in the Bible, you will notice that the authors were careful to name foreign rulers, and these were always historical characters. But in the Book of Jonah, we aren't told the king of Nineveh's name, which is unusual. Even more odd, the story tells us that this capital of a pagan empire repented just because of the preaching of one Hebrew prophet. The book gives many people the impression that it did not take place in history but in the land of "Once upon a time . . ."

> The world's most famous book about whales, *Moby-Dick,* includes a chapter titled "Jonah Historically Regarded."

Defenders of the book (those who believe it actually happened) like to point out that Jesus himself referred to Jonah's story, saying that just as Jonah was three days in the belly of the fish, so Jesus himself would be three days in the earth, then resurrected (Matthew 12:38–41). Of course, the fact that Jesus referred to the story does not prove it literally happened. In fact, it doesn't even prove that

Jesus himself believed it literally happened. He may have just used the story as an illustration of the point he was trying to make about his own death and resurrection.

And while we are on the subject of resurrection, let's deal with the whole matter of miracle. Normally, a man does not survive being swallowed by a whale (or a "great fish"). But miracles are, by definition, *extraordinary* occurrences, something outside the norm. It does stretch the imagination to believe that this truly happened to Jonah. But it also stretches the imagination to believe Jesus was raised from the dead, that Elijah was carried into heaven, that God destroyed Sodom and Gomorrah with fire from heaven, and so on.

Let's get back to science, though. For Jonah to have actually endured this ordeal, four things would be required: (1) a creature large enough to swallow him, (2) the person passing safely over the creature's teeth, (3) the person surviving its digestive juices, and (4) enough oxygen for three days. We know that a large sperm whale can swallow something as big as eight feet in diameter. It could, in theory, swallow a man in one gush of water without biting him. If the whale was sick or had died, the person could be (as the Bible says) vomited out.

One well-known case involves James Bartley, who was on the whaling ship *Star of the East.* In February 1891, men from the ship's longboats pursued a sperm whale near the Falkland Islands off South America. One of the men harpooned the whale, which submerged, then resurfaced suddenly, under one of the boats, scattering the men into the air. As it happened, the harpoon did its work and the whale died, surfacing near the ship. It was hoisted alongside the ship and cut up into smaller pieces. When the whale's stomach was laid on the deck, it was moving slightly. The ship's doctor cut the stomach open—and inside it was James Bartley. He was curled up and unconscious, but alive. He had been inside the whale for a total of fifteen hours. In that span of time, the whale's digestive juices had removed all the hair from his body and bleached his skin white. He was also nearly blind. It was a month before he came to his senses enough to relate what had happened. He recalled being flung in the air when the whale surfaced, seeing the whale's mouth come toward him, and being dragged across the whale's teeth. Then he slid down the animal's slimy esophagus and slipped into unconsciousness because of insufficient air.

Oddly enough, this happened on Bartley's first day as a sailor. Understandably, it was also his last. He lived out his life as a cobbler in Gloucester, England, where he is buried. His tombstone bears the words A MODERN JONAH.

Well, obviously a man can be swallowed by a whale and survive. But after three days and nights? There is no record of anyone surviving that long . . . unless Jonah did, that is. Probable? No. Possible? Yes—particularly if you admit that miracles are possible.

6

Falling for Each Other After Dinner

"Adam and Eve's 'original sin' was sex."

It used to be common knowledge what "original sin" was. But we live in an age of biblical illiteracy, so a little explanation is in order. The word *original* meant, originally, "first" or "root" or "at the origin." So *original sin* meant "first sin" and "root sin."

What was it? In one sense, it was disobedience. Adam and Eve existed in this beautiful garden, Eden. God told Adam, "You may surely eat of every tree of the garden, but of the tree of the knowledge of good and evil you shall not eat, for on the day that you eat of it, you shall surely die" (Genesis 2:16–17). This sounds like a very minor restriction.

However, there was that snake in the garden. (He is described as "crafty" in most modern versions of the Bible, though the word *subtil* in the King James Version has a nice ring to it.) The serpent teased Eve with a question: "Did God actually say, 'You shall not eat of any tree of the garden?' " The serpent was planting a disturbing notion in Eve's mind: God likes to withhold good things. Eve, however, gave the serpent the correct answer: No, only one tree was off-limits to her and Adam. If they ate its fruit, they would die. The serpent told her, "You will not surely die. For God knows that when you eat of it your eyes will be opened, and you will be like God, knowing good and evil" (3:5).

In one old version of the Bible, the serpent says, "Tush, ye shall not die."

We all know what that led to. Eve "saw that the tree was good for food, and that it was a delight to the eyes, and that the tree was to be desired to make one wise." So she ate some of the fruit and gave some to Adam.

Suddenly their whole world changed. Before, they were "both naked and were not ashamed." But now, "the eyes of both were opened, and they knew that they were naked." So they created the first human wardrobe (made of all-natural fibers, since nothing else was available), the infamous fig-leaf coverings.

Not only were they now looking at each other in a different way, but things had changed in regard to God, too. God was "walking in the garden in the cool of the day," and Adam and Eve hid among the trees. When God asked, "Where are you?" Adam answered that he hid because "I was afraid because I was naked." Clearly this was not the only reason Adam was afraid. He knew he had disobeyed God, and he feared what would follow. When God asked him directly if he had eaten the forbidden fruit, Adam shifted the blame to Eve: "The woman whom you gave to be with me, she gave me the fruit of the tree, and I ate." Eve, too, passed the buck: "The serpent deceived me, and I ate."

The threatened punishment for eating the fruit was death. God withheld this, for the time being, anyway. But he did punish Adam, Eve, and the serpent as well. The serpent was cursed to crawl about on its belly and "eat dust." We have to assume that, prior to this, the serpent was a more elevated animal. Eve was cursed in two ways: she would have to endure great pain in bearing children, and she would be under the rule of her husband. Adam was cursed with hard work: the ground would bring forth thorns and thistles, and man would labor hard to bring forth his food. Then, a general curse on all mankind: "You are dust, and to dust you shall return." They did not get what the serpent promised. Instead, they got pain, toil, and, eventually, death. God then clothed the couple with animal skins and expelled them from the garden of Eden.

Back to the original sin: obviously the couple had disobeyed God. They had but one rule to follow, and they broke it. But Jews and Christians had added another interpretation: they disobeyed out of *pride.* They believed the serpent when he said, "You will be like God." They had been put in this blissfully happy place but wanted more. They wanted to be independent from God.

This is called, in theology, the Fall or the Fall of Man. The sin wasn't in the fruit itself. (See pages 7–10 for more about that "apple.") The sin was in disobeying God's command, and in wanting to be gods themselves.

In Christian tradition, every human being "inherits" Adam's original sin. It isn't "genetic" or in any way biological. It is inherited, you might say, spiritually. Everyone born into the world finds themselves guilty of disobedience and pride. The apostle Paul expressed this in Romans 5:12: "Sin came into the world through one man, and death through sin, and so death spread to all men because all sinned."

You might say that Adam, the first man, is also the Bible's first villain (unless you count the snake). The assumption in Genesis is that everything would have gone on just fine, if only earth's original couple had not loused everything up.

So where does sex fit into this? It doesn't. The Bible is pretty clear that the Big Sin that caused all the trouble was the combination of disobedience and pride.

But interestingly enough, it happens that right after Adam and Eve are expelled from Eden, the Bible has these words: "Now Adam knew Eve his wife, and she conceived and bore Cain" (Genesis 4:1). You are probably aware that *knew* in this context means "had sex with." There is no mention of sex while Adam and Eve were still in Eden. The first mention of childbearing is when God curses Eve with the pains of birth.

A lot of question marks are floating around. Was there sex before the Fall? Would Adam and Eve have lived forever if they had not sinned? (If so, then there would have been no need to reproduce, right?) If there was sex before the Fall, did it, for some reason, not result in conception? Since sex is only mentioned after the Fall, is sex basically a kind of "fallen" activity?

We don't know. No one knows for sure—not that this has kept people from some wild speculations. Nevertheless, we can probably draw a few sensible conclusions: the Fall somehow loused things up between man and woman. Before, they were "naked and not ashamed." Afterward, they felt the need to cover themselves—not to avoid just God's sight, but each other's as well. The innocence was gone. Somehow a feeling of *indecency* had entered the picture. If there was sexual intimacy before the Fall, things changed. Once God put his curse on Eve, things changed a lot: childbirth, something most woman desire, is terribly painful. (And until relatively recent times, it was often fatal to the mother.) The woman will desire her husband, but (as one translation puts it) "he will lord it over you." This seems pretty clear: after the Fall, sex is no longer an innocent thing, and there is tension in the man–woman relationship.

This interpretation of Genesis, which seems to be the correct one, has always had its critics. People opposed to Christianity have said that the Fall was a fall *up*—to knowledge, to independence, to sexual enjoyment. In their view, Adam and Eve in Eden were a couple of naive fools, blindly obeying God and stupidly not indulging in the joys of sex. The smartest thing they ever did was to listen to the serpent. Afterward, man could "do his own thing," which included the pursuit of sexual ecstasy.

This spin on the story assumes that God and the Bible are anti-sex. (For more on that, see pages 62–67.) An amusing notion, and an interesting interpretation of the garden of Eden story. But it happens to be wrong.

7

Family Ties—or Were They?

"Mary remained a virgin, so the 'brothers' of Jesus mentioned in the Bible were not his real brothers."

If you ever walked through an art museum, you probably saw paintings of Mary, Joseph, and the baby Jesus. (In art, they are called the Holy Family.) Almost always, Mary is an attractive young woman while Joseph is an older man. Why?

To begin with the Bible itself, we don't know much about either Mary or Joseph. According to Matthew's and Luke's Gospels, Mary was engaged (but not yet married) to Joseph when she learned she was to give birth to the "Son of the Most High." Mary, being a virgin at the time, asked the obvious question: "How?" She was told by the angel Gabriel that "the power of the Most High will overshadow you." In other words, the Son of the Most High would not be conceived in the normal way. He would be the child of Mary, but not the child of any human father.

This is what Christians have always called the virgin birth. It is mentioned in only two books of the New Testament, but early Christians considered it important enough to include in their creeds. The fact that Jesus was "born of the virgin Mary" became one of the basics of the faith.

Now, regarding Joseph: Matthew's Gospel tells us nothing about Joseph's age, but it does tell us that Joseph was descended from the great King David himself. At the beginning of the story, Joseph and Mary were engaged, and Mary was "found to be with child from the

Holy Spirit." A potentially embarrassing situation, but in a dream an angel told Joseph to go ahead and marry Mary, for this wondrously conceived child would "save his people from their sins." Joseph, who is described as a "just man," married Mary, "but knew her not until she had given birth to a son." If you've read much of the Bible, you know that *knew her* is a polite way of saying "had sex with."

So here are the basics of the birth story: Mary was a virgin, about to be married to Joseph. We can assume that she was probably very young, since women married young in that culture. She conceived Jesus through the power of God, not through the usual way. At the time Jesus was born, she and Joseph had not had sexual relations.

Can we assume they had normal marital relations after Jesus was born? The Bible seems to say, definitely, yes. Jesus is mentioned as having both brothers and sisters (Matthew 12:36–50, 13:55, Mark 6:3, Luke 8:19–21, John 2:21, 7:3). All of this seems pretty straightforward. Mary conceived Jesus miraculously, then afterward she and Joseph settled down to a normal family life with several children. Strictly speaking, since Jesus was not the son of Joseph, his siblings would only be half brothers and half sisters (since they all have the same mother, Mary). After Jesus began his ministry as an adult, there is no mention of Joseph, so we can probably assume he had already died. This could mean he was older than Mary (think again of the older man in the paintings), but does not necessarily mean that.

So what is the source of the idea that Mary had no other children? Why does the Catholic Church officially teach that the "Blessed Virgin Mary" not only gave birth to no other children, but also maintained her virginity throughout her life? Why does it teach that the references to Jesus' brothers in the Gospels are actually to cousins or other relatives?

With all respect to the Roman Catholic tradition, no one can prove the "perpetual virginity of Mary" from the Bible. The Gospels mention Jesus' brothers and sisters. You have to assume these are literal blood brothers and sisters—unless you have already made up your mind that Mary bore no other children. And in that case, you would have to do some mental gymnastics and think, "Ah, it must mean 'brothers' in a broader sense, like 'cousins' or 'relatives.' "

Or they might be children of Joseph, but not children of Mary. This possibility is what is behind all the artworks showing Mary as young and Joseph as old. Joseph could have married at a young age, fathered several children, become a widower, then taken Mary as his second wife. In that case, their household would have included several older children, who would be (legally) Jesus' brothers and sisters.

That is precisely the theory of a story known as the Protevangelium of James, written sometime around the year 150. The story claims to be written by James, the son of Joseph and the (legal) brother of Jesus. The story relates that Joseph was already a widower with several children when he married the virgin Mary. After they married, he continued to respect her virginity. The story makes it clear that Mary had dedicated herself to perpetual virginity even before she conceived Jesus.

It's an interesting story—and almost certainly a piece of fiction. Some well-meaning Christian found the concept of virginity so attractive that he wrote this story to make Mary an example of his favorite virtue.

The story was not immediately accepted. Some scholars and even one of the popes (Innocent I) believed the story was completely false. But it struck a chord with many Christians. There have always been people—probably more women than men—who are very attracted to the idea of "virgin mother." It is, you might say, woman at her best: the purity and innocence of the virgin, the compassion and nurturing quality of the mother. In Mary, they had both. But then, if she went on after the birth of Jesus to have a normal married life with Joseph, well, that somehow made her less appealing.

Protestant Christians, of course, have had no problems accepting that the virgin Mary who gave birth to Jesus went on to give birth to other children. Protestants admire Mary, but not so much as Catholics have done. Sticking with the New Testament, Protestants are aware that Mary did not always seem to understand or appreciate Jesus (see Luke 2:50, Matthew 12:46–50). In the Protestant tradition, she is not the perfect human that Catholics make her out to be.

The Catholic view of Mary is rooted in more than just the Protevangelium of James mentioned above. It is rooted in something that happened fairly early among Christians: the urge to invent stories about characters in the New Testament. The Gospels tell us very little about Jesus' life between his birth and his adult ministry—a long stretch of about thirty years. Pious Christians remedied that by inventing lots of "Infancy Gospels," telling stories about the miracles Jesus worked as a child, details about Joseph and Mary, and so forth. Joseph became an important figure, but Mary even more so. Since Jesus was the Savior of mankind and the Son of God, then the person who gave birth to him was of vital importance. Some people began to teach that since Jesus himself was sinless (a belief taken from the Bible), he had to have been born of a sinless woman, so Mary herself must have been without sin.

> The belief that Mary was conceived without sin is known as the doctrine of the Immaculate Conception.

Couple this with a growing appreciation among Christians for celibacy. Jesus was (so far as we know) never married. Neither was the great apostle Paul (though he might have been widowed). Paul said that the celibate state was fine for people like himself, who had devoted themselves the Lord's work. But he admitted that most Christians would do well to marry and give their sexual appetite what it needed within the bonds of marriage. But later generations of Christians, however, placed a much higher priority on celibacy and virginity. As the honor given to virginity increased, so did the honor given to Mary. In time, Catholics came to refer to the "Blessed Virgin Mary" and honor her so much that Protestants have accused them of treating her like a goddess.

None of this is intended to offend or deride Roman Catholics. Millions of people over the centuries have found great comfort in honoring and praying to Mary. But truthfully, if Christians take the Bible to be the basis of belief, there isn't much foundation for all the reverence that has been given to Mary. The Catholic Church celebrates marriage as a sacrament and has given its approval to producing children and raising them in a godly home. If Mary and Joseph had several children (which is pretty obvious from the Bible), they were probably excellent parents, and to most people this is more commendable than Mary maintaining her virginity throughout her life.

8

How Mary Magdalene (Might Have) Made a Living

"Mary Magdalene, the follower of Jesus, was a former prostitute."

Our word *maudlin* means "sickeningly sentimental or emotional," and the word is rooted, curiously, in *Magdalene,* that is, the woman Mary Magdalene, one of the most appealing female characters in the Bible. How did she, one of the first followers of Jesus, come to have a connection with *maudlin?*

It all comes from the "prostitute with a heart of gold" myth, the wayward woman who is basically good on the inside despite the way she earns her living. The Bible has a few golden-hearted prostitutes of its own, the most famous being Rahab, the harlot of Jericho who aided the invading Israelites in their takeover of the pagan city. While the Old Testament's Book of Joshua goes largely unread today, some readers still remember the gallant Rahab, who hid the Israelite spies in her home. When the king of Jericho sent a posse to ferret out the spies, Rahab would not betray them. They rewarded this courage and loyalty by allowing her and her family to be the only survivors when they sacked the city. According to the New Testament, Rahab married an Israelite and became one of the ancestors of King David (and thus also an ancestor of Jesus), and the Epistle to the Hebrews lists Rahab in its "Faith Hall of Fame," commending her courage and faith. (At the risk of shattering the myth of the golden-hearted prostitute, some Bible scholars believe that Rahab may actually have been an innkeeper, not a prostitute.)

And while the Old Testament gives us Rahab, the New Testament gives us Mary Magdalene, the prostitute won over to a life of virtue by the kind and merciful Jesus. Artists have had a field day with Mary Magdalene, showing her tearful and sorrowing, lamenting her wicked life as she turns in repentance to the Lord. The many depictions of her tear-streaked, agonized face are the reason *Magdalene* eventually evolved into *maudlin.* (The English, incidentally, pronounce *Magdalene* the same as we pronounce *maudlin.*)

In our own day, the belief that Mary Magdalene was a reformed prostitute found new life in the rock opera *Jesus Christ Superstar,* with Mary in the role of a dedicated "camp follower" of Jesus and his disciples, attending to their needs, being a comforting mother-sister figure. Her famous song "I Don't Know How to Love Him" exposes her emotions as she laments having "had so many men before," while Jesus affects her in a much deeper way. At the same time that *Superstar* was affecting pop culture, the much-loved TV movie *Jesus of Nazareth* also followed the tradition of showing Mary as a reformed harlot.

But was she? The Gospels do not say so. They tell us that Jesus cast seven demons out of her (Mark 16:9, Luke 8:2) and that she became one of his devoted followers. She was present at the crucifixion, followed the body of Jesus to the grave, and, on the first Easter, had the privilege of being the first person to see the risen Jesus (Matthew 28:1–8). Beyond this, we know nothing, and whether she ever resembled the teary Magdalenes of paintings and sculptures is anyone's guess. She, like many other people Jesus encountered, benefited from his power to drive out demons. But there is certainly no connection between demonic possession and living as a prostitute. So how did she come to be portrayed as one?

It happens that one of the few mentions of Mary Magdalene, found in Luke 8:2, follows one of the most touching stories in the Bible: Luke 7:36–50 tells of a dinner where a "woman who had lived a sinful life" anoints Jesus' feet with perfume, weeping all the while. Jesus' host is aghast that Jesus registers no protest at this sinful creature touching him. Jesus explains that "her many sins have been forgiven—for she has loved much." And he tells the woman,

"Your faith has saved you; go in peace." It is probably safe to say the woman was a prostitute—or at least a "loose woman"—in her past life. But who was she? Her name is never mentioned, and it seems odd, since Luke's Gospel mentions Mary Magdalene in other places, that he would not have referred to her by name here. Still, tradition identified the two women as being one and the same; thus Mary Magdalene was—so people assumed—the weeping woman with an immoral past, mercifully forgiven by the Lord.

The story is complicated because in another place in the Gospels, a certain Mary anoints Jesus' feet with expensive perfume. In this case, the Mary was the sister of Lazarus, the man Jesus brought back from the grave. According to John 12, Mary anoints Jesus' feet, "and the house was filled with the fragrance of the perfume." No mention is made of her being a sinful or immoral woman, so we can probably assume that she and the immoral woman of Luke 7 are two different women, and these are two different occasions when Jesus' feet are anointed with perfume. In John 12, Judas Iscariot objects to this "waste" of expensive perfume, saying that the cost of it could have benefited the poor. *Jesus Christ Superstar* has Judas directing these words to Mary Magdalene. For the record, there are a *lot* of women named Mary in the New Testament, but Mary the sister of Lazarus was not the same person as Mary Magdalene. (*Magdalene,* by the way, probably means she came from a village named Magdala, on the shores of the Sea of Galilee.)

> In time past, a "magadalen home" was a home or refuge for reformed prostitutes.
>
> 

In brief, Mary Magdalene was a woman whose demons were cast out by Jesus, but we have no reason to believe she had been a prostitute. Still, the world of art—and the devotional lives of people who have been touched by pictures of the repentant Magdalene—has been enriched by the image of the flagrantly immoral person given a new life by a forgiving, merciful Christ. If an artist occasionally overdid it, creating a *maudlin* picture, perhaps it was due to the problem of using paint and canvas to depict something as profound as repentance.

9

Two by Two (or More) Into Noah's Ark

"Noah took two of each animal into the ark."

Any trip through an art museum makes it pretty obvious that, for hundreds of years, Christianity dominated Western art. Throughout the long period called the Middle Ages and on into the Renaissance, artists spent most of their time and energy depicting scenes from the Bible. While the emphasis was on showing situations involving, obviously, *people,* a favorite story that allowed for the painting of animals was the tale of Noah, his ark, and the loading of the multitude of animals into it. Even today, artists love to paint the scene, with the enormous boat at the center and a fascinating parade of birds and beasts into the open doorway, with Noah supervising the operation. And of course, the animals enter the ark in pairs—male and female—allowing for the species to continue once the cataclysmic flood has subsided. The ark scene is the closest painters come to depicting a biblical zoo. They frolic in the riot of animals, even allowing themselves some whimsy such as painting mythical beasts like unicorns. (Obviously these became extinct at some point.) In many species, the contrast between the male and female is interesting in itself—such as the famous eclectus parrots, with the flaming red male bird and the bright green female bird.

Aside from the pleasure in seeing so many creatures crowded onto one canvas, the scene touches us in another way: God was choosing to destroy the world by flood because of human sin. The flood was both a punishment and a cleansing. God told Noah, "I am going to put an end to all people, for the earth is filled with violence because of them. I am surely going to destroy both them and the earth." But the righteous Noah, along with his wife, his three sons, and their wives, alone would survive—along with the animals, which, after all, were sinless, so the beasts survived, while the sinful among humankind are wiped out. Though God declared that "Everything on earth will perish," the presence of male and female creatures on the ark ensured that life would regenerate once the flood has done its work.

The problem is, this charming scene is wrong—according to the source, the Book of Genesis. Observe what instructions God actually gave Noah regarding the ark's cargo: "Take with you seven of every kind of clean animal, male and its mate, and two of every kind of unclean animal, a male and its mate, and also seven of every kind of bird, male and female, to keep their various kinds alive throughout the earth" (Genesis 7:2–3).

"Clean" and "unclean"? The author of Genesis could only have been thinking of the kosher laws—first written down during the days of Moses, many generations after Noah lived. Assuming Noah understood the distinction between clean and unclean animals, the ark would have had seven cows (cattle are "clean" according to the kosher laws found in Leviticus) but only two pigs. Seven deer, but two rabbits (except of course that with rabbits, there wouldn't be just two of them for very long). Seven chickens, but two storks. Seven zebras, two geckos.

How exactly would one divide seven into male and female? Three males and four females, or four males and three females? Perhaps the alternative translation of *seven* solves the problem: the alternate is "seven pairs."

Most of us, even observant Jews, have no idea how all the animal species of the world would be divided into clean and unclean. Some—the pig, for example—are pretty well known, but how about the many species that were not mentioned in the kosher laws? The artists who painted Noah's ark—and the people who wrote the Broadway musical *Two by Two,* based on the story of

Noah—probably saw no point in fussing over the "seven of clean, two of unclean" distinction. Most likely people will go on continuing to believe that Noah's ark—whether it was real or merely part of a cautionary tale about how God views human evil—contained two of every creature. Happily, in the book you are reading, this ranks as one of the least bothersome misperceptions about the Bible.

For the record, here is an explanation of why Genesis refers to the "seven of clean, two of unclean" pattern: in the original Noah story, repeated from one generation to another, Noah took two of every creature into the ark. By the time Genesis was actually written down (obviously a *long* time after the events it describes), the Jews were very fastidious about keeping to the laws of kosher. The distinction between clean and unclean creatures was very clear to them (if not to us), and so the author(s) of Genesis must have thought, "Well, clearly God did preserve both clean and unclean creatures in the ark, but clearly he would not have wanted them to be *equal.*" So as a way of indicating that even in Noah's time the earth's creatures were not quite equal in God's eyes, the ark would contain more pairs of clean animals than unclean ones. Thus, when the ark finally found its dry resting place atop Mount Ararat, there would emerge from it a male and female pig, but seven (or seven pairs of) cattle.

In the original Broadway musical *Two by Two,* comic Danny Kaye played Noah.

One other interesting item: the detail that there are seven of every clean creature is important because, after Noah left the ark, he built an altar to God and sacrificed on it *clean* birds and animals. If there had only been one pair of these, then, obviously, they could not have reproduced on the earth.

10

Investing Yourself in Faith

"The Bible teaches the 'prosperity gospel,' the idea that believers will prosper in this world."

A few years ago, a religious magazine ran an article with the title, "Would Jesus Wear a Rolex?" It is an interesting question, isn't it? Read on.

Every person wants to be a success—the question is, a successful *what?* Spouse? Parent? Businessperson? Athlete? The envy of everyone you know? While there is nothing wrong with setting goals in life and pursuing them, the Bible takes a rather different view of success. The only real success, ultimately, is being a good and moral human being. While achieving this will never merit a cover story in *Time* or *Money,* it may bring the greatest satisfaction of all. There are plenty of true stories of people who sought and achieved worldly success but then found themselves unsatisfied and restless. What about the stories or people who sought to live in a loving relationship with their fellow man and with God? The stories of those anonymous people are rarely told, but perhaps they should be.

Having said all that, we turn to what some people call the prosperity gospel. In a nutshell, this is the idea that God's people, if they are faithful to him, will prosper in this world as well as in the next. Those who follow this teaching can find lots of passages in the Bible to back it up. All of these are found in the Old Testament, for the ancient Hebrews did not, frankly, believe in an afterlife. Life was limited to this world, and it was here that you fellowshiped with

God and with man. The best you could hope for was to follow God's commands, living a moral life, and enjoying your honest gains and the companionship of as many children as possible.

The Hebrews were supposed to be in a *covenant* relationship with God, a covenant being an agreement, a contract. Essentially it took this form: if you obey the commands of God, your land will be fertile, your crops will grow, your wealth will increase, you will be at peace, et cetera, but if you forget God's commands, your crops will fail, your enemies will triumph over you, you will slip into poverty, and so forth. This agreement is repeated, with minor variations, throughout the earliest books of the Old Testament. (You can find one statement of it in Leviticus 26.) There is no promise of heaven, no threat of hell. Your obeying, or disobeying, of God's commands will determine your condition here in this world.

But there are other voices heard in the Old Testament. One of the loudest is the Book of Job. Here a very saintly and very wealthy man has just about everything he possesses taken away. Yet he refuses to curse God. He also refuses to accept his friends' statements that his sin has brought his calamities upon him. His friends are, of course, simply repeating the covenant idea: if you were righteous, Job, these horrible things would not have happened to you. But Job isn't buying it. At the end of the book, God restores Job's wealth, but not until after Job has made the point that sometimes the wicked do prosper and sometimes the saintly do suffer.

The Book of Psalms contains both ideas. Psalm 1 echoes the old idea: those who follow the Lord's commands will thrive: "In all that he does, he prospers." But some Psalms, like 73, dwell on the idea that the wicked and proud do often prosper in this life. Psalm 49 offers the faint consolation that evil men who prosper will perish like everyone else. According to Psalm 37:16, "A little that a righteous man has is better than the riches of many wicked."

The Book of Ecclesiastes puts another spin on prosperity. Its author claims to have been amazingly prosperous—yet found it all somehow unfulfilling. Like so many of life's pleasures, wealth is just "vanity," a meaningless "chasing after the wind."

The Hebrew prophets put yet another spin on it: the rich often got where they are by exploiting the poor. Instead of wealth being a sign that the person is following God's commands, it may be a sign that he is a heartless exploiter. Using their wealth for bribes, the rich can buy their way out of court.

Summing up the Old Testament: there is much here to support the idea that moral living will lead to prosperity. But there is also much against the idea, for some of the authors of the Old Testament were aware that in a sinful world, the winners are not always those who put God first. Good people can be poor and exploited, and bad people can reach the top rung of the ladder.

The New Testament tosses away the belief that good people prosper. Look who is the central character here: Jesus, a working-class man who wandered about from place to place with no permanent home and, we assume, not much more than the clothes on his back. While he gained a measure of fame, it never led to wealth. And he ended up dying in what was considered the most degrading and dishonorable execution imaginable. Not exactly a prosperous or successful man.

But then, the key event of the New Testament is the resurrection of Jesus. A new life begins after death. The saintliest man of all achieves not worldly success but something much better, eternal life.

During his ministry, Jesus had some wealthy acquaintances. But he never had a kind word to say about wealth or the people who pursue it. Rather, his attitude was more like this: "Woe to you that are rich! For you have received your consolation. Woe to you that are full! For you shall hunger" (Luke 6:24). He also said, "Take heed, and beware of covetousness, for a man's life consists not in the abundance of the things he possesses" (Luke 12:15). And perhaps the most famous quote of all regarding worldly success: "What is a man profited, if he shall gain the whole world, and lose his own soul?" (Matthew 16:26). Does any of this sound like a "prosperity gospel"?

Jesus told his followers, "I have come that they might have life, and that they might have it more abundantly" (John 10:10). If you took this out of context, you might make a case for the prosperity gospel. But fit it in with the rest of the New Testament and it's pretty clear that "abundant life" is not the same as "material comfort."

Paul, the great apostle, earned his living as a tentmaker and frequently had to remind Christians to work hard and not be lazy. But he never even hinted that prosperity or wealth was the goal. In fact, as in 1 Timothy 6:17, he issued warnings to wealthy Christians, telling them not to be proud and remember that they should trust in God, not in their wealth. In the same vein, the Letter of James states that God has "chosen the poor of this world to be rich in faith" (2:5).

Jesus' promise of "abundant life" had nothing to do with material goods.

I could go on listing examples from the New Testament, but you get the idea: Christians set their sights on the next world, which means that all the things people pursue in this world seem less important.

Having said all that, is there anything wrong with a Christian investing wisely and planning for his family's future? No, not a thing. Christians are not so otherworldly that they forget about work, food, and shelter. But they are otherworldly enough to see that money and material possessions are not as important as others believe.

PART II

WHAT THE POLITICALLY CORRECT CROWD SAYS

JESUS AND THE WOMAN TAKEN IN ADULTERY
Jesus the tolerant and nonjudgmental modern man . . . or was he?

11

Jesus and the Unstoned Woman

"The story of Jesus and the woman about to be stoned for adultery teaches the virtue of tolerance."

In the age of Political Correctness, tolerance reigns as the supreme virtue. This is definitely a pretty modern view of virtue, because in times past tolerance wasn't given much thought. Every community had certain moral standards—standards that were maintained by either law or custom. If you played by the rules and stuck to the standards, you were doing fine. If you did not, you suffered the consequences, either socially or legally, or both. The law could penalize you in various ways (legal punishment), or your neighbors could snub or abuse you (social punishment).

This doesn't mean that every society in the past was totalitarian, taking pleasure in witch-hunts. There were (and still are) such societies, but most societies gave a certain amount of freedom to individuals. As long as you obeyed the basic rules, you were free to do as you liked. And as long as you agreed with the people around you about what "acceptable behavior" was, there was no problem.

Let's jump back two thousand years to the locale known as Judea, homeland of the Jews. It was a conquered territory of the Roman Empire, an empire stretching from as far west as Spain to as far east as Persia. Rome had conquered tribes and nations with literally hundreds of languages and religions. One of the conquered nations had been known, historically, as Israel, a nation that worshiped only one god (which ancient peoples considered pretty odd), a nation with its moral laws written down in the books that today we call the Old Testament. The Roman Empire has a reputation in history for being pretty footloose in regard to morals. Certainly the Romans were more relaxed and tolerant about sexual morality than the Jews were. Roman sexual morality (or lack of it) was much closer to our standards today than it was to the moral standards of the Jews.

But even the Romans had their limits. While they were highly tolerant of male promiscuity, they liked their women to be more restrained. There are plenty of tales of high-class Roman women with low-class morals. But in fact, the Roman men (like most men throughout history) generally preferred their women (or their wives, anyway) to be monogamous and loyal.

> There is nothing in the Bible to indicate that stoning a person for adultery was an everyday occurrence.
>
> 

That was even more true of the Jews. Adultery was not something they took lightly. One of the Ten Commandments specifically prohibited adultery. And other laws in the Old Testament mandated the death penalty for it. A man or woman guilty of it could be stoned (Deuteronomy 22:22–24). Marriage was a serious relationship, not to be taken lightly. The whole community had an interest in seeing that two married people remained faithful to each other.

How often were people actually stoned to death for adultery? Probably not very often. In most cases, the offended spouse probably forgave—or at least overlooked—the offense.

We have no information on that, any more than we have information about how many people committed adultery. Human nature being what it is, we can safely assume that both male and female Jews sometimes broke the law and committed adultery.

The most famous adulterer in the New Testament is an unnamed woman. Her story, found in John 8, is often referred to today.

According to John 8, Jesus was teaching at the Jerusalem temple when some "scribes and Pharisees" brought to him "a woman who had been caught in adultery." The Bible scholars assure us that "caught" here means she was literally caught in the act—that is, she was probably found actually engaging in sexual relations with a man. This is important, because the woman was not being accused on the basis of idle rumor. We can safely assume that, yes, she was guilty as charged.

Her accusers say to Jesus, "In the Law, Moses commanded us to stone such women. So what do you say?" What was their motivation here? According to the Gospel, "This they said to test him, that they might have some charge to bring against him." In other words, these scribes and Pharisees, people who had a reputation for a very strict morality, were trying to put Jesus in the position of appearing too lax about morals.

Jesus finally gave his famous reply: "Let him who is without sin among you be the first to throw a stone at her." And, "when they heard it, they went away one by one . . . and Jesus was left alone with the woman standing before him."

How often have you heard someone refer to "let he who is without sin cast the first stone"? It is heard often in our time, and in all likelihood the person using those words has only a vague feeling that they are somehow connected with the Bible and with Jesus. The story, in the age of Political Correctness, seems to teach a wonderful lesson: Jesus, whom the Christians claim to honor, actually was a tolerant man, one who sided with an adulterous woman, not with her accusers. So Jesus was on the side of the "sinners," not people who are self-righteous. In fact, the Politically Correct side says, Christian conservatives today are the bad guys, since they are as self-righteous as the adulterous woman's accusers. The story, it seems, tells us that sexual sin isn't sin at all—rather, self-righteousness is the *real* sin.

That might be a logical interpretation of this story—if it ended with Jesus' words to the woman's accusers. But it doesn't end there. Jesus said to the woman, "Woman, where are they? Has no one condemned you?" The woman replied, "No one, Lord." Then Jesus said, "Neither do I condemn you." So far, this story still seems to be preaching tolerance, doesn't it? But Jesus added the words, "Go, and sin no more." That doesn't quite fit the usual view of tolerance, does it? If Jesus was truly tolerant (in the modern sense), he would have *condoned* the woman's adultery. He definitely did not. He told her, very plainly, not to do it again. So he believed—just as the scribes and Pharisees did—that adultery was wrong. The early Christians, with their very strict sexual morality, certainly would not have included this story in the New Testament if they believed it showed Jesus condoning adultery.

Bible readers still puzzle over this story. Why did Jesus *appear* (at least briefly) to side with the woman? The key to it probably lies in the motivation of the accusers: the story says the woman was brought to him "to test him." They were not motivated primarily by concern for the sanctity of marriage. They were trying to make Jesus look bad, and he knew that. Though the woman was probably guilty as charged, Jesus knew they were just using her as a tool to get at him.

12

The Burden That Personkind Bears

"The Bible is anti-woman."

Who would have predicted, thirty or forty years ago, that paganism and witchcraft would have a revival? Granted, paganism and witchcraft never died out, but for a long time they were "underground." Now, however, there are plenty of people, both women and men, who hold steady jobs, live in respectable neighborhoods, and readily identify themselves as "pagans" or "Wiccans." How times change.

And no one doubts that contempt for Christianity has helped these other movements grow. Christians have been accused of most or all of the world's ills—sexism, racism, homophobia, environmental damage, and more. Paganism and Wicca, on the other hand, are held up as models of enlightenment, particularly in regard to women. These new (or very old) religions heartily condemn sexism and patriarchy.

In the meantime, millions of women continue to attend church and read the Bible. Are they all fools? The dupes or doormats of men? Or do they simply not believe that the Bible is anti-woman?

Well, the obvious thing is to begin at the beginning. First of all, the ancient Middle East, where the Bible originated, was patriarchal. Men dominated society and the family. Women had less power and less importance. Sons were valued more than daughters. A man desired to marry a virgin, even though his own virginity was not important. When a man preceded his wife in death, his brother or some other male relative took responsibility for the wife.

In Genesis, man was created before woman. Afterward, God stated that it was not good for the man to be alone, so he created Eve as "helper, suitable for him" (Genesis 2:18). If this sounds sexist, consider this: she was the man's helper, not his *property.* Both man and woman were told to fill the earth and subdue it (Genesis 1:28). Both parents, not just the mother, were told to discipline and teach the children (Ephesians 6:1–4).

What about work? Yes, in the Bible most women assumed the usual roles of homemaker and child rearer. But the ideal woman depicted in Proverbs 31 works outside the home as well as inside, making garments and selling them to merchants. In Acts, Lydia is a businesswoman (Acts 16:14), and the often mentioned Priscilla was a tentmaker (Acts 18:2). (There is a flip side to this, too: men are urged not to neglect their home and family to pursue their careers. See 1 Timothy 3:4, 12.)

What about property? In Numbers 27, the daughters of Zelophehad could inherit and own property—if there were no sons to inherit it. While this strikes modern minds as pretty sexist, consider this: in many cultures, a woman could not inherit property, period.

Was Jesus himself patriarchal? Well, certainly he called God "Father." (Israel never, ever thought of God in female terms, so Jesus could not have done otherwise.) But Jesus frequently showed a high regard for women. He referred to Jewish women as "daughters of Abraham" (Luke 13:16), acknowledging that their spiritual status was equal to that of men. (Abraham, "father of the faithful," was considered both the spiritual and physical ancestor of the Jews.) Luke 8:1–3 and Mark 15:40 list women who were traveling companions of Jesus and his disciples, which tells us that though Jesus had chosen twelve male disciples, there were women involved with his ministry. Jesus had a deep emotional attachment to the sisters Mary and Martha and their brother Lazarus, the man he raised from the dead (John 11). It is clear from his conversations with these two women that he did not regard them as inferior beings.

So Jesus, in regard to women, had a rather *non*patriarchal approach. The apostle Paul, however, author of a large chunk of the New Testament, has often been held up as the poster boy for Christian Patriarchy. Does he deserve this bad reputation?

> According to John 20, it was a woman, Mary Magdalene, who was first to see the risen Jesus.
>
> 

It is true that Paul made some statements that make feminists say "ouch!" In 1 Corinthians 11:3, he states that the head of a man is Christ, while the head of a woman is her husband. While that does seem pretty blatantly sexist, note that the husband is not the final authority—he himself is subordinate to someone, Christ. In Ephesians 5:22, Paul tells wives to be subject to their husbands. Another "ouch!" There are not many women today in North America or Western Europe who warm to the idea of being "subordinate" to man.

But there is more to Paul than the subordination of women. He makes it clear (Ephesians 5:21) that there is *mutual subordination*—a man should sacrifice his own interests and desires for the sake of his wife. He may even be called upon to give up his life for his wife, just as Christ gave up his life (Ephesians 5:25).

Paul definitely saw the husband as head of the family. But this wasn't the same as being a tyrant. To be a good head of the family, the husband has to love it and protect it, not tyrannize it.

Paul was actually pretty modern in some ways. Consider: the Greek and Roman world in which he moved was extremely sexist. Among the Greeks, women and men generally did not eat together or sleep in the same quarters. Men spent most of their waking lives outside the home, the women inside. For the most part, men and women did not converse much together, certainly not on an intellectual level. But Paul encouraged wives to discuss spiritual matters with their husbands (1 Corinthians 14:35). He rejected separation of the sexes at home or in the Christian fellowship (1 Corinthians 11:11). It is pretty safe to say that the first Christian fellowships were much less sexist than the world of the Greeks and Romans.

And of course, Paul made his grand statement on Christian equality: "There is neither Jew nor Greek, there is neither slave nor free, there is neither male nor female, for you are all one in Christ Jesus" (Galatians 3:28). In the Christian fellowship, traditional barriers were broken down. This didn't mean that Paul considered everyone to be the *same*. But he clearly believed that, spiritually speaking, there was a "level playing field."

Paul was unmarried (it is possible he might have been widowed) but clearly had some close female friends among the Christians. At the end of the Epistle to the Romans, he tells the Roman Christians to welcome "our sister Phoebe." He greets the married couple Priscilla and Aquila (naming the wife first, incidentally). While it is true that there were no women ministers among the earliest Christians, it is also true that women were very active. (A visit to any church today would confirm that, even if ministers are men, women pretty much dominate the fellowship.)

Obviously none of this is going to convert a dedicated pagan or Wiccan to Christianity. The matter of sexism in Christianity is a hot-button issue, one that has generated a flood of books and articles. Whether anyone on one side has changed the mind of someone on the other side is questionable. It so happens that the author of the book you are now reading believes that the Bible is *not* sexist, and *not* anti-woman. So here we have added a few more drops to the ocean of ink spilled over one of the key religious and social issues of our time.

13

Jewish Writers Who Didn't Like Themselves?

"The New Testament is anti-Semitic."

Anti-Semitism has been around as long as there have been Semites to be anti. Specifically, hostility toward Jews goes way back before the beginning of Christianity. In the Old Testament period, nations were in the habit of hating other nations for no particular reason. Today we call it xenophobia, the irrational fear of what is strange or foreign. Most people throughout human history thought it was normal to hate—or at least to be suspicious of—people different from themselves. (Most people still do, frankly.)

And the Jews were different in one very important respect: they worshiped just one God. And they would not make statues or any kind of images of this one God. In the ancient world, this was very peculiar. Then there was the Jews' habit of taking one day out of seven and doing nothing on that day but worshiping and resting. As you may have noticed, all three of these peculiarities are mandated in the Ten Commandments. What the Jews took to be the vital task of being a "holy" people, the rest of the world took to be a determination to be a *strange* people.

These worshipers of one God had come to believe that God would send them a Messiah, the Anointed One who would be their political (or perhaps spiritual) savior. Sometime around the year 30, a Jew from the region called Galilee began preaching, performing healings and casting out demons, and convincing some of his fellow Jews that he himself was the Messiah they had expected. But most of his followers were the common folk. The Jewish leaders, those known for their expertise in the Jewish law and their connections with the priesthood in Jerusalem, were not impressed with this Jesus person. They had known of plenty of false Messiahs over the years. Here was just one more. The Messiahs came and went, but the Jewish laws and the Jewish temples remained.

This Jesus let some of the Jewish teachers know that he thought them to be hypocrites. He made a shocking prediction that the great temple would be torn down, with not one stone left on another. The Jewish leaders, especially the priests, wanted Jesus out of the way, but they bided their time, fearing his followers might cause a ruckus. One of Jesus' own disciples offered to lead the priests' soldiers to Jesus by night. Dragged before the priests, Jesus was declared a blasphemer. They turned him over to Pilate, the Roman governor, to be executed. Pilate, a cynical bureaucrat, had no use for the Jews or their bickering. He saw no political threat in Jesus, but to pacify the Jewish leaders he ordered Jesus crucified. Shortly after his death, Jesus' followers swore they saw him alive again. Until the year 70, the tension between Jewish Christian and Jewish non-Christian continued. In that year, a Jewish revolt against Rome led to the destruction of the Jewish temple. The Jews ceased to rule over Israel, and over time Christianity outgrew its parent religion.

That, in a nutshell, is what the New Testament tells us about the Jews and the Christians. A well-established religion (Judaism) had to deal with a splinter group (Christianity). The Jews in the splinter group believed they were faithful Jews, accepting the Messiah that God had promised. To other Jews, they were heretics or blasphemers. Some of the Jewish leaders worked to bring Jesus' execution about, and we read in the Book of Acts that some of the Christian leaders were executed or imprisoned.

Where does anti-Semitism come into the picture? The earliest Christians were Jews. Jesus was a Jew, his twelve disciples were Jews, and the great apostle Paul was a Jew. They firmly believed that they were faithful to their religion, not heretics. Their "Bible" was the Old Testament, the same books that all Jews honored and studied. When the faith spread to non-Jews, they, too, accepted the Old Testament as their own. When you think about it, it's remarkable that pagans who had been brought up to bow down to statues of Zeus and Apollo could somehow learn to cherish the Jewish books about Moses and the prophets and the kings of Israel. Pagans mostly looked down on Jews and their "primitive" sacred books, but some of those pagans became Christians and learned to love those same books. Does any of this sound anti-Semitic so far? You might get the opposite impression: as Christianity spread, respect for the Jews' God and the Jews' sacred books spread as well. Thanks to Christianity, people in every corner of the globe have heard of Noah, Abraham, David, Solomon, Elijah, Isaiah, Jeremiah, and other figures from the Jewish tradition.

Tragically, over time Christians forgot about their Jewish roots. (They never forgot the Old Testament, of course.) As Christianity became legal, and then the predominant religion, Christians unfortunately did what majorities often do: look down on, and persecute, the minorities. It was not unusual for Christians in the Middle Ages to refer to Jews as "Christ-killers." Ferdinand and Isabella, the Spanish rulers who sent Columbus to America, did a religious housecleaning in Spain and forced Jews to either convert to Christianity or leave the country. Spain's Inquisition harassed and persecuted converted Jews who were suspected of being insincere Christians.

And the twentieth century, alas, gave us Nazism and the Holocaust, a horror no Jew or anyone else can ever forget. Nor can most people forget that the German people who allowed—and even aided—the Nazis were supposedly Christians. How could it have happened? Some have wondered if there is something in Christianity that is basically anti-Semitic. Some have claimed they see it in the New Testament.

Well, I've already said that Jesus and the first Christians were Jews. And the first Christians were deeply attached to the Jews' sacred books (now called the Old Testament). The anti-Semitism that some people claim to find in the New Testament lies in the way it presents Jesus' death. Some people claim that all the blame is placed on "the Jews" while the Romans get off lightly. Pilate, the Roman governor, is presented as not really desiring Jesus' death, but simply caving in to Jewish pressure. There is a suspicion that the New Testament writers wanted to spread the faith among the Romans, so they make the Romans look good and the Jews look bad. This is a possibility, and if it is true, then the lie "The New Testament is anti-Semitic" is no lie at all. But the other possibility is this: the New Testament portrays pretty accurately how the Jews reacted to the first Christians.

Here is something crucial to keep in mind if you read the New Testament: when it refers to "the Jews," it never means *all* the Jews. The New Testament writers, remember, *were* Jews. They were aware that many Jews, like themselves, believed in Jesus or at least did not despise him. Look at this verse from John's Gospel: "The Jews had already agreed that if anyone should confess Jesus to be the Christ, he was to be put out of the synagogue" (9:22). Clearly "the Jews" does not refer to all Jews nor to a majority. It is referring to the Jerusalem establishment, the small but powerful elite that opposed Jesus. If you read John's Gospel, you may have to pause to remind yourself of this, because John uses "the Jews" often, and "the Jews" in his gospel come off looking very bad. But remember: John is a Jew himself. He doesn't hate his religion or his fellow Jews. But he is painfully aware that most of them did not accept Jesus as their Messiah.

John's Gospel uses "the Jews" often, while the other three Gospels almost never do. They refer to Jesus' opposition as being the priests, the Pharisees, the Sadducees, and so on, but never "the Jews." So clearly John is using "the Jews" as his shorthand way of saying "the religious establishment in Jerusalem." When you read of Jesus telling the Samaritan woman that "salvation is from the Jews" (John 4:22), you can safely conclude that John's Gospel is *not* anti-Semitic.

What about the accusations that the Romans are treated too kindly in the New Testament? That does not hold water. The Gospels tell of the Roman soldiers mocking Jesus, hitting him, and spitting on him, which hardly depicts Roman military men in a favorable light (see Luke 27:27–31). Although the Gospels indicate that Pilate wanted to set Jesus free, Pilate is not presented as an admirable character. The Roman officials who dealt with Paul in Acts were not exactly saints, either. Acts says that the Roman governor Felix kept Paul in prison while he hoped for a bribe (Acts 24:26).

If you are determined to find anti-Semitism in the New Testament, you will. The New Testament is definitely pro-Christian, and for some people that is enough to categorize it as anti-Jewish. But there is nothing whatever in the New Testament to indicate that the authors hated Judaism or hated themselves for being Jews. When they present the Jerusalem elite as being opposed to Jesus, there is no doubt they were right on target. Establishments do not like to change, and the Jewish establishment saw Jesus as someone who might rock the boat, might agitate the people, might irritate the Romans, and, worst of all, might result in the establishment losing its privileges. That fear of losing one's position is not a Jewish trait, but a human trait. And if you say that the first Christians were opposed to a hidebound religious elite that preferred that things stay "as is," you are correct.

14

Polluted by Religion?

"The Bible is anti-environment."

No doubt you have seen the LOVE YOUR MOTHER bumper stickers. The "Mother" is, of course, Mother Earth. Obviously the owner of the vehicle is pro-environment. But then, isn't *everyone* pro-environment now? Have you ever met anyone who actually claims not to care if the air and water are polluted? Of course not. Every person wants clean air and water, and everyone wants plants and animals to flourish on the earth. So how is that Christians—and the Bible—are taking a lot of heat for being "anti-environment"?

Well, as one of the characters on the TV series *Picket Fences* observed, "Hating Christians is Politically Correct." Christians have been accused of being racist and sexist. They are also accused often of being exploiters of the natural world. In 1967 (back when we talked about "ecology" instead of "environment"), UCLA professor Lynn White published an essay in *Science* magazine. In it, he claimed that the root problem for ecology was religious, and that the solution must be religious. "Christian" views of nature had to be overthrown and replaced. His essay was reprinted in the 1970 *Environmental Handbook*. From then on, the Bible and Christianity have been prime targets.

What is the Bible's view of nature? To begin at the very beginning, God creates the earth and all the creatures that inhabit it. "And God saw everything that he had made, and behold, it was very good" (Genesis 1:22). This hardly sounds anti-environment. It sounds as if the created world (which includes man, by the way) is "very good."

An obvious delight in the created world crops up often in the Bible. It is clear that the various people who wrote the Bible were nature lovers. As one example, Job 37:14: "Stop and consider the wondrous works of God." In Chapters 38 through 41 of Job, God himself, speaking "out of a whirlwind," orders Job to consider all the wonders of nature. Whoever penned the Book of Job would have been a superb writer for *National Geographic*. He certainly could not be accused of being insensitive to the earth.

The Psalms, the hymnbook of the Bible, are full of praises of the beauties of nature. Psalm 8 praises God for "your heavens, the work of your fingers, the moon and the stars, which you have set in place." Some of the Psalms speak of God riding upon the thunderclouds with the lightning flashing. Obviously the "storm chasers" of today were not the first to marvel at dramatic displays of thunder and lightning.

In the New Testament, Jesus himself showed an appreciation for natural beauty. "Consider the lilies, how they grow: they neither toil nor spin, yet I tell you, even Solomon in all his glory was not arrayed like one of these" (Luke 12:27). It is just a small step from this to St. Francis of Assisi speaking to "Brother Sun, Sister Moon."

So far, so good. None of this would offend even the most committed environmentalist. But there is more to the Bible than appreciation of nature. For one thing, the main object of all the praise is not nature, but God. The Creator, not the creation, is the focus. We learn in Chapter 1 of Genesis that the people of the Bible did not see nature as creating itself, nor existing for itself. Whether you take the creation story literally or not, the key idea in it is that things exist because God created them. No cosmic accidents here.

And no idolatry either. One of the Ten Commandments specifically forbids the people from creating idols: "You shall not make for yourself a carved image, or any likeness of anything that is in heaven above, or that is in the earth beneath, or that is in the water under the earth" (Exodus 20:4). The author of Exodus was obviously familiar with the religions of the peoples that surrounded Israel. They created idols that looked like people, like animals, and like some grotesque merging of the two. (The Egyptians, as you probably know, were noted for having gods with human bodies and the heads of birds and animals.) The Hebrews worshiped an invisible God who had specifically told them not to make any visual image of him. The main idea: focus your attention on the real God, not on an idol, and not on any part of the created world. We can only assume that Moses, who delivered the Ten Commandments to Israel, would not have been too pleased with the LOVE YOUR MOTHER bumper stickers.

But this is not the main problem that environmentalists have with the Bible. The main bone of contention is the idea of *human dominion*. This idea appears very early. When man is created, God says, "Let us make man in our image, after our likeness. And let them have dominion over the fish of the sea and over the birds of the air and over the livestock and over all the earth and over every creeping thing that creeps on the earth" (Genesis 1:26). You can almost hear eco-radicals saying "ouch!" Another "ouch!" statement is found in Genesis 9, where God is speaking to Noah and his sons after the great flood subsides: "Be fruitful and multiply and fill the earth. The fear of you shall be upon every beast of the field and upon every bird of the heavens, upon everything that creeps on the ground and all the fish of the sea. Into your hand they are delivered."

Not only has God repeated the "have dominion" command that he gave to Adam, but he has told human beings to "be fruitful and multiply." Here, in Genesis 9:1–2, is the one item in the Bible that environmentalists use to beat Christians with. God's words to Noah, so they say, give people free rein not only to exploit the earth, but to overpopulate it as well. In nations that have been historically Christian, pollution and overpopulation are due to those words in Genesis 9.

Is it true?

It *is* true that Americans and Europeans have at times been careless with the environment. It's also true that Americans and Europeans have had the most advanced technologies. We have no way of knowing whether non-Christians, if they'd had access to the same technologies, would have been equally careless with the earth. The former Soviet Union, a nation that was explicitly atheistic and anti-

Christian, was home to the notorious nuclear accident at Chernobyl. We can hardly blame that on Genesis 9. We cannot blame Genesis 9 for the pollution that occurs in nations that are Hindu, Muslim, or Buddhist. Rene Dubois, a noted scientist and social philosopher, observed that "Judeo-Christian civilization has been no worse and no better than others in its relation to nature." But it is certainly getting more blame at the moment.

In fact, we really cannot blame any environmental problems on Genesis 9. Factories that used to dump their chemicals into lakes and rivers were not motivated by the Bible's command to "have dominion" over the earth. They were motivated by the convenience of the lake nearby. It is human nature to exploit everything—nature, other human beings, whatever. Christians at least have the Bible to remind them that they do not *own* the earth. People are, according to the Bible, only God's *tenants* on earth. While people are to "have dominion" over the earth (which includes such necessary things as farming, of course), it all belongs to God.

15

A Cold Shower on an Old Misbelief

"The Bible is anti-sex."

On a "Jay-walking" segment of the *Tonight Show,* host Jay Leno took to the streets to ask people some basic questions about the Bible. He asked one woman if she could name any of the Ten Commandments. Her reply: "Well, um, they say that—well, you can't do anything." This got a laugh from the audience. But it probably reflects a pretty common view of the Bible: the Bible is an "anti" book, a book that tells you "you can't do anything," a book that tells you that everything you like to do is sinful. In this view, God is the great Cosmic Killjoy, and the Bible is the Killjoy Book. Especially in regard to sex.

Is it really anti-sex? Consider a few passages:

"Your two breasts are like two fawns, twins of a gazelle that graze among the lilies."

"Behold, you are beautiful, my love . . . your eyes are like doves."

"Your lips are like a scarlet thread, and your mouth is lovely."

"His body is polished ivory, bedecked with sapphires. His legs are alabaster columns, set on bases of gold."

"Your stature is like a palm tree, and your breasts are its clusters. I say I will climb the palm tree and lay hold of its fruit."

"His left hand is under my head, and his right hand embraces me."

You may have guessed that these are from the Song of Solomon in the Old Testament. This is one of the most curious books in the Bible, since it never mentions God and seems to have no religious meaning at all. It seems to be nothing more than exchanges of sentiments between a man and woman who are about to be married and who feel a powerful erotic attraction for each other. It's true that both Jews and Christians have tried to find a "deeper" meaning in it. Jews have said that it is "really" a book about God's love for Israel. Christians have said it symbolizes God's love for the church. Both Jews and Christians have said it symbolizes God's love for the human soul.

Maybe. But sometimes we have to go with the obvious. And obviously the Song of Solomon is about the attraction of a man and woman. Much of that attraction is physical. And it is part of the Bible. So if the Bible is anti-sex, it isn't *all* anti-sex.

It certainly is not anti-children, and in the ancient world people definitely connected the two. Birth control wasn't very advanced in ancient times, and most people didn't want it to be. You don't have to read too far in the Old Testament to learn that women are horrified at not being able to bear children. Most parents want as many as possible. The patriarch Jacob is the father of twelve sons, and that large number is not at all unusual. And we can assume that, human nature being what it is, they did not regard sex as just a burdensome duty done for the sake of producing children.

The Bible never once says that sex itself is a bad thing. In fact, it takes a pretty earthy and practical view: people want sex, both because they enjoy it and because it leads to children. In the Old Testament Law, we find this: "When a man is newly married, he shall not go out with the army or be liable for any other public duty. He shall be free at home one year to be happy with his wife whom he has taken" (Deuteronomy 24:5). In other words, among the Israelites a man got a "marriage leave." His marital bliss was, for one year anyway, more important than military service.

The Book of Proverbs has a down-to-earth view of sexuality. "Rejoice in the wife of your youth, a lovely deer, a graceful doe. Let her breasts fill you at all times with delight; be intoxicated always in your love" (5:18–19). Doesn't sound anti-sexual, does it? In fact, the Proverbs don't say much about sex at all, but what they do say is pretty positive. However, the book does contain warnings about adultery and prostitution. Chapters 5 through 7 are a stern warning about what befalls the man who pursues an adulterous relationship.

That brings us back to the beginning of this chapter, and to the woman who says the Bible tells us "we can't do anything." Well, "anything" is a pretty broad category. But in fact, the Bible does tell us we can't commit adultery. It is one of the Ten Commandments (Exodus 20:14). You could hardly call that anti-sex. Even the tacky TV "scream shows" confirm the fact that people today still condemn adultery. No one particularly likes to learn that his or her spouse is sleeping with someone else. We may not take it quite as seriously as the Israelites did (it could lead to the death penalty), but it is still serious. Most married people still believed that sexual pleasure isn't totally "footloose and fancy-free"; it ought to have some restrictions.

Some of those restrictions involve incest. You will find these in the Old Testament (see Leviticus 18), but in fact they are pretty much universal. No society, no matter how loose its sexual standards, has smiled upon incest. The various brother–sister, mother–son, father–daughter pairs that show up on TV scream shows are loudly booed by the audiences. In some ways, things have not changed so much since ancient times. There is still the powerful feeling, down in the gut, that there are some things that are just plain *wrong*.

What about premarital sex? We have to admit that the Old Testament does have a kind of double standard. (So has most of the world, until very recently.) Men were not necessarily expected to be virgins when they married, but women were. Female virginity was prized, as shown by the law that Israel's priests could only marry virgins (Leviticus 21:13–15). A woman was expected to guard her virginity, and if a man tried to force himself on her, she had to cry out for help. If she did not, she became a party to the rape and was held to be as guilty as the man (Deuteronomy 22:23–24).

If you comb through the Bible looking for passages that deal with sex, you may be surprised: there isn't that much there. The Book of Leviticus, for example, consists of 27 chapters of rules governing Israel. Only one chapter (18) deals with sexual relations. Of the 34 chapters in Deuteronomy, only a section of Chapter 22 is devoted to sexual matters. I've already mentioned that Proverbs, that wise and practical book about daily life in the world, says nothing about sex, except to enjoy it within marriage and stay away from adultery and prostitution.

What about the Prophets? This last section of the Old Testament, from Isaiah to Malachi, presents these men as speaking the word of God to the people. Sometimes they speak comfort and hope, but often they denounce the people's sins and order them to repent. Did the prophets say much about sex? Frankly, no. They do condemn, very often, people of Israel who worshiped false gods. Sometimes that worship involved practices that you might call "religious orgies." Sex with "shrine prostitutes," both female and male, was often a part of pagan religion. When the prophets spoke out against this, they weren't so much anti-sex as anti-paganism. Far from being obsessed with sexual matters, the prophets spoke out more often about how the rich exploit and deceive the poor. They also spoke out against hypocrisy—talking the religious talk without walking the walk. People who observed the correct religious rituals but then abused and exploited their neighbors were a prime target for the prophets.

Summing up: the Old Testament (which, remember, includes the Song of Solomon) is neither anti-sex nor obsessed with sex.

What about the New Testament? A couple of major differences: for one thing, Christians view this world, and the next, differently from the Jews of the Old Testament. The Old Testament pretty much focused on life in this world, without much thought for the afterlife. So for the Jews, lots of children—the more the merrier—were good. Not so for Christians. They believed they would live forever in heaven. That didn't make life in this world unimportant. But it did mean that living well in this world, surrounded by a brood of children and grandchildren, wasn't so important.

Another difference: the Old Testament Jews inhabited their own nation, governed by the Law that God had given to Moses. The Christians of the New Testament lived in the Roman Empire, a pagan nation that often mocked Jews' and Christians' moral standards. If you want to understand the difficulty of Christians living in a pagan world, read 1 Corinthians, Paul's long letter to Christians in the Greek city of Corinth. The city was so notoriously immoral that the word *Corinthian* meant "prostitute." Even in the morally lax Roman Empire, Corinth had a bad reputation. So it is not surprising that in giving advice to Christians in Corinth, Paul inevitably had to talk about sexual morality. Chapters 5–7 of 1 Corinthians make up the New Testament's longest section dealing with sex. In the section, Paul does claim that Christians would be better off like himself—single and free to devote themselves fully to Christian service. But Paul is too sensible to demand celibacy of everyone. "If they cannot exercise self-control, they should marry. For it is better to marry than to be aflame with passion" (7:9). Not exactly pro-sex, but hardly anti-sex. In fact, Paul instructs married Christians "Do not deprive one another" of sexual relations (7:5).

Paul is not, by the way, responsible for the Catholic Church's insistence on celibacy for its priests. Granted, he did say that it is "better" for pastors to be single, free of family entanglements. But elsewhere in his letters he assumes that most of these men are married with children (see 1 Timothy 3:1–13, Titus 1:5–6).

The Roman Empire was home to more than just lustful pagans. There were also many religious cults that really were anti-sex—not only anti-sex, but anti-body and even anti-matter. Some of these are called by the broad name of *Gnostic.* Most of the Gnostics taught that matter itself was plain evil, that the best that people could do was to divorce themselves as much as possible from the material world. So Christians were living among people who offered them some interesting alternatives: the lustful pagans ("If it feels good, do it—don't be so uptight") and the anti-material Gnostics ("You call yourself religious and you engage in *sex?* Yuck!") Paul, though he was single himself, had no use for these anti-material types. Raised as a Jew, he believed that the world was God's creation and that material things were not evil in themselves. So he warned Christians to have nothing to do with the false anti-material religions: "Do you submit to regulations—'Do not handle. Do not taste. Do not touch'—according to human precepts and teachings?" (Colossians 2:21). Avoid such things, Paul commanded. He also warned against false teachers "who forbid marriage and require abstinence from foods that God created to be received with thanksgiving. . . . For everything created by God is good, and nothing is to be rejected if it is received with thanksgiving" (1 Timothy 4:1–5). So "everything created by God is good"—including the human sexual appetite. That is the view of the New Testament. It is also the view of the New Testament that the sexual urge is to strictly kept (by both men and women) within the bounds of marriage. That doesn't always please people today, but you can't really call it "anti-sex."

16

A Great Story for a Buddy Movie

"David and Jonathan were homosexual lovers."

Not so long ago, the subject of homosexuality wasn't discussed much in religious circles. Christians generally believed that the practice was condemned in both the Old and New Testaments, that it had been condemned throughout Christian history, that it was and always will be a sin in God's eyes, case closed. But the rise of the gay rights movement reopened discussion of the subject. The traditional Christian view was put on the defensive for the first time in centuries. Many Christians, including many clergymen, came forward to condemn the traditional view of homosexuals. In doing so, they had to face the problem of the Bible. Could the Bible be interpreted so as to tolerate—or even approve of—homosexual behavior?

The prospects did not look good. The first reference to homosexuality in the Bible is in the sordid tale of the wicked cities of Sodom and Gomorrah, places so evil that God destroyed them with fire and brimstone from heaven (Genesis 19). Living in Sodom with his two daughters, Lot is rescued from the city's destruction by two angels, whom he has invited to his home. The men of Sodom demand that Lot bring the visitors out "that we may know them"—and *know* in this context clearly means "carnal knowledge." This story is, of course, at the root of the term *sodomy.*

The Old Testament Law is pretty clear in denouncing and prohibiting homosexual relations. The nations surrounding Israel had a different view, however. Sexual relations with "sacred prostitutes" was a feature of fertility religions, and the "sacred prostitutes" were both male and female. The people of Israel sometimes strayed into these pagan rites, but Israel's prophets always condemned such behavior.

In the New Testament, we find no word from Jesus himself regarding the subject. We have to assume that, as a devout Jew, he accepted and approved the Jewish standard of sexual morality. We definitely know that the apostle Paul did, for Paul made it clear in his epistles that homosexuality was an abomination in the eyes of God (see 1 Corinthians 6:9). In Romans 1:26–27, Paul claimed that homosexual behavior is a sign of just how depraved human beings are. Traveling as a Christian missionary around the Roman Empire, Paul was clearly sickened by the sexual practices of the Greeks and Romans. He made it clear to Christians that they had to steer clear of such loathsome behavior. Such vile people could not, Paul said, enter heaven.

So homosexuality in the Bible is treated pretty consistently: it is wrong.

But what about David and Jonathan? Theirs is one of the great friendships in human history, certainly the most famous friendship in the Bible. "The soul of Jonathan was knit to the soul of David, and Jonathan loved him as his own soul. . . . Then Jonathan made a covenant with David, because he loved him as his own soul" (1 Samuel 18:2–3). Jonathan was the son of Israel's first king, Saul. David was the shepherd boy who gained fame by slaying the giant Philistine warrior, Goliath. Jonathan was apparently deeply impressed by the spunky David. So was Jonathan's father, but in a different way: Saul was jealous of David's fame, so jealous that on more than one occasion Saul tried to kill David. David married Saul's daughter Michal, but his position as son-in-law did not endear him to the peevish Saul. Jonathan did whatever he could to protect David from his father's wrath. When both Saul and Jonathan died after fighting the Philistines, David mourned their deaths—especially

Jonathan's. "I am distressed for you, my brother Jonathan; very pleasant have you been to me, your love to me was extraordinary, surpassing the love of women" (2 Samuel 1:26).

"Surpassing the love of women"? Hmmm. Yes, that does sound pretty deep. So, were these two men homosexuals? One thing that is certain about David: he certainly loved women—a *lot*. He had numerous wives and concubines, and his lust for the married Bathsheba led him to arrange her husband's death so he could have her. Jonathan himself married and had children. People today are wise enough to know that men can marry and father children and still be homosexuals. Was this the case with David and Jonathan? Obviously we cannot know for certain. But consider this: the ancient Israelites had, obviously, a horror of homosexuality. Given this, how likely is it that the Old Testament would have recorded this extremely deep friendship . . . if it had been more than a friendship? If there was any suspicion that David and Jonathan had engaged in sexual relations, the author of 1 Samuel would have been wise to delete any references to the love of the two men.

There was, obviously, some deep male bonding here. The two men were courageous warriors, brothers in arms. Jonathan gave David not only brotherly affection, but also unselfishness, loyalty, and helpfulness. He saved David's life, and somehow managed tactfully to be Saul's faithful son while being David's faithful friend. He did so despite Saul's prediction (which proved true) that David would one day be king instead of Jonathan. This is the friend most men could only dream of having.

But what about David's statement that their love "surpassed the love of women"? Well, 1 and 2 Samuel make it pretty clear that the amorous David had many wives and many children—but not much satisfaction on the home front. His children were most often a thorn in his side; ditto for some of the wives. (Polygamy pretty much rules out having your wife as your best friend.) Jonathan, while he lived, was the most reliable and loyal person in David's life. David had several wives and concubines, but only one supreme "buddy."

17

Executing Justice

"The commandment 'Thou shalt not kill' means we should prohibit capital punishment."

You might say that Christianity got its start with capital punishment. Jesus was executed by crucifixion, and the Book of Acts records that James, one of Jesus' disciples, was executed by beheading. Tradition has it that the apostles Paul and Peter both were executed during persecution of Christians by the vile Roman emperor Nero. Good men and women died for their faith. Thus Christians had martyr-heroes to honor, and this willingness to die impressed many unbelievers, some of whom became Christian converts.

If you think this is ancient history, think again. In many parts of Africa, Asia, and the Middle East, Christians are being executed today. The nations and cultures that kill them have no qualms about capital punishment.

But Americans and Europeans do. Europeans have pretty much ruled out the death penalty. In fact, many Europeans regard America as a barbaric place, a place that still executes criminals. When George W. Bush was running for president in 2000, he got a lot of flak over the number of executions in Texas, the state where he was governor. Liberals liked to portray Texas—and its governor—as relics of a bygone era. We should not kill criminals, so the sentiment goes. We should try to rehabilitate them or, as a last resort, give them life imprisonment. Just as civilized people no longer whip people publicly or put them in stocks or mutilate them, so they should no longer take life.

A lot of Christians have lent their support to the crusade against capital punishment. In their view, killing another human being is wrong, even if that human being has committed horrible crimes. A number of well-known church figures, including many Catholic bishops, have stated that the death penalty should be abolished. At the same time, many Christians believe that in the case of truly loathsome crimes, the criminal should suffer the ultimate penalty. Particularly in the case of multiple murderers, there is a feeling that the criminal has taken so many lives that he has forfeited his own right to live. The debate continues, and there is no final court of appeal to decide what *the* Christian position on capital punishment should be.

One thing is for sure: the Old Testament cannot be used as a weapon against capital punishment. If you browse through the first five books of the Bible, you will see that God himself actually commanded the death penalty for certain crimes—not just for murder (which fits the "eye for an eye" pattern) but also for blasphemy (Leviticus 24:13), adultery (Leviticus 20:10), striking a parent (Exodus 21:15), laboring on the Sabbath (Numbers 15:32), witchcraft (Exodus 22:18), and other offenses. These were not just "paper laws"—executions were actually carried out. Stoning, in which the community itself carried out the execution, was the preferred method. Israel took its position as God's chosen people very seriously. They were told to be holy, for God was holy. They could not be holy if they were "soft on crime."

What about those famous words in the Ten Commandments, "Thou shalt not kill"? This is what the King James Version has in Exodus 20:13. With all respect to the King James translators, this was a poor choice of words. The meaning of the Hebrew here is not "kill" but "murder," which is what all modern translations have. Of course, anyone could probably figure this out from the context. It is quite obvious in Exodus that "killing" in the sense of "executing" is allowed in some instances, but "murder" is not. In short, the Ten Commandments do not prohibit us from killing—they prohibit us from murdering, which is quite a different thing.

Since the teaching of Jesus is supposed to set the standard for

Christians, we have to ask: what did Jesus think of capital punishment? Well, we know that he allowed himself to suffer it, ordering his disciples not to resist those who arrested him. Guilty of no crime, he accepted the death penalty. Jesus' crucifixion is a painful reminder that sometimes "justice" is injustice. Good people can be legally destroyed. But whether Jesus would have approved of the execution of, say, a serial killer, we simply don't know.

Jesus' crucifixion is a painful reminder that sometimes "justice" is injustice.

The Bible records one case in which Jesus was confronted with an almost-execution. This is the famous story in John 8 of the woman caught in adultery. As her accusers reminded Jesus, under the Jewish Law she could be legally stoned to death. Jesus uttered the famous words, "Let him who is without sin among you be the first to throw a stone at her" (John 8:7). Her accusers walked away one by one, and Jesus told her to go and "sin no more." Does this indicate he disapproved of the death penalty altogether? Hard to say.

And the debate goes on.

18

Saying "Punish My Enemies, God" With a Smile

"The Bible is vicious and mean-spirited, as you can see in several of the Psalms."

Many of the Old Testament's Psalms are lovely hymns of praise to God—many, but not all. A few of the Psalms call for God's swift vengeance upon an enemy. These are called the *imprecatory* Psalms (the word means "calling down a curse"), and they are Psalms 2, 37, 69, 79, 109, 137, and 143. In today's lingo, they are "mean-spirited"—the rantings of someone who believes he is righteous, calling for God's brutal smashing of his enemies. Consider one of the most famous imprecatory rants, Psalm 137, written as a lament of people conquered by the cruel Babylonians: "O daughter of Babylon, doomed to be destroyed, blessed shall he be who repays you with what you have done to us! Blessed shall be he who takes your little ones and dashes them against the rock!" (137:8–9).

Christians have for centuries been bothered by these Psalms. They seem cruel and vindictive—not exactly "Christian." But stop and consider: the author of these Psalms was not taking vengeance into his own hands (which the Bible forbids). He was asking God, the Righteous One, to reward the good and punish the wicked—something that Christians can agree with. While we may not like the stark tone of these Psalms, they remind us of something: God will ultimately destroy evil.

19

The Silliness of Sacrificing Tofu

"The Bible's emphasis on blood and sacrifice proves its authors were insensitive and inhumane."

There is no point in denying the obvious: the Bible says a *lot* about sacrifice and blood. The idea that Jesus Christ offered himself up as a sacrifice for human sin is a key belief of Christianity. That belief is evidenced by the millions of crucifixes in homes and churches around the world. It shows up in thousands of hymns, which speak of the "precious blood of Jesus" and the "fountain filled with blood" that cleanses sinners. In the Christian Communion service, people take wine (or juice) and bread to remind them of Jesus' body and blood. Until relatively recent times, none of this shocked or offended many people.

Nowadays, many people, including many Christians, believe they are more sensitive. Many churches no longer sing the old hymns about the blood of Jesus. Crucifixes are less common than they used to be. Our squeamishness about blood and sacrifice is kind of amusing when you think about the video games and movies that revel in violence and death.

One reason that blood offends us is that we are pretty far removed from it. The animals we eat are usually not killed in front of us. Animal rights groups like to publicize the unpleasant conditions of slaughterhouses, but most people manage not to think about it. We see animal flesh on our plates, usually bloodless. We don't make much of a connection between that food and how it got there.

But people in biblical times did. For them, animal sacrifice and killing an animal for food were the same thing, a thing they saw often. If animals are eaten, obviously they have to be killed. In the Bible, and in many other cultures, the necessary killing got coupled with the notion of sin: a lamb is killed on your behalf, and before you eat it, its bleeding and death are a reminder that you sinned in some way. Sacrifices were a kind of "visual aid," putting together something pleasant (eating meat) with a profound thought (something gave up its life so you could have food) and another profound thought (this creature's death was done on your behalf, because you sinned).

Sacrifice was more than a sin offering. It could be a "thank-you" to God. The first mention of sacrifice in the Bible is after Noah leaves the ark. He builds an altar and sacrifices animals to God. Afterward, God tells Noah that all creatures are to be food for mankind. (Does this mean people were vegetarians before that? We aren't sure. See pages 229–232.) At any rate, God is pleased with the animal sacrifice. Now, clearly, God himself does not eat animals. People who offered up animals "to God" ate the animals themselves (or gave them to the priests, in some cases). There was a sense of "sharing a meal with God."

But it is the "sin offering" of the Jewish religion that concerns us most, because this is the sort of sacrifice the New Testament gives so much attention to. In the sin offering, the guilty person laid his hands on the head of the sacrificial animal (it was either a bull or goat). This touching identified the person with the animal victim. The beast became his substitute—not that folks actually believed that they "passed on" their sins to the animal; you might say the animal died "on their behalf." After the priest killed the animal, its blood was sprinkled on the altar. The purpose of the ritual: purify the sinner and reestablish the relationship with God.

The animal used in the sin offering had to be "unblemished." Naturally, the early Christians believed that the sinless Jesus was the perfect sin offering. He, the sinless victim, died on behalf of sinners. And while the sacrifices of animals had to be repeated again and again in Judaism, the sacrifice of Jesus was the final sacrifice (Hebrews 10). No more sacrifices were required, which is why Christianity has no animal sacrifices. However, the Communion service is a kind of reminder of Jesus' sacrifice, since the bread and wine remind the people of his death.

You might say the whole New Testament is overflowing with blood—Jesus' blood, to be specific. The people living in those days would have had no trouble connecting with the idea of Jesus as sacrifice. Not just the Jews, but Greeks and Romans and others, were familiar with sacrifice. The basic idea was the same for everyone: we need to "get right" with God (or the gods), and something has to die to make it right. In the Christian view, the thing that died to enable us to "get right with God" was the perfectly sinless human being—who also happened to be God's Son (Romans 3:25, 8:3).

Worth noting: the Jews did not practice human sacrifice. Neither did the Greeks or Romans (usually, anyway). Human sacrifice has been common in some places, notably among the Aztecs, who might slaughter hundreds of human victims at a single ceremony. But the first Christians were not horrified at the idea of Jesus being a sacrifice because he *volunteered.* He was not only an innocent victim (like the bull or goat) but a victim who *chose* to die on behalf of others. That choice is mentioned many times in the New Testament.

If the Bible is "dripping with blood," the New Testament at least did away with the old system of animal sacrifices. This was long overdue. Non-Jews who converted to Judaism were deeply impressed with the Jews' morality and their teachings about the one loving God. But when these converts came to pay their respects to the holy city of Jerusalem, they saw that the Jewish temple was a slaughterhouse. Where, they wondered, did all this animal killing fit in with that highly ethical religion that had attracted them? And then there was the hypocrisy factor: long before Jesus, Israel's prophets proclaimed that honoring God and loving your neighbor were really more important than the system of sacrifices. The prophet Amos spoke out against people just "going through the motions" of the rituals, claiming that God did not accept the offerings of hypocrites (Amos 5:21–24). And consider the words of Micah: "Will the LORD be pleased with thousands of rams, with ten thousand rivers of oil? . . . He has told you, O man, what is good; and what does the LORD require of you but to do justice and to love kindness and to walk humbly with your God?" (6:7–8). The prophets were aware of what can happen with any religious ritual: people do it out of habit and forget the meaning it is supposed to have.

Back to the beginning of the chapter: were the Bible's authors a bunch of crude, insensitive slobs? No. The New Testament does mention the blood of Jesus many times, but not because the authors were inhumane. They took Jesus' death *very* seriously. They spoke often of his blood and the cross to remind Christians of something important: Jesus wasn't just another wise teacher walking around saying beautiful words—he died the nastiest kind of death that people at that time could imagine. Jesus did not save people through his preaching. He saved people because, in some way no one can fathom, he made things right with the God who is angry at human sin. There are other ways of describing how Jesus made us "right with God." But it happens that the Bible uses images people were familiar with: sacrifice, blood, death.

A culture that allows children to play video games in which they continually annihilate other beings is in no position to sneer at the crudeness of the Bible.

PART III

WHAT THE REAL SKEPTICS SAY

NOAH AND THE ARK
The flood story is just another rehash of ancient myths . . . or is it?

20

Are More Witnesses Better, or Just Confusing?

"The Gospels aren't reliable because they report details of Jesus' life in different ways."

The phrase *he said, she said* has become part of our language. Kevin and Brittani split up, each has a different version of why. In movies and TV, a familiar comic device is to have the same event told and retold by different people who experienced it. Naturally the stories are wildly different. People do tend to tell about events so as to reflect well on themselves. It's hard to be objective, particularly when your own ego is involved.

In fact, it's hard to be objective about anything. You know this if you have ever been in a courtroom. Witnesses who saw something happen can vary a lot about the details, even when they themselves have no stake in the trial's outcome. A car runs a stop sign and crashes into another car; four people on the sidewalk see it. In court, their stories are very similar but never quite the same. What was the weather like that afternoon, witnesses? "Sunny." "Somewhat overcast, as I recall." "Cloudy, because I remember it rained later that day." "I'm not sure." Four liars? Three liars and one person telling the truth? Or four basically honest people who saw an event in slightly different ways?

The Bible presents us with four Gospels. No, scratch that—the church has never believed there were four Gospels. There is only *one* Gospel, *gospel* being the "good news" about Jesus Christ. You catch this idea in the titles of the four: the Gospel According to Matthew, the Gospel According to Mark, et cetera. Just one Gospel, as reported by four authors.

Why four? One would have sufficed, of course. You could get the basic facts from any one of the four: Jesus is the Son of God, the Messiah (Christ) sent by God to save humans from their sins. He taught, performed miracles, angered the religious establishment, and was killed by crucifixion. He was buried but raised to life by God, then afterward ascended into heaven. All four Gospels have that in common.

> Among the four Gospels, each includes valuable tidbits that the others leave out.
>
> 

But then, none of them is quite like the other. Each one has details the others lack. Take the birth of Jesus, for example: Mark and John have nothing to say about the subject. Matthew and Luke do, but the details are different. Both say Jesus was born in Bethlehem, but Luke reports the visit of the shepherds while Matthew reports the visit of the wise men. Thanks to both accounts we have a fuller image of what the first Christmas was all about. If you were the judge in the courtroom, you would be thankful that there were two accounts of an important event instead of just one.

You don't need to be bogged down by all the terminology the Bible scholars use. But one useful term is *Synoptic Gospels*. Matthew, Mark, and Luke are known as the Synoptics. The Greek word *synoptikos* means "see together." These three do "see together," reporting most of the same acts and teachings of Jesus, often using the same wording. The three differ in many ways from John, which records a number of events and teachings that the Synoptics leave out.

But the problem that rattles many skeptics, and many Christians, is this: when the Gospels report the same event, the details do not always match. I can give a few examples here, but there are lots more. You can find at a library or bookstore a reference book known as *Gospel Parallels* that sets Matthew, Mark, and Luke in three columns so you can see at once how they differ in the details.

One example: Matthew and Luke report how Jesus healed the servant of a Roman centurion (Matthew 8:5–13, Luke 7:1–10). In both accounts, the story takes place in the village of Capernaum. In both accounts, the centurion believes that Jesus can perform the healing without even setting foot in the man's house. In both accounts, Jesus is deeply touched by the man's faith. In Luke's account, Jesus says, "I tell you, not even in Israel have I found such faith." Matthew has those words, too, but adds something else: "I tell you, many will come from east and west and recline at the table with Abraham, Isaac, and Jacob in the kingdom of heaven, while the sons of the kingdom will be thrown into the outer darkness. In that place there will be weeping and gnashing of teeth." Why the difference? Matthew might have remembered a detail that Luke did not know of. Or Luke might have known of those additional words but chosen not to include them. Obviously the Gospels do not include everything that happened to Jesus. The authors had to pick and choose. Examples like the one here don't show contradiction. It is a matter of one author (Matthew, in this case) leaving in some detail that another author (Luke) left out.

This is the main reason why John's Gospel is in the New Testament. If you compare it with the other three, you immediately sense that John is giving a lot of information that the other three did not include. One example: the well-known story of Jesus turning water into wine at a wedding (John 2:1–12). This story does not contradict the other Gospels. It supplies a beautiful story that they, for whatever reason, did not include. As in the courtroom, we are glad there are four witnesses, not just one. We get more information that way.

What about outright contradictions? Some of these are, everyone admits, extremely minor. Take the famous story of Jesus casting out the demons from a violent man who lived among tombs. In Mark 5 and Luke 8, there is one man possessed by demons. Jesus sends the demons into a herd of pigs nearby. The frenzied pigs rush into the water. Matthew 8:28–34 reports the same event, but with a noticeable difference: there isn't one demon-possessed, but two. Hmmm.

Why the difference? Was Matthew lying? Or were Mark and Luke wrong? The bigger question: does it make any difference, since the main point of the story is that Jesus worked a miracle in the life of a pathetic and dangerous man—or perhaps two men? You will find several of these "numerical" difficulties in the Gospels. Most of them are pretty petty.

But we have to admit there are some contradictions that are bothersome. Take the incident known as the cleansing of the temple. All four Gospels tell us that Jesus visited the temple of Jerusalem, where he was offended at seeing the courtyard filled with livestock and money changers. Using a whip made of cords, he overturned the money changers' tables and drove them out of the temple. The importance of the story: Jesus affirms that the temple is a place of worship, not a place of commerce. But the chronology is the problem: in Matthew, Mark, and Luke, the event occurs toward the end, shortly before Jesus is crucified. But John's Gospel has it near the beginning of his public life. Possibilities: there were two such incidents, or John has the chronology right, or John has it wrong, or John placed it near the beginning of the story for reasons of his own. Which option? We don't know.

Another contradiction that troubles some readers: there are two genealogies for Jesus, and they don't match. The one in Matthew traces Jesus' line all the way back to the patriarch Abraham. Luke's goes farther, all the way back to Adam. Both genealogies trace Jesus through Joseph, since Joseph was Jesus' legal father. But beyond Joseph, the genealogies are way, way different. Joseph's father in Matthew's version is Jacob; in Luke's version, he is Heli. Going back farther still, the names differ a lot. Both genealogies trace Jesus' family back to King David, but in Luke's version the line goes through David's son Nathan, while in Matthew's version the line goes through David's son Solomon. The scholars have spilled a lot of ink over this problem. There is no painting over the main problem, which is that the two family trees do not match. By the time Matthew and Luke wrote, Joseph was probably dead, so the two authors did the best they could to piece together family traditions about his descent.

If you are a real skeptic, you might conclude that Matthew or Luke—or both—was simply inventing the genealogy to make the point that Jesus was descended from Israel's great king, David. But considering how many wives and children David had, it isn't far-fetched to assume that a *lot* of Jews were descended from him. A good possibility is that Jesus had been taught that Joseph, his legal father, was a descendant of David, and that Jesus' disciples knew of this. Faced with a long gap between David and Joseph, Matthew and Luke might have "filled in" as best they could. Either author would have called this discussion nitpicky, since their main point is that Jesus was descended from David (Israel's most famous king) and Abraham (the ancestor of all the Jews). You can believe the Bible is divinely inspired without having to place much importance on the many tiresome genealogies found in it. (See 1 Chronicles 1–9 for the longest and most tedious of them all.)

People have been looking at the four Gospels through a microscope for close to two thousand years. If you are a believer, this is your position: *Yes, there are some differences in the Gospels, and even some contradictions, but they don't matter.* If you are a skeptic, or outright opponent, this is your position: *There are major differences and serious contradictions, and they do matter, because they mean that Christianity is based on lies.* There is no impartial judge to decide which position is best. As stated earlier, generations of Christians have been glad, not sad, that there are four Gospels instead of just one, since the four give us a powerful three-dimensional portrait of Jesus. Most of the differences of details are very minor matters that a courtroom judge would size up and say, "Well, that is to be expected when you have four different witnesses."

21

Check Your Calendars, Folks

"The New Testament is unreliable because it was written many centuries after the events."

Hairstyles change, clothing styles change, and idea styles change, too. Just as there is trendiness in shoes and skirts, there is trendiness in beliefs. This is definitely true in regard to beliefs about the Bible.

There was a period in the 1800s when liberal thinkers came up with a novel idea: Jesus never existed, and the whole New Testament was pure fiction, so Christianity was based on a pack of lies. No one seriously believes this today; even the fiercest enemies of Christianity believe Jesus did exist. But for a certain period in history, it was trendy to claim that you believed Jesus never existed.

Around one hundred years ago, there was a growing trend to believe that the New Testament was not what generations of Christians had believed it was. Traditionally Christians believed the New Testament had been written by the first generation of Christians—Matthew, Mark, Luke, and John (the authors of the four Gospels, the stories of Jesus' life), and Paul, Peter, James, and Jude (the Epistles and the Revelation). It was assumed that when readers picked up the New Testament, they were getting faithful reports written by eyewitnesses. In the case of Matthew's and John's Gospels, the stories had been written by two of Jesus' actual disciples. In the case of Mark's and Luke's Gospels, their stories were based on reports from the disciples. And the apostle Paul, the author of a huge part of the

New Testament, was well known as one of the earliest Christian missionaries.

But in the late 1800s and early 1900s, a trend arose against this traditional view. According to trendy thinkers, the New Testament was written later—*much* later—than anyone had thought. In fact, it was unlikely that any of it had been composed during the lifetimes of Jesus' original followers. It came much later, and since it was later, it was unreliable, because the original eyewitnesses of Jesus' activity had died off. Thus a lot of legend and even outright lies had crept into the Bible. The upshot of all this: the book that Christians kept as their standard of belief was basically unsound, unreliable. While there might be some kernels of historical truth in the New Testament, what we are stuck with is a perplexing mix of a little fact and a lot of myth.

To some extent, this view is still around. The group that calls itself the Jesus Seminar, composed of academic types with numerous degrees, meets to discuss which parts of the Gospels might be true. Their finding: not much.

But the winds of change continue blowing. One sign of this was in 1976 when an English bishop, John A. T. Robinson, published his book *Redating the New Testament.* Bishop Robinson had a reputation as quite a liberal. He had authored a very controversial book, *Honest to God* (published in 1963), in which he pushed for a "demythologized" Christianity that had cast aside the traditional view of the Bible. Somewhere between 1963 and 1976, however, Robinson changed course. He studied not only the New Testament itself, but also the various trends connected with its interpretation. He decided to overlook all the liberal trends in New Testament studies and try to determine just *when* the New Testament books were written. His conclusion: the whole New Testament had been completed by the year 70. Assuming Jesus was crucified around the year 30, it had been completed within forty years. Meaning: The New Testament was completed when there were still numerous people around who had known Jesus or known his disciples personally. So the authors were not free to make up stories, for there were people alive who could say, "Wrong! That never happened! I was there!"

Bishop Robinson never claimed that the New Testament was absolutely reliable in every detail. What he did claim was that it was composed within the lifetime of eyewitnesses. It was not written nearly as late as people had assumed. Put another way, he pretty much had come around to the traditional view of the New Testament. More conservative Christians probably said to themselves, "Yes, exactly what we have believed all along."

Robinson had his critics, of course. There are still plenty of liberal scholars who prefer the view that the New Testament was written much later than the lifetime of the apostles. But it's harder to maintain that view now than it was a hundred years ago.

Is the New Testament *true*? The scholars cannot decide that, of course. Faith is an important element. What scholars can do—as Robinson did—is examine the evidence carefully. In doing so, many of them reached the same conclusion Robinson did: the New Testament is very old, probably composed by the disciples of Jesus or by their immediate followers.

22

Galileo, the Earth, the Sun, and Some Really Stubborn Men

"The Bible says the earth is the center of the universe, a belief that led to persecution of great scientists like Galileo."

Mercy, this long-standing conflict between science and religion shows no sign of ending. It has been going on since the 1500s, and one of the key figures in the conflict was the Italian scientist Galileo, who taught the shocking theory that the earth was *not* the center of the universe. He locked horns with the Catholic authorities, who ordered him to be silent or suffer the consequences. Religion won the battle then, though now everyone knows Galileo was right. Galileo is still held up as an example of the enlightened scientist confronting stubborn, stupid religious folk. Somehow his ordeal is believed to symbolize science versus the Bible. It doesn't. Read on.

Let's begin with some basics: we all know that the earth revolves around the sun, and not vice versa. We know that—but we don't talk that way. We talk about the sun "rising" and "setting" just like ancient folks did. Why? Because, like them, we don't feel the earth moving. We feel we are perfectly still, so it *looks* as if the sun, stars, and planets were moving around us. We can forgive the people of ancient times for not knowing any better. How could they?

The man whom many people considered the greatest thinker and scientist of ancient times was Aristotle. He believed that the heavenly bodies moved around the earth, just as the common man believed. He added the detail that the planets and stars moved in transparent spheres around the earth.

An often forgotten fact about Christianity is that in the Middle Ages, theologians fell in love with Aristotle. He was "the Philosopher," the fount of most (but not all) wisdom. It was believed that the Bible taught man the way to salvation, and the writings of Aristotle taught everything else. One of the goals of medieval thinkers was to somehow merge Aristotle's wisdom with the divine wisdom of the Bible. Here is a Very Important Point: the Bible says very little about the earth and the solar system. What little it does say can be interpreted in different ways, so that you cannot really say the Bible "teaches" anything about the movements of sun and earth. Aristotle said much more, and he made it clear he believed the sun and stars moved around the earth. These beliefs were seconded several centuries later by the scientist Ptolemy, which is why we apply the name *Ptolemaic* to the view that the earth is the unmoving center of the universe.

In 1543, the Polish scientist Copernicus published his brilliant book proving that the earth moved around the sun, not vice versa. The book was published the year Copernicus died. Refining and defending his theory fell to a later generation, which included Galileo.

Back to the Bible: what does the Bible say about earth's movements? In the very beginning, Genesis 1, we are told only that God made the sun and moon (the "greater light" and the "lesser light") to separate day and night. God "set them in the expanse of the heavens to give light on the earth" (1:17). Nothing is there to indicate an earth-centered or sun-centered view of things.

But consider Joshua 10:12–14. Israel is fighting a battle with its enemies. Joshua, Israel's leader, prays, "Sun, stand still at Gibeon, and moon, in the Valley of Aijalon. And the sun stood still, and the moon stopped, until the nation took vengeance on their enemies." In short, Joshua prayed that time would "freeze" for a while. Did time miraculously "stand still" that day, or was there something so dramatic in the battle that time *seemed* to stand still? We can't decide that here, obviously. But the big question is, does the passage prove that the people then believed the earth was center of the universe? Not really.

Psalm 19:6 speaks of the sun: "Its rising is from the end of the heavens, and its circuit to the end of them." Anything shocking here? No. We still talk about the sun rising and setting. Psalm 19:6, like the passage from Joshua, doesn't prove much.

The Bible does have a couple of passages that hint that people believed that the earth moved through space. Job 9:6 speaks of God moving the earth, and Job 26:7 says that God "hangs the earth on nothing." Scientifically, those statements are true. Interestingly, when Galileo was on trial before the Catholic authorities, he cited both these verses as proof that his views could be squared with the Bible. His accusers did not buy this. In their condemnation of his views, they wrote, "The proposition that the sun is at the center of the world and does not move from its place is absurd and false and heretical, because it is expressly contrary to Holy Scripture."

Those words are important. As representatives of the Catholic Church, they could not state that Galileo's idea was "expressly contrary to the Greek philosopher Aristotle." But it was Aristotle, not the Bible, that guided their thinking, because, as we just saw, the little that the Bible tells about earth's location in the universe isn't much to go on.

Galileo's accusers were wrong. Galileo's belief that the earth rotated around the sun was right. But Galileo never tried to convince anyone that the Bible was wrong. In a letter to a friend, Galileo wrote that "the Holy Bible can never speak untruth—whenever its true meaning is understood." Galileo made no attempt to defend Aristotle's view of the earth, because he knew that Aristotle was just plain wrong. Still, the Catholic Church was at that time very attached to Aristotle. His science was quickly going out of style, but the church was slow to catch on. From 1633 on, Galileo was under house arrest and absolutely forbidden to publicize his views. Of course, his views won out eventually.

Summing up: the church court that condemned Galileo in 1633 said that his views were contrary to the Bible. They were mistaken. The church stubbornly held to the idea that the sun moved around the earth, not because of the Bible, but because of the outmoded teaching of Aristotle.

Galileo was not the victim of the Religion-versus-Science war. He was a victim of Outdated Science versus Corrected Science.

23

Keeping the Skeptics Amused

"The Bible claims that the world was created in 4004 B.C."

If you think the "creation or evolution" controversy has been settled for good, you haven't kept up with the news. Christians have pushed (sometimes successfully) to have "creationism" taught in schools, not necessarily replacing the teaching of evolution, but at least presented as an alternative. To give these people their due, most of them have been willing to accept that some species (not necessarily human beings) evolved over the centuries. And darn near everybody accepts the fact that the world was *not* created in 4004 B.C. That date still gets mentioned sometimes, mostly by people who like to use it to show how ignorant Christians are.

Well, in the first place, the Bible itself contains no dates within it. You will find them in footnotes and margins, but the Hebrew and Greek originals make no reference whatever to B.C. or A.D. They couldn't, since that method of numbering years did not exist in ancient times. The usual way of dating something was to connect a date with the reign of a certain ruler. Something happened in "the fifth year of the reign of Pharaoh Necho" or "the tenth year of the reign of Caesar Augustus" or "the year that King Uzziah died." For the people of the times, those dates were precise enough, though they pose problems for us now, centuries later.

The Bible begins, logically enough, with the creation of the world—"In the beginning," as Genesis 1:1 puts it. Not too many people now, whatever their religious beliefs might be, would care to fix a date to Genesis 1:1. Scientists seem certain that the earth is *millions* of years old. They also seem certain that it was not created in six days, as Genesis would have us believe. About the only common ground is that Genesis and the scientists both affirm that plants and animals existed before humans did.

So where did this date of 4004 B.C. come from? It came from the mind of a man who was both brilliant and saintly. His name was James Ussher, and he was born in Dublin, Ireland, in 1581. He became a minister and in time became the archbishop of Armagh, meaning he was head of the church in Ireland. Ussher took his duties seriously and was considered a model of Christian charity. He also wrote (in Latin) a curious book, *Annales Veteris et Novi Testamenti*—"Chronicles of the Old and New Testaments." Ussher hit upon an idea: since we know for certain the dates for a few key Bible events (such as the Babylonians' conquest of Jerusalem in 586 B.C.), we can work backward from there and figure out the dates for everything else in the Bible—including the creation of the world. How? Well, if you thumb through the Old Testament, you notice there are a lot of genealogies. In many of these, we are told how long the person lived. Ussher attempted something that, before computers, would have short-circuited most people's brains. Using the life spans of various men in the Old Testament, he determined that the world had been created in 4004 B.C.

Now, here is the shocker: he was correct—that is, he was correct *if* all the life spans mentioned in the Book of Genesis are correct. The most important of these is Adam, who is mentioned as living 930 years (Genesis 5:5). Ussher was able to work backward to Adam because he knew the ages of Jacob, Abraham, Noah, and so on, back to the Original Man himself. Knowing that Adam was 930 when he died, and knowing that Adam was created on the sixth day of creation, Ussher pegged the creation of the world to 4004 B.C.—more precisely, to October 23, 4004 B.C. (Adam, coming later that same week, was born/created on October 28.)

When Ussher published his book in the 1650s, no one was shocked or amused. The science of archaeology did not exist, carbon-14 dating did not exist, and most people who knew about his book applauded his brilliance. That included some Jews, who had earlier attempted to do the same thing Ussher did and came up with the date of 3761 B.C. The two dates are extremely close. In the Middle Ages, some Christian scholars attempted to calculate the date of the world's creation and came up with 3962 B.C. Some books written in the Middle Ages contain phrases such as *in the year of the world 5375, the year of our Lord 1413.*

No one bothered to improve on Ussher's amazing work, and many people believed the date deserved to be included in Bibles. And so it was, beginning in 1701 and continuing until relatively recent times. It could be found in footnotes to Genesis 1, in introductions to Genesis, or in general introductions to the whole Bible. And let us admit the obvious: until science began to prove otherwise, the date did no harm at all. (It did no particular good, either. Whether or not you know that Jesus was crucified around the year 30 has no bearing on your life, does it? Dates are useful for academic purposes, but the purpose of the Bible is to change lives, not to prepare you for *Jeopardy!*)

So to clarify: printed Bibles in the past *did* sometimes include the date 4004 B.C. in footnotes or marginal notes. The Bible itself—the actual text that the authors wrote in ancient times—contained no such date. Ussher was wrong, but wherever he is now, he is probably not too concerned.

24

The World's Most Recycled Story of Wetness

"The story of Noah and the flood is just a rehash of Middle Eastern myths."

First of all, be warned: I'm not going to try here to answer the question "Was there really a flood that covered the whole world?" But while there is some doubt about the flood being universal, there is no doubt that *stories about the flood are almost universal.*

Take ancient India, for example. Several centuries B.C., people were telling the tale of Manu, who is warned by a small fish that a great flood is about to occur. Manu builds a ship, and the fish (which has grown a lot) tows the ship to a mountain. When the waters subside, Manu comes out of the ship and offers the gods a sacrifice of butter and milk. From the sacrifice springs a woman, who becomes the mother of the human race.

The ancient Greeks had a more elaborate version. Zeus, chief of the gods, decides to destroy the human race. King Deucalion, warned by the half-god Prometheus of what is to come, builds an ark for himself and his wife, Pyrrha. Zeus floods the world (or at least, in some versions, all of Greece). Deucalion's ark floats for nine days and winds up on Mount Parnassus. When the waters subside, Deucalion exits the ark and makes a sacrifice. Zeus is pleased with the sacrifice and offers Deucalion whatever he wishes. Deucalion asks that he be allowed to multiply the human race. He throws stones over his shoulders, and these become men. His wife throws stones over her shoulders, and these become women.

Notice any similarities? A great flood, a big boat, a sacrifice, then the beginnings (or second beginnings) of the human race. Sound familiar? It should. It is strikingly similar to the story of Noah in Genesis.

These two aren't the only ones that are similar. Flood stories were told in America from Alaska to the tip of South America. They were told in Australia and the Pacific Islands. They were told in most parts of Asia and in many parts of Europe. (In Africa, for reasons we don't fully understand, there was a lack of flood stories.)

If you believe the Bible is inspired by God and that there was an actual Noah and an actual flood that covered the world, you probably have a good explanation for why these stories are universal: because it happened. From this point of view, the Noah story in Genesis is the original (and true version) of the story, while the other versions around the world are later (and distorted) versions.

On the other hand, if you are skeptical about the Bible in general, or skeptical about the oldest parts of Genesis in particular, you might have another explanation: the Noah story is just one of those common myths that crop up around the world. There are plenty of these. The familiar fairy tale of Cinderella, for example, is found around the world. The details vary, needless to say, but the core of the story is pretty constant. Ditto for the Noah story—so the skeptics say.

The skeptics especially like to point to a really old story from ancient Assyria, the tale of Gilgamesh. This myth has been found on clay tablets that may date back to 1900 B.C. In this story, the gods decide to destroy mankind. One of the gods warns the man Ut-napishtim, who builds a huge vessel and brings into it his family and animals. (In dimensions, his ark is considerably smaller than the one in Genesis.) The earth is submerged in the flood. Seven days later, the ark comes to rest on Mount Nisir. In another seven days, a dove, then a swallow, then a raven are sent out. The raven does not return, which is the signal it has found a place to alight upon. So the survivors come out of the ark and make a sacrifice, upon which the gods descend. The story says the gods "crowded like flies around the sacrifice."

Let's make some connections here: Assyria was fairly close to Israel. Of all the various flood stories in the world, its story is most similar to the one found in Genesis. It has not only the flood, the ark, a small handful of human survivors, and a sacrifice when the water subsides, but also a dove and a raven that are sent out to determine if dry land is yet available. Since the Gilgamesh story is so extremely old, skeptics assume that the Hebrews who wrote Genesis simply borrowed the Gilgamesh tale and altered it a bit. This means that the skeptics also assume that the Noah tale is as completely fictional as the Gilgamesh tale.

Archaeologists have a different take on the flood stories. Digging around in the clay of the Middle East, they've learned a lot from how various kinds of soil "layer" themselves. And they have learned that sometime between 4000 and 3000 B.C., there really was a phenomenal flood (or maybe a series of floods) in the area called Mesopotamia. (The area is Iraq today, Assyria and Babylonia in ancient times.) The archaeologists had no trouble believing that the great flood, or floods, could have caused such devastation that only a few people might have survived. And obviously those people would have found refuge on mountains somewhere.

Archaeologists have also found inscriptions that refer to "the flood." These inscriptions are not referring to legends but to actual events. The impression is that there was a flood (or floods) that was so devastating to human life that later generations referred to it as *the* flood. Skeptics and believers can find some common ground here: there really was a flood so amazing that human and animal life over a large area was destroyed.

Now, back to Noah. We have already seen some similarities between his story and the Gilgamesh story. But the differences are even more striking. To begin with, the story is set in a *moral* framework. "The LORD saw that the wickedness of man was great in the earth, and that every intention of the thoughts of his heart was only evil continually. And the LORD was sorry that he had made man on the earth, and it grieved him to his heart" (Genesis 6:5–6). God resolves to destroy the human race. "But Noah found favor in the eyes of the LORD." So, corrupt though the human race is, God is going to save Noah and his family from the disaster. "I will establish my covenant with you, and you shall come into the ark, you, your sons, your wife, and your sons' wives with you." And of course, the animals too. (But not *two* of everything. See pages 36–38.)

At the ripe age of six hundred, Noah sees the whole earth flooded. The flood continues forty days. The waters rise so high that even the mountains are covered. The waters "prevailed on the earth 150 days" (7:24).

Then the ark came to rest "on the mountains of Ararat." Noah opens a window in the ark and sends out a raven. We are not told what becomes of it. Noah sends out a dove, which returns to the ark because there is no place to alight. In another week, he sends out the dove again and it returns with a freshly plucked olive leaf. "So Noah knew that the waters had subsided from the earth." In another seven days, he sends the dove out again, and it does not return. Noah and his family and the beasts exit the ark, and are told by God to "be fruitful and multiply" (8:17).

Noah builds an altar and makes sacrifices to God. "And when the LORD smelled the pleasing aroma, the LORD said in his heart, 'I will never again curse the ground because of man. . . . While the earth remains, seedtime and harvest, cold and heat, summer and winter, day and night, shall not cease' " (8:21–22).

In the pagan flood stories, there is no connection between immorality and the flood. The gods decree a flood for no particular reason, and one man receives a warning about it for no particular reason. In the Noah story, the human race survives because of one good man. We aren't told, by the way, that Noah's sons were righteous. God declares that he will never destroy the world again, but he does so in the full awareness that human sin continues (8:21).

The story's Big Moral, which most people miss, is this: the human race survived because one man was righteous. You can see why the early Christians liked the Noah story so much: they saw the similarity between Noah and Christ, the righteous man who is the salvation of a sinful world.

Now, some would say that the morality of the Noah story proves it is *better* than the other flood stories. Does that necessarily make it any *truer?* Well, historically speaking, no. We have no way of proving with absolute certainty that the author of Genesis was not familiar with the Gilgamesh story. We also have no way of proving that the Gilgamesh story did not borrow from the Noah story. Both stories are ancient, so ancient that the evidence does not allow us to say, "Yes, this one is definitely older." The skeptics prefer to believe that the Gilgamesh tale came first. That way, the author of Genesis is not only uninspired but unoriginal, too. Let us admit that "the jury is still out" on this issue. But we can wrap up this chapter with an affirmation: no one has been able to prove that Genesis borrowed the flood story from the Gilgamesh story.

25

Legends Too Pretty to Throw Away

"The Bible says there were unicorns, just one more proof it is full of errors and legends."

Ah, unicorns. The lovely beast of legend, horselike, with its one long horn spiraling from its forehead. For an animal that never existed, it still has a powerful hold on people's imaginations. You can buy stuffed unicorns, statues, pillows, stationery, and whatnot. And yes, there are unicorn Web sites, which tells us that there are many collectors of unicorn bric-a-brac out there.

Unicorns go way back in history—way, way back. Unicorns have been found pictured on ancient Assyrian buildings. Many Greek and Roman authors described them and (even though they had never seen one, obviously) believed they were real. In one Greek document from about 400 B.C., the author claimed that a certain beast of India was the size of a horse, with a white body, a purple head, blue eyes, and, on its forehead, a long red horn pointed at the tip. Those who drank from its horn were protected from stomach ailments, epilepsy, and poison. Naturally, such a beast is fleet of foot and practically impossible to capture. Other Greek authors described such a beast, which they called, in Greek, *monoceros,* "one-horned." In Latin, it is *unicornis.*

Now, what about the Bible? Several places in the Old Testament mention a creature with the Hebrew name *re'em* (Numbers 23:22,

Job 39:9, Psalm 92:10). Whatever animal this referred to was horned and strong. The ancient Hebrews probably knew exactly what animal this was, but we do not. When the Hebrew was translated into Greek, the word chosen was *monoceros.* Making its way later into Latin, it was *unicornis.* And sure enough, the King James Version of 1611 has *unicorn.*

No, the King James translators were not idiots. But they were living in the 1600s, well before *National Geographic* magazine and the Discovery Channel. They were probably familiar with the wildlife of their native England, maybe the rest of Europe, too, and vaguely familiar with such exotic beasts as lions and leopards. But they really had no clue what the Hebrew *re'em* referred to. So they leaned on the old Greek and Latin versions and gave the English-speaking people a Bible with unicorns.

Do we have any clearer idea now of what the *re'em* was? It may have been the rhinoceros, a strong beast with a prominent horn on its nose. Many modern translations have *rhinoceros* where the King James Version had *unicorn.* But in all likelihood, the *re'em* was the creature known as *aurochs,* or wild ox. You will probably find most versions today using *wild ox.*

It is more correct, though certainly less interesting, than *unicorn.* However, it does disarm the scoffers who snicker at the Bible referring to creatures that never existed. (Of course, it is a leap of faith for anyone to say unicorns *never* existed. Numerous species have become extinct over the centuries. Why not unicorns? Scientists haven't dug up any unicorn fossils—yet.)

The old Bible versions were wrong in including unicorns. But the innocent error led to some colorful stories. The mythical beast came to have all kinds of Christian meanings. As the unicorn's amazing horn could, legend said, neutralize poison, so Christ neutralized man's sin. Paintings and tapestries from the Middle Ages show a unicorn standing by a lake with its horn in the waters. It is using its horn to purify the water so other creatures can drink from it. Legend had it that there was only one unicorn in the entire world—like Christ, the unique Son of God, the unicorn was one of a kind.

Worth mentioning: a favorite subject for painters has been Noah and the ark, with the fascinating train of animals stretching across the landscape. Next time you see a picture of this subject, look closely: in all likelihood, there are unicorns in the picture. Since the Bible mentions unicorns, this gave the artists freedom to paint the legendary creature.

Before we leave the unicorn, we should mention some other mythical beasts from the Old Testament. One of these is the satyr. In Greek mythology, satyrs were weird creatures of the wild places, having a manlike torso and arms, but with the hind legs, ears, and horns of a goat. The prophet Isaiah mentions them twice (13:21, 34:14)—in the King James Version, that is. The Hebrew word that the old versions translated as "satyr" referred to some shaggy creature of the wild, and most modern versions have "wild goat" instead. (Since the satyrs were supposed to be half goat, the King James Version was half right.)

Then there is the cockatrice. "The suckling child shall play on the hole of the asp, and the weaned child shall put his hand in the cockatrice's den" (Isaiah 11:8—King James Version, naturally). In the realm of legend, a cockatrice was a kind of serpent that could kill with its glance. It appears several times in the King James Version. As you might have guessed from this quotation from Isaiah, the Hebrew word was referring to some kind of snake. Most modern versions have *viper* or *adder* or a similar word.

And finally, dragons. Well, the wicked red dragon of the Book of Revelation really is supposed to be a dragon. But the King James Version of the Old Testament has several dragons, too—as in "Praise the LORD from the earth, ye dragons, and all deeps" (Psalm 148:7). Translators still puzzle over these "dragons"—the Hebrew words *tannim* and *tannin.* Whatever these were, they were unpleasant and frightening beasts, mentioned more than twenty times in the Old Testament. As proof that we still aren't quite sure what they were, consider the different words used in the modern versions instead of *dragon: serpent, whale, wolf, sea monster, sea creature,* and even *jackal.* You might wonder if some translation in the future will simply say "big nasty critter" and leave it at that.

26

The Name That Resembles *Hobbits*

"The Hittites mentioned in the Old Testament never even existed."

We often think of the Victorian period as an era of family-oriented entertainment, conventional morality, and religious conformity. But this same period was also a period of doubt. Many people, particularly intellectuals, were starting to doubt things that everyone took for granted. This included Christianity. Charles Darwin, the scientist who popularized the concept of evolution in the world, was a Victorian Englishman. In London, the same city where Charles Spurgeon attracted swarms to hear his sermons, a German named Karl Marx was putting together an atheistic philosophy that would later shake the world. The great mass of people still believed in the truths of Christianity and the Bible. But the intellectuals were doubting everything—the Bible, Christianity, and God.

Since the Bible was the foundation for Christianity, skeptics figured that if they could prove the Bible was full of errors, Christianity would fade away in embarrassment. The skeptics were relying on a new science, archaeology, to come to their aid. Archaeologists would (so the skeptics believed) be able to confirm that certain people and places in the Bible never existed. This would prove that the Bible was nothing but a collection of legends and fairy tales.

Of course, the skeptics overlooked one important factor: it is extremely difficult to prove something did *not* happen. It is fairly easy for a historian to prove that King Henry VIII lived in England in the 1500s. But it is difficult to prove that Tom Tyler, a farmer in northern England, lived in the same period—and also difficult to prove Tom did *not* exist. Archaeologists can only deal with what they do find, not with what they don't. The fact that archaeologists have never found the tomb of Israel's King Solomon does not prove that Solomon never existed. It simply means his tomb has not been found—yet.

But the skeptics thought they had found a major error in the Bible: the Old Testament refers many times to a nation called the Hittites. These were not one of the many minor tribes mentioned in the Bible. In fact, after the Egyptians, Babylonians, and Assyrians, they are probably the most important group in the early part of the Old Testament. According to Genesis, Abraham bought his future tomb from the Hittites (23:3–20) and Esau married Hittite wives (26:34). Later Israelites married Hittites (Judges 3:5–6, 1 Kings 11:1). The most famous Hittite in the Bible was David's great warrior Uriah, whose wife, Bathsheba, caught David's eye. More important for the archaeologists, Joshua 1:4 refers to a large chunk of the Middle East as "all the Hittite country."

What made the skeptics happy was that, with all the Bible's references to the Hittites, not one bit of evidence had been found to prove they ever existed. The diggers were turning up piles of evidence that the Egyptians, Babylonians, Assyrians, and Persians were real. But the Hittites? Not a particle. So, the skeptics claimed, they were an invention of the Bible's authors, just as the screenwriters for the *Star Wars* movies invented Wookiees and Ewoks. Amusing, but not real. And if the Bible's authors lied about the Hittites, couldn't they have lied about many other things?

But archaeology is a science, and science has to be open to new data. Just when the skeptics had written off the Hittites as completely fictional, a German archaeologist named Hugo Winckler struck a gold mine. More accurately, he found a treasury of clay—clay tablets at a site called Bogazkoy in Turkey. When all these tablets—written in the peculiar script called cuneiform—were deciphered, they confirmed that the site was the capital city of the "land of the Hatti." Further finds made it clear that the "Hatti" were the Hittites of the Old Testament. Even more important, the geographic details that the Old Testament provides about the Hittites have been pretty much confirmed by excavations.

Skeptics have learned over the years not to rely too heavily on archaeology to disprove the Bible. In fact, quite a few archaeologists are devout Christians and Jews. More often than not, what they find serves to build up faith instead of tear it down.

PART IV

THE PROBLEMS THE TRANSLATORS CAUSED

MOSES WITH THE TEN COMMANDMENTS
After he had been on Mount Sinai with God, Moses had horns on his head . . . or did he?

27

Truly Bare, or Barely?

"The Old Testament prophets Isaiah and Hosea walked around naked."

Did you ever wonder why people speak of being "stark naked" or "buck naked"? Isn't naked just, well, plain naked?

Not necessarily.

Let's take the word *bald*. If you say "Kevin is bald," you might mean "Kevin has some hair on the side but none on top" or "Kevin's head is as slick as a peeled onion." So if you said "Kevin is bald," someone might reply, "Totally bald?" Why? Because there are, yes, *degrees* of baldness.

But how could there be *degrees* of nakedness?

Very simple: in past times, our English word *naked* could mean "stark naked" but could also mean "inadequately or inappropriately clothed." The same is true of the Hebrew and Greek words that we translate "naked." The key idea is of being in a condition of shame and embarrassment. You would be ashamed at being seen at a mall totally nude. You would also be ashamed at being seen at a mall in your underwear. (Most people would, anyway.)

Take two steps backward, one step culturally, the other step chronologically: it is ancient Israel, and though the climate is warm much of the time, people do not walk around in shorts and tank tops. In fact, even when the weather is warm, men and women usually have their arms and legs pretty well covered. Men sometimes strip to the waist when they work, but rarely does a woman see a man in this condition.

While the ancient world had its equivalents of pornography, there was nothing like today's Internet and cable TV. People's imaginations could do whatever they liked, but they had to do so without visual stimulation. As we see in Genesis 9:20–27, people were expected to keep their bodies concealed, even around close family members. It may seem terribly prudish and repressive to us today, but it was part of their culture. Today, in the same part of the world, conservative Jews and Muslims have pretty much the same view as the ancient Hebrews had. We are familiar now with how strict Muslims are about female flesh being exposed. They are almost as strict with men, opposing games such as soccer because men go barelegged. (Closer to home, visitors to many Caribbean islands, including Puerto Rico, notice that tourists walk around in shorts and skimpy tops but the natives mostly do not.)

Until recently, Americans were fairly reserved about such matters. When Columbus and his men sailed to the New World, they described the Natives they met as "naked." (In fact, it was the Europeans who were inappropriately dressed for the climate they had entered.) Europeans in general found Native Americans to be too scantily clad for their taste, especially in warm regions. It wasn't until fairly late in history that people thought it acceptable to swim together, men and women, with men's torsos bare. When mixed bathing first began, an older generation complained about young people "going naked" in front of each other, and what they meant was not "nude" but "not adequately dressed."

So when the Bible says a person was "naked," just how naked was he? Usually you can determined from context. Mankind's First Parents, Adam and Eve, are described as "naked and not ashamed" (Genesis 2:25). This condition of innocence did not last, however. After listening to the serpent and disobeying God, "the eyes of both were opened, and they knew that they were naked" (3:7). Suddenly feeling a new sensation (shame), they hastily assembled the first human wardrobe, loincloths (or aprons) made of fig leaves. We can safely assume from this story that the two had been, yes, *stark* naked.

What about other cases of nakedness? John 21:7 relates that the disciple Peter, at his work of fishing, was "naked." But the same verse indicates that he then put on an outer garment, so he was not stark naked, but, in all probably, working in just his loincloth. Mark's Gospel relates that when Jesus was betrayed by Judas, a young man followed after Jesus, a young man wearing nothing but "a linen cloth about his body." The arresting soldiers seized him, "but he left the linen cloth and ran away naked" (Mark 14:51–52). Bible scholars assume that, in all likelihood, he was probably wearing his loincloth under the linen cloth.

Now back to the "naked" prophets of the Old Testament. Two of them, Isaiah and Micah, are spoken of as going naked. According to Isaiah 20:2, the prophet was ordered by God to walk around "naked and barefoot." He was to be a walking symbol of shame and humiliation. It is very, very unlikely that he was *stark* naked, however, considering the loathing that the Jews had of nakedness. He was probably in his loincloth. Ditto for the prophet Micah (see Micah 1:8), who went "stripped and naked" as a symbol of lamentation and mourning.

Keep in mind that most people in the ancient world did not have a surplus of clothes. The great mass of people had one everyday outfit and perhaps one finer outfit for special times such as weddings. To be seen without one's outer garments meant the obvious: you were poor, robbed, or otherwise in a dire condition. Far from sending a sexual message, being scantily clad sent quite another message: something horrible had happened. A prophet walking around stripped to his underwear got people's attention: why was he doing this? What had happened to him? Had he been robbed? If not, why was he choosing to walk around this way in public?

So titillating as it might be to think of God's prophets walking around nude, it wasn't so.

28

What Happens After Prolonged Divine Exposure

"Moses had horns."

One of the most famous religious statues in the world is Michelangelo's *Moses*. Millions of people have seen it, or at least seen pictures of it. Housed in Rome, this impressive piece of marble shows Moses as an elderly but very sinewy, muscular man. He is holding the stone tablets with the Ten Commandments carved on them. He has a long flowing beard. And he has horns on his head.

Yes, horns.

Now, Michelangelo was one of the greatest artists of all time. And he was a highly intelligent man. He could, however, make mistakes. For example, his famous statue of *David* shows the spunky shepherd boy naked—and uncircumcised. Didn't Michelangelo know that the Hebrew boy David would have been circumcised? This is one of the best-known artworks in the world, yet it is, historically speaking, incorrect.

And what about the horns on Moses' head? Did Michelangelo just dream those up? No, indeed. Michelangelo was carving a Moses based on the description of him in the Bible.

A quick review of Moses' career might be appropriate here. If you have read Exodus, or saw movies like *The Ten Commandments* or *The Prince of Egypt,* you might recall that Moses' career had two main parts. In the first part, he was Moses the Liberator, confronting the Egyptian pharaoh with God's command, "Let my people go." In the second part, he is Moses the Lawgiver. Following their exit from Egypt, the mass of Hebrew slaves takes a full forty years to reach their destination, the land of Canaan. Not surprisingly, people who have been held in slavery for years are not exactly good at governing themselves. They constantly grumble against Moses and against God. But God gives to Moses the Law—first the Ten Commandments, then the other laws found in Exodus, Leviticus, Numbers, and Deuteronomy. These laws become the foundation for the spiritual and social life of Israel.

If you saw Charlton Heston as Moses in *The Ten Commandments,* you might recall the dramatic scene in which God first delivers the Commandments. Moses is alone with God on Mount Sinai, with the people camped out at the base of the mountain. With his own "finger," God writes the Commandments on stone tablets. (In the movie, this is shown as a literal finger of fire, cutting into the stone of the mountainside.)

But in the movie, as in the Bible, Moses is not pleased with what he finds when he comes down from the mountain. The people know he has gone up to the mountain to meet with God. But he stays a long time, and the people become so restless that they force Aaron, Moses' brother, to make them a golden calf idol to rally around and worship. When Moses descends from the mountain, he witnesses something akin to a religious orgy in progress. "And as soon as he came near the camp and saw the calf and the dancing, Moses' anger burned hot, and he threw the tablets out of his hands and broke them at the foot of the mountain" (Exodus 32:21). He proceeds to destroy the calf idol and gives the people the scolding of a lifetime.

So the original Ten Commandments, the ones written by God himself, are destroyed even before anyone has seen them. God then commands Moses to carve out new tablets of stone. Moses goes back up to Mount Sinai and God once again writes the Commandments in stone. He is on the mountain forty days and forty nights, and, according to Exodus 34:28, during that time neither eats nor drinks.

He certainly makes an impression when he comes down again. "Moses did not know that the skin of his face shone because he had been talking with God. Aaron and all the people of Israel saw Moses, and behold, the skin of his face shone, and they were afraid to come near him." To tone down the radiance, Moses puts a veil over his face (Exodus 34:29–33).

Most Bible translations, like the one quoted here, state that Moses' face "shone" or "was radiant." That is exactly what the Hebrew text means. But this wasn't the Bible that Michelangelo read. The only Bible available for many centuries was the Vulgate, a translation of the Bible into Latin. Jerome, who made the translation from Hebrew into Latin, understood that the Hebrew words describing Moses' face meant something like "giving off hornlike rays." Jerome rather clumsily translated it to mean "having horns." So for centuries, people got the impression that Moses came down from Mount Sinai with horns on his head. Michelangelo was not the first or last artist to show Moses with horns, as you will notice in any art museum with paintings from the Middle Ages and Renaissance. Had Jerome done a better translation of the passage, Moses might have been shown with rays of light coming from his head, perhaps like the spokes of a wheel.

Old Sunday school joke: Moses was so long on the mountain, he turned into a mountain goat.

Perhaps the old Sunday school joke bears repeating here: "Teacher, why does Moses have horns on his head?" "Well, he stayed so long on the mountain, he turned into a mountain goat."

29

So Many Meanings for *Adultery*

"The prophet Hosea was married to a prostitute named Gomer."

Poor Hosea. Not only did he have the task of making sinful Israel see the error of its ways, but he also had a family with the most hideous names in the whole Bible. His wife was named Gomer, and his children were Jezreel, No Mercy, and Not My People. The most that people remember about him is his wife's profession: "Ah, yes, Hosea—the one married to a prostitute."

But she wasn't.

A little background is in order: Hosea's book is in the Old Testament, the first in the collection known as the Minor Prophets. (*Minor* refers to their books being fairly short, not to any assessment of their value.) Hosea's book is unusual in that it provides us a lot of information about the prophet's home life, something the Bible usually doesn't give. But it does this for a reason: Hosea's rocky marital life is intended to symbolize the rocky relationship of God and Israel.

The book begins with a rather unpleasant command from God to Hosea: "Go, take to yourself a wife of whoredom and have children of whoredom, for the land commits great whoredom by forsaking the LORD" (Hosea 1:2). Whoredom? Meaning that she is a prostitute, correct? Not quite. Read on.

In short order, Hosea's wife (with the lovely name of Gomer) gives birth to three children: Jezreel, No Mercy, and Not My People. These names are chosen by God, not Hosea himself. As you might have guessed, the names have meaning. The daughter No Mercy is so named because God declares he will have no mercy on Israel and will not save them from foreign oppression. The boy Not My People is so named because God declares that Israel is no longer his people.

All of this sounds pretty harsh. Yet it is followed, oddly, by this: "In the place where it was said to them,'You are not my people,' it shall be said to them, 'Children of the living God.' " This is pretty typical of the Old Testament: God's wrath is never far away from mercy and consolation. In fact, as Chapter 2 of the book shows, Hosea is to plead with his country to mend its ways, otherwise the name *Not My People* really will apply.

What exactly were the people doing that riled God so? Mainly, they were worshiping false gods. Ever since the Israelite slaves had left Egypt and settled in Canaan, they were constantly tempted to worship other gods. In so doing, they broke two of the Ten Commandments ("No other gods" and "No idols"). One reason they so often fell into idolatry is a human trait: people like to worship what they *see*. Israel was forbidden from making images of God. Other religions had no qualms about idols. There were plenty of images of Baal, the Canaanite fertility god.

Speaking of Baal, this is a good time to explain the "whoredom" matter. Most of the fertility religions in that part of the world involved what the anthropologists called "imitative magic." If you wanted something to happen cosmically, you acted it out on earth. If you wanted the clouds to drop rain upon your fields, the way to act that out was . . . well, through sex. If you were a man, you went and had intercourse with a woman who was a "ritual prostitute"—not someone who made her living as a whore, but a woman who, for the occasion, was playing the role of the consort of the fertility god. For the duration of your encounter, you were Baal and the woman was the goddess Ashtaroth. It had nothing to do with love, it had something to do with religion, and, obviously, it had a lot to do with sex. Israel's prophets were not fools—they could see that part of the attraction of fertility religion was that people could be promiscuous (and in the name of religion!). Fertility religions offended God on two counts: idolatry and adultery. His people were pursuing false gods, and they were engaging in wild, abandoned sex.

Hosea's wife, Gomer, was not a prostitute in the sense we use the word. She was, most likely, a ritual prostitute, doing what she did in the service of fertility religion. (For this reason, some Bible translations have *adulterous wife* instead of *whore* or *prostitute.*) Outside of Israel, her behavior would not have been considered shocking. But among the Israelites, it was scandalous. She was not only committing adultery, but serving a false god as well.

There is another possibility: instead of being a ritual prostitute, she might simply have been a Baal worshiper. Spiritually speaking, that was enough to make her a "whore" or "adulterous."

If you read the Old Testament prophets, you learn quickly that words like *adulterous* and *whoredom* and *unfaithful* get used frequently. To the prophets, God was Israel's loving husband, while Israel was always going "a-whoring" after false gods. Hosea's marriage is an object lesson in what was happening on the spiritual level. Just as it must have grieved Hosea to see his wife, the mother of his children, being a whore, so it grieved God to see Israel serving other gods. The Book of Hosea is full of stern warnings, but it also overflows with love. If the people will change their ways, God says, "I will heal their apostasy, I will love them freely, for my anger has turned from them" (14:4). God is a jealous husband, but he does not hold a grudge.

Unfortunately, Hosea's words went unheeded. He has been called "Israel's deathbed prophet," because he was the last man to prophesy there before the country fell to the Assyrians in 722 B.C. His book has continued to be read because of its message: no matter how rotten your life has been, God will take you back.

30

Joseph and the What-Shall-We-Call-It? Dreamcoat

"Joseph wore a 'coat of many colors.'"

Generations of Bible readers have smiled at the familiar story of Jacob giving his favorite son Joseph a "coat of many colors" (Genesis 37:3). It has served as the basis of numerous paintings, as well as the popular musical *Joseph and the Amazing Technicolor Dreamcoat.* But frankly, *coat of many colors* in the King James Version is probably not accurate. Most likely (though the scholars aren't absolutely certain), the item given to Joseph was a fine robe with long sleeves. (*Coat* is definitely wrong, the garment being more of a robe.) Such a fine garment is the sort of thing that would be worn by a man's designated heir. So Joseph's jealous brothers weren't envying the robe's beauty but, rather, what it symbolized: Joseph, the next-to-the-youngest brother, was being elevated above his older brothers. "When his brothers saw that their father loved him more than all his brothers, they hated him and could not speak peacefully to him" (37:4). In the ancient world, birth order was extremely important, and the oldest son was always supposed to be the most special.

Still, though the wonderful old King James Version was quite as accurate as it could have been, it does seem a shame to part with "coat of many colors," doesn't it?

31

Ask Your Dermatologist

"The beggar Lazarus in Jesus' parable was a leper."

Ever heard of a "lazaretto" or a "lazar house"? In times past, these were places where people with leprosy lived. The places take their name from Lazarus, a beggar mentioned in one of Jesus' parables. People have assumed that Lazarus the beggar was also a victim of leprosy. This wasn't so. Read on.

You can't read very far in the Bible without encountering the disease called leprosy. It was a serious problem in the ancient world. And in a time when medicine was, to put it mildly, quite primitive, people had no idea how to treat the problem. But they did understand that the disease was contagious. This is why the Jewish Law had strict rules about keeping lepers (people with leprosy, that is) isolated from others.

Just what is leprosy, anyway? Scientifically, it is Hansen's disease, caused by the microorganism *Mycobacterium leprae.* It causes brownish red spots on the face, ears, arms, thigh, and posterior. These develop into thick nodules that lose their skin covering and become sores (or "ulcers"), which in time look horribly deformed. In some cases, the person's fingers become like claws as a result of paralysis and muscular wasting away. (The name *leprosy,* by the way, comes from the Greek word *lepra,* meaning "scaly.")

It doesn't sound pretty, and it isn't. The attitude of humans everywhere was to expel the person with leprosy, cutting him off from the community. This reaction was partly a result of the person's appearance, but also a gut feeling that the condition was contagious. Leprosy is spread by skin-to-skin contact, so isolating lepers from the community did have the effect of keeping down epidemics.

If you want to know how the Israelites treated lepers, the subject is treated at great length in Leviticus 13–14. Under these rules, the person with the skin disease is examined by a priest, who is given the authority to pronounce the person "clean" or "unclean." The priest also has authority to examine the person's clothing and home. If the priest determines that the clothing or home are "unclean," they can be destroyed. Detailed rules are given for offering sacrifices that will purify the person.

This section of the Bible isn't exactly a "fun read." Perhaps most unpleasant of all is Leviticus 13:45–46, which mandates that the leper must wear torn clothes, let his hair be unkempt, cover the lower part of his face, and cry out "Unclean! Unclean" as he approaches people. Worst of all, he is required to live alone, "outside the camp." There was such a loathing of leprosy that the leper could not even be buried with other people. Uzziah, the king who was afflicted with leprosy, was buried apart from his royal relatives (2 Chronicles 26:21–23).

This sounds terribly inhumane to us, but these laws were written in the days before sanitation—or dermatology. We now know that the Hebrew word translated as "leprosy" in the King James Version is actually a kind of blanket term that refers to many different skin diseases. Not all of these were contagious, but the ancient Israelites did not know that. Many modern translations of the Bible have discarded the word *leprosy* and instead use *infectious skin diseases* or *leprous diseases*. (The word *infectious* is probably not accurate, since many of the skin diseases were not truly contagious.)

Obviously a person with "leprosy" (whether true leprosy or some other nasty skin ailment) did not have a pleasant life. You have to understand this to appreciate the occasions when Jesus healed lepers. Lepers were society's outcasts, people not only poor but also unattractive, sometimes horribly so. Mark 1:40 relates that a leper came and begged Jesus to "make him clean." Jesus was "filled with compassion" for the man and healed him. The leper told everyone about what happened and helped to spread Jesus' fame. On another occasion, Jesus healed ten lepers at once. Luke's Gospel tells us that they "stood at a distance" and called out to Jesus to have pity on them. Jesus was able to heal them at a distance. He told them to go and show themselves to a priest (following the rules of Leviticus), who would pronounce them "clean" (Luke 17:11–19).

Now, what about the most famous leper of all, the beggar Lazarus? He appears in a parable of Jesus, found in Luke 16:19–31. In the parable, he is a beggar at the gate of a rich man, hoping that he will receive some scraps from the rich man's table. When Lazarus dies, he is taken to "Abraham's bosom" (heaven, that is). The rich man also dies, but he goes to hell. Seeing Lazarus at the side of Abraham, the rich man begs for a drop of water to cool his tongue. Abraham reminds the rich man that he had good things on earth, while Lazarus had nothing—and now the situation is very much reversed.

This parable is curious for this reason: it is the one parable in which a character is actually given a name. (Jesus' parables otherwise refer to "a farmer" or "a king" or "a merchant," but these people are never given names.) Why exactly he chose to name the beggar is not known. *Lazarus* was a fairly common name at the time, and an even better-known Lazarus is the dear friend whom Jesus raised from the dead (John 11). But it is the Lazarus in the parable whose name wound up in *lazar house* and *lazaretto*.

Yet, oddly, Lazarus was *not* a leper. In the parable, he is described as "a poor man named Lazarus, covered with sores." He is not only poor and loathsome, but to add insult, "even the dogs came and licked his sores." But no mention of leprosy. Luke refers to the ten lepers in the following chapter, but does not say that Lazarus was a leper. Considering that Luke was supposed to have been a physician, this is an interesting omission. Obviously he intended us to know that Lazarus was a beggar with sores—but not a leper. In fact, following the Jewish Law, Lazarus could *not* have been a leper, for a leper, being "unclean," would not have been allowed to hang out at the rich man's gate.

Even so, Christians chose to apply the name of the beggar with sores to homes for lepers. It is a credit to Christian compassion that, over the centuries, Christians have ministered to these outcasts from society.

32

Burdened With Contradictions

"The Letter to the Galatians contradicts itself, telling people to 'bear one another's burdens,' then saying that 'each man shall bear his own burden.'"

Nothing delights critics of the Bible more than finding contradictions in the Bible itself. Let's be upfront and admit that these exist. Happily, really *glaring* contradictions aren't very common. But even small ones perplex the Bible's defenders. Those who believe the Bible is both inspired (by God, that is) and inerrant (no mistakes!) agonize over contradictions. Sometimes they refer to the original autographs. No, not the kind of autographs that are the signatures of famous people. *Original autographs* means the very first Bible writings—that is, the copy of Jeremiah written by Jeremiah, the original copy of Paul's Letter to the Romans, and so forth. Where are these? Nowhere. Even if archaeologists could dig up some very old manuscripts (older than the ones we already have, that is), there is no way of proving that they were from the actual hand of Moses, David, Paul, Luke, et cetera.

However, many people who believe the Bible is inerrant ("without error") claim they believe that the Bible *in the original autographs* was totally error-free. The flip side of this belief: minor errors may have crept in over the centuries due to the carelessness of copyists. Saying you believe in the original autographs is a way of having your cake and eating it, too. You can say that the Bible is completely error-free, and if someone points out an error, you can say, "Yes, but the original autographs had no errors." End of discussion.

I mean no disrespect to people who hold to this belief. But the belief in original autographs isn't for everybody. Even if you do believe the original Bible was inerrant, you still probably puzzle over some of the contradictions.

Still, some of the so-called contradictions really aren't. One that many Bible readers stumble upon is in the Letter to the Galatians. Here is 6:2: "Bear ye one another's burdens, and so fulfill the law of Christ." Here is 6:5: "Every man shall bear his own burden." Hmmm. Here is a rarity in the Bible: a blatant contradiction (so it seems) only three verses apart. Paul tells the Galatian Christians in one place "one for all, and all for one" then suddenly tells them "every man for himself."

But it isn't so. Here is the problem that crops up again and again in this book: the wonderful old King James Version is not perfect. It certainly isn't in Galatians 6. Here the translators were clearly having a "bad pen day." They chose to use the same word, *burdens,* to translate two different Greek words. In 6:2, Paul tells the Galatians to gently aid those who struggle with sin; to help carry their *bare,* meaning "weights" or "burdens." Just as a physically strong person helps out a physically weak person, so the spiritually strong Christian aids the weaker Christian. This is something Paul repeats often: no solitary Christians—you are all part of a great spiritual fellowship so *think about each other.*

In Galatians 6:5, Paul shifts the emphasis a little. While we are a Christian fellowship, each of us will be judged individually by God. Each person will have to bear (future tense) his own *phortion,* which can mean "freight" or "load" or even "burdens." Paul used two different Greek words, but they are pretty similar, and the King James men were correct about one thing: both *phortion* and *bare* can be properly translated "burdens."

Here is the whole passage in a modern version: "Brothers, if anyone is caught in any transgression, you who are spiritual should restore him in a spirit of gentleness. Keep watch on yourself, lest you too be tempted. Bear one another's burdens, and so fulfill the law of Christ. For if anyone thinks he is something when he is nothing, he deceives himself. But let each one test his own work, and then his reason to boast will be in himself alone and not in his neighbor. For each one will have to bear his own load" (6:1–5). Note the verb in the last sentence: *will have to bear.* Paul is talking about the future, not the present. In all likelihood, he is talking about the Last Judgment, when each person gives account to God. At that stage, we will no longer be able to "bear one another's burdens."

You can see that, even when using two different English words, *burdens* and *load,* this is still a ticklish passage. You can almost picture Paul dictating the passage to a scribe. After saying "each one should carry his own load," Paul sees the scribe raise an eyebrow. "Um, respectfully, Paul, don't you think they might think you just contradicted yourself?" Paul, anxious to get on with the letter, says, "No contradiction at all! I told them to help each other out! And I told them that at the Final Judgment, each person is responsible for himself! So what's the problem?"

No problem at all.

33

The Great Verse on Procrastination

"The Roman official Agrippa told Paul he was 'almost persuaded' to be a Christian."

If you ever attended a revival or an evangelistic crusade, you might have heard the hymn "Almost Persuaded." It's popular as a song for the "altar call," the time when people are asked to come forward if they wish to commit (or recommit) themselves to Christ. It has a pretty, haunting tune, and the theme is that "almost" is not enough; that you should not put off making the decision that will change your entire life.

It's a beautiful song, and one that probably has helped nudge many fence-straddling people off the fence. But the words are based on a very old *mis*translation of a Bible verse.

It comes from the Book of Acts, where one of the chief players is the apostle Paul. The man made enemies, but no one who ever met him forgot him. Paul was made of solid brass, never lacking in courage and never afraid to preach what he thought was the true faith. He was the great missionary of the new faith.

In his travels, Paul was stoned, imprisoned, beaten, shipwrecked, often loved, and often hated.

He had a dream: he wanted to take the gospel to Rome, the hub of the empire that sprawled around the Mediterranean Sea. He got what he wanted, though perhaps not in the way he had planned. In Jerusalem, the seat of Judaism, Paul ran into trouble with the Jewish authorities: he was accused of trying to escort a non-Jew into the temple area, which was strictly forbidden. A mob might well have killed him if the Roman authorities hadn't intervened. Paul was given the chance to defend himself before the Jewish authorities, but another riot ensued, and the Roman soldiers again had to intervene. The Jews plotted to kill Paul, and when the Romans got wind of it, they moved him out of Jerusalem. By this time, Paul had been given a revelation from God: he would witness for Christ in Rome.

Paul was moved to the town of Caesarea. As you might guess from its name, the town was the Roman headquarters in that region. There Paul had to stand trial before a corrupt Roman official named Felix. He was kept in custody a full two years by Felix, who was hoping for a bribe. Felix was succeeded by Festus, who had a little more integrity. Paul was a citizen of the Roman Empire, which gave him a legal option: he could ask to be tried before the emperor himself. So to Festus he uttered the fateful words, "I appeal to Caesar."

While awaiting his trip to Rome, Paul met with one other official: King Agrippa, of the famous Herod family. Agrippa and his sister Berenice had come to Caesarea to pay their official respects to Festus. Apparently Festus thought it might be amusing to have Agrippa meet the Jewish troublemaker Paul. (A bit of historical gossip: Berenice and Agrippa were rumored to be closer than brother and sister.) Paul defended himself eloquently, as always, using the encounter, as all others, to witness to his faith in Christ. Paul was probably aware of Agrippa's immorality, but Agrippa was a Jew, and Paul passed up no opportunity to convince a fellow Jew that Jesus was the Messiah they had all awaited.

Paul asked Agrippa, "King Agrippa, do you believe the prophets? I know that you believe." Agrippa's reply: "In a short time you would persuade me to be a Christian?" (Acts 26:27–28). You can almost imagine the cynical ruler barely concealing a sneer as he said the words. Needless to say, the Book of Acts does *not* report that he became a Christian.

In the King James Version, Agrippa's words are: "Almost thou persuadest me to be a Christian." Quite a difference, yes? The modern translations are almost certainly correct: Agrippa was telling Paul, almost in jest, "Don't be silly enough to think you can convert me to this heresy of yours." The King James translators were, unfortunately, not correct. Agrippa was *not* hinting that Paul had come close to persuading him.

Still, as pointed out elsewhere in this book, the King James Version has influenced Christians for more than three hundred years. For Christians who are inclined to witness to their faith, Agrippa's "almost persuaded" is unforgettable. The world is full of people who might be "almost persuaded" and just need a gentle nudge and a prayer. The verse has been encouragement to hundreds of preachers, especially evangelists. And it is at the root of the song "Almost Persuaded." It just happens that "Almost thou persuadest me to be a Christian" was not what Agrippa actually said to Paul.

Agrippa was, by the way, the last of the immoral and corrupt Herod dynasty. Historians might well say, "Good riddance!"

34

Humanly High, or Devilishly Low?

"The Bible condemns wickedness in high places."

In Ephesians 6:12, Paul speaks of Christians doing battle against "wickedness in high places"—or so it reads in some translations. It is clear in the context that Paul is talking about the realm of the supernatural—specifically, war against the devil and his forces. Yet some people have quoted the section on "wickedness in high places" and used it to criticize big government, big business, and the like. The English Standard Version, which has "evil in the heavenly places," is less misleading. (Of course, no one need rule out the possibility that big business and big government might indeed by influenced by demonic forces . . .)

35

When the Going Gets Tough, Is Patience Enough?

"Job was praised for his patience."

People have been talking about the "patience of Job" for centuries. "Poor Betty. To put up with that family of hers, she must have the patience of Job." The phrase gets tossed around so often that you wonder if any of the people who use it have any idea who Job was. If they did, it might occur to them that *patience* is not the right word to apply.

If you turn to the first two chapters of the Book of Job, the action unfolds quickly. Job is a man who is "blameless and upright, one who feared God and turned away from evil." He is living well: he has seven sons and seven daughters, seven thousand sheep, three thousand camels, and an estate full of servants. He is the kind of man whom people in ancient Israel aspired to be: wealthy, devout, and well stocked with children.

The fly in the ointment is Satan. The Satan in the Book of Job is not quite the nasty Satan later in the Bible. He is a sort of cosmic observer, one in the habit of "going to and fro on the earth." God mentions to him Job, a fine specimen of a man. Satan replies that, yes, indeed, Job is good—and why not, since he has so much to be thankful for? God allows Satan to test Job. Horrible things happen in quick succession. All Job's livestock is rustled. His servants are all killed. A storm strikes the house, killing all of his children at once.

Job tears his robe in agony, shaves his head as a sign of grief. But he is not angry at God. "The LORD gave," Job says, "and the LORD has taken away, blessed be the name of the LORD." Satan is irritated. He goes one step farther and afflicts Job with loathsome sores all over his body. Job's wife urges Job to "curse God and die." But Job will not.

The worst test of all is when his three old friends come to give him comfort. They are so affected by the sight of him that they tear their robes and weep. But then they try to comfort him—or, more plainly, they try to rationalize what happened. They use the usual explanation: horrible things happen to you because you sin. You do bad things, bad things happen to you. Most of the Book of Job is a dialogue between Job and the three friends. Job will not accept their wisdom. He knows he has done nothing to bring his calamities on himself, and his friends are sure that he has.

If you read the exchanges between him and the three friends, you learn very quickly that Job is *not* patient—not with them, anyway. He gets very irritated with them, and they with him. They are sure that their view of God and justice is the traditional one, and that they are right. Job knows that bad people often suffer, but he himself learns the painful lesson that good people suffer, too, and that there is no way to explain it.

The book ends happily. God restores Job's fortunes to him. But before doing so, God drives home an important point: your finite human minds are not big enough to grasp everything.

Christians and Jews have both treasured the Book of Job. For people who are suffering, the book provides some comfort. In the New Testament, the Letter of James reminds suffering Christians of the "patience of Job" (James 5:11). But this word *patience* (in the King James Version, but also in most later versions) does not communicate what the Letter of James meant, nor the quality that Job possessed. The quality of Job that James referred to is better translated "perseverance," having the fortitude (and reliance on God) to endure tough times—something that *patience* does not really communicate today. The Greek word James uses is *hypomone,* which means something like "enduring courageously." James was reminding people who suffer to be like Job, a combination of saintliness and toughness.

36

Some Great Words for Flag-Waving

"The Bible says that 'Where there is no vision, the people perish.'"

Church signs are often inspiring, sometimes amusing. You may have noticed around patriotic holidays like the Fourth of July that many church signs will say WHERE THERE IS NO VISION THE PEOPLE PERISH. Patriotic days are obviously a proper time for the pastor to preach on those words from Proverbs 29:18. The words have been quoted, and preached on, countless times, and most people would accept the message as true: where a culture lacks a vision for itself, the people perish, spiritually speaking. This is a message that anyone, whatever their religious beliefs, could agree with.

However, our use of the word *vision* here is not quite what the author of Proverbs had in mind. He meant something more like "oracle from a prophet" or "revelation." Some modern versions of the Bible have replaced *vision* with *revelation.* Or consider this version, which is pretty accurate: "Where there is no prophetic vision, the people cast off all restraint." Closer to the real meaning, but preachers have certainly gotten a lot of mileage out of "Where there is no vision, the people perish."

37

Do Spirits Ever Tire?

" 'My Spirit shall not always strive with man' means that God gives up on certain people."

Ever seen a TV broadcast of one of Billy Graham's crusades? Most people have. It might surprise a lot of people under the age of forty, but this type of preaching used to be extremely common in America and elsewhere. The American frontier was the scene of religious "camp meetings," where a traveling evangelist (sometimes more than one at a time) would visit the area and preach for several days and nights in a row. With people on the frontier living so far apart, the camp meetings served a social purpose as well as a religious one. People from a wide area could gather together, swap news and stories, eat together, and have a break from the normal routine of frontier farm life. They could also hear some very colorful and dramatic preaching. Some of the frontier preachers were "stars," well-known names to people who found entertainment, socializing, and a religious experience in the same place.

Billy Graham's style is pretty typical of the camp meetings. There is a lot of singing of hymns, of course, some with the whole congregation, some with soloists. Then the preacher himself takes center stage and focuses on some basic themes from the Bible: people are sinners, Jesus is the Savior from sin, God wants you to repent and live as a Christian. At the end of each sermon is the "altar call," in which people can leave their seats and come forward to acknowledge their repentance. Then, or later, they would be baptized and would join a church.

In preaching repentance, evangelists have always had a lot of Bible passages to draw from. According to Mark's Gospel, when Jesus began his public ministry, his first words were, "The time is fulfilled, and the kingdom of God is at hand. Repent and believe in the gospel" (Mark 1:15). You don't have to read too far in the New Testament to figure out that *repenting of your sins* is one of the main themes. One thing Jesus and his apostles made clear: no matter how rotten a life you have led, you can repent at any time, and God will love and accept you.

Is it ever too late to repent? The usual Christian answer has been, "No, never too late." In fact, it is possible to be saved just before dying. Luke's Gospel states that when Jesus was crucified, two thieves were crucified with him. All three men were, of course, in excruciating pain, but one of the thieves found the energy to mock Jesus. The other, however, said, "Jesus, remember me when you come into your kingdom." And Jesus replied, "Truly, I say to you, today you will be with me in Paradise." Jesus died shortly after uttering those words, and presumably the thief did also—and went to Paradise, as Jesus promised. So Christians, when speaking about the possibility of salvation at the very last moment, sometimes say, "Remember the thief on the cross." (Since the other thief never repented, some people ask, "*Which* thief?"—for obviously some people do not repent, even at the bitter end.)

For obvious reasons, evangelists have never been fond of quoting this story in their sermons. If you have an audience of people whom you want to repent *now,* you certainly don't want to remind them that they can put off repentance until the moment of death, right? There is, in fact, another verse in the Bible that says—or at least *suggests*—that God may eventually give up on unrepentant sinners.

This verse is, frankly, one that gives translators fits. The Hebrew words are darn near impossible to translate, and no one is quite sure just what is the *correct* translation. To show you the difficulty of translating Genesis 6:3, consider these different versions of it:

- My Spirit shall not abide in man forever. (English Standard Version)
- My Spirit shall not contend with man forever. (New International Version)
- I will not allow people to live forever. (Good News Bible)
- My spirit must not be for ever disgraced in man. (Jerusalem Bible)
- My spirit shall not abide in mortals forever. (New Revised Standard Version)
- My Spirit will not put up with humans for such a long time. (New Living Translation)

Now, you might ask, what does this verse have to do with evangelism and repentance? The answer is: not a thing. In the context of Genesis 6, the verse is explaining that God chooses to limit man's life span. Genesis 5 traces human genealogy from Adam to Noah, and we learn that people lived a long, *long* time—notably the famous Methuselah, who lived 969 years. (Adam, in fact, lived to be 930.) In Genesis 6, we find, suddenly, that humans will no longer have such phenomenal lifetimes: "My Spirit shall not abide in man forever, for he is flesh; his days shall be 120 years." To paraphrase: "God's divine spirit—which gives people life—will no longer remain in people for hundreds of years. Human life will now be much shorter." We have to admit this is the *likely* interpretation.

But the different Bible translations quoted above are modern translations. In the days of the frontier evangelists, and well into the twentieth century, there was only one English Bible, and that was the beloved King James Version, published in 1611.

Here is what the King James Version has for Genesis 6:3: "My spirit shall not always strive with man." And that is the verse that evangelists liked. If you take the verse out of context, it seems to be saying that God's spirit will finally give up on a person. Christians have always believed that God's spirit (or Spirit, as in Holy Spirit) acts inside the person to lead him to repent. So if you're attending an evangelistic meeting and listening to the preacher talk about sin (*your* sin) and the need to repent (*your* need to repent), then the

Spirit is working on you, too—on the inside, that is. Of course, you can resist the Spirit—you are a human with free will, not a puppet. You can delay repentance. But then, if you keep putting it off . . . what might happen? You have heard preachers and others repeat it time and time again: "My spirit will not always strive with man." If you keep procrastinating, perhaps there will come a time when the Spirit will no longer lead you to repent. So, better to do what the evangelist is calling you to do: repent now.

Taking Bible verses out of context has been going on ever since the Bible existed. To the evangelists' credit, their hearts were in the right place. They wanted to stress the urgency of repentance. In fact, there are plenty of verses in the New Testament that make it clear that *now* is the best time to repent of one's sins. Why exactly people chose to lift Genesis 6:3 out of context and make it a plea for repentance, no one knows. There were probably plenty of preachers in the past who might have said, "Well, if it helped people make a decision to repent, what's the problem?"

38

Lawyers, the Usual Targets

"Jesus condemned lawyers."

The world abounds with lawyer jokes, and the law is certainly one profession that people feel free to mock and despise. Jesus himself had harsh words to say about "the lawyers and the Pharisees," as the King James Version has it. But the "lawyers" he preached against were not attorneys in our modern sense. They were (as newer versions have it) "experts in the law"—people well versed in the Old Testament Law and how to apply it to daily life. Jesus denounced them, along with the Pharisees, for focusing too much on the Jewish Law's details and missing the "big picture"—loving God and our fellow men. The long "anti-lawyer" passage can be found in Luke 11:45–54. Jesus tells his famous parable of the Good Samaritan in response to a lawyer who asks him, "What shall I do to inherit eternal life?" (Luke 10:25–37).

What Jesus would have thought of lawyers today is anybody's guess. Since he reached out to the despised tax collectors in his own time, perhaps he would reach out today to attorneys?

39

Well, Creating an Entire Universe Is Quite a Task

"God had to rest after the six days of creation."

Anti-Semitism has been around for centuries (see pages 53–57). One habit of the Jews that people in times past laughed about was the Sabbath. To non-Jews, taking one day out of seven and devoting it to rest and worship seemed wasteful. The Romans sneeringly referred to the Sabbath as "the day of the Jews." But if you read the Old Testament, you learn quickly that this habit was taken very seriously. Sabbath keeping is one of the Ten Commandments. Centuries after those Commandments were given, we can appreciate the wisdom. People do need to break regularly from their daily grind. While not that many people today use the Sabbath to *rest* in any meaningful sense, at least it is a respite from work. People who are neither Jews nor Christians ought to feel at least a bit of gratitude for the Sabbath, for without it, there would be no weekends.

According to Genesis 1, the Sabbath goes all the way back to the beginning. God created the whole universe in six days. Whether these "days" were twenty-four-hour days or something else is still being hotly debated. The point of Genesis 1 is that God makes everything, declares that it is "good," and does it all for a purpose.

Then what happened? "On the seventh day God finished his work that he had done, and he rested on the seventh day from all his work that he had done. So God blessed the seventh day and made it holy, because on it God rested from all his work that he had done in creation" (Genesis 2:1–3). Those words are echoed in the Ten Commandments. Humans resting on the Sabbath is connected to the original Sabbath, the day that God rested.

Now, we know people need rest. Did God? After all, it does say he "rested" on the seventh day, right? It does indeed. But the experts in Hebrew tells us that the word we translate as "rested" means something more like "ceased activity"—not from being tired, but from choice. Human beings need rest, but God does not—although we might assume that creating the entire universe must have been quite a task.

40

Marital Bliss, or the Fiery Hiss?

"The Bible says it is better to marry than to burn in hell."

Well, if it came down to a choice, most people would obviously choose to marry, wouldn't they? In the King James Version, 1 Corinthians 7:9 reads, "It is better to marry than to burn." Over the centuries, many readers have assumed that this means it is better to marry than to burn in hell. But the verse has nothing to do with hell. The fire is not hell, but lust. Newer translations are more accurate: "It is better to marry than to be aflame with passion."

The New Testament's classic statement on marriage is in 1 Corinthians 7. Paul, the single man and the devoted missionary, thought that the single life was best for people spreading the gospel. But he was realistic enough to see that most Christians needed the comfort of a spouse, comfort that included physical intimacy. For those who could live without this, good. For the vast majority who cannot live without it, do the honorable thing and marry. Otherwise you will do a lot of lusting in your hearts or (more likely) throw your self-control to the winds and indulge in immorality.

So, the Bible does not actually say that it is better to marry than to burn in hell. But then, it *is* better, isn't it?

41

The Consolation of Not Being a Beautiful Princess

"Psalm 45:13 teaches that inward beauty is more important than outward."

To begin, let's say that the Bible is much more focused on the inside than the outside of human beings. "The LORD sees not as man sees; man looks on the outward appearance, but the LORD looks on the heart" (1 Samuel 16:7). That attitude is at odds, to put it mildly, with the video age, where the visual image is everything. Man not only looks on the outward appearance, but sometimes seems capable of looking *only* at the outward appearance. Try dropping the phrase *inner beauty* at the health club or any place where singles gather, and you will probably get a laugh.

You figure out pretty quickly from reading the Bible that it focuses *on what endures*. In the Old Testament, this takes the form of creating a family—on extending your life (and your reputation for being a good person) through generation after generation. In the New Testament, it takes the form of focusing on heaven, eternity. In either the Old or New Testament, the present is never quite as important as the future. Put another way, your present life matters only in relation to what comes afterward. Unlike animals, humans *can think ahead*. That is very useful in life. The woman who says, "Wow, Scott is so handsome!" could also say, "Sure, he's attractive now, but in twenty years he'll be a philandering middle-aged man, probably ready to dump me for his secretary or . . ." A nice ability God gave us, don't you think?

The Bible isn't anti-physical or anti-sex (see pages 62–67), as you can see from the Song of Solomon. There are plenty of deeply spiritual people who still have eyes and still appreciate someone's physical beauty. But the Bible has in it this wise voice, like some aunt or uncle you respect, whispering in your ear: "Don't let that pretty face or body lead you into something you might regret." Consider 1 John 2:16–17: "All that is in the world—the desires of the flesh and the desires of the eyes and pride in possessions—is not from the Father but is from the world. And the world is passing away along with its desires, but whoever does the will of God abides forever." Underline the word *forever* and you have a fair idea of the Bible's view of beauty.

The Bible's authors were aware of something that modern psychology confirms: men are more motivated by physical attraction than women are. Not surprisingly, the Bible has more warnings to men than to women about the shallowness of outer beauty: "Like a gold ring in a pig's snout is a beautiful woman without discretion" (Proverbs 11:22). "Charm is deceitful and beauty is vain, but a woman who fears the LORD is to be praised" (Proverbs 31:30). And then there is Peter's famous advice to Christian women: "Do not let your adorning be external—the braiding of hair, the wearing of gold, or the putting on of clothing—but let your adorning be the hidden person of the heart with the imperishable beauty of a gentle and quiet spirit, which in God's eyes is very precious" (1 Peter 3:3–4). *Imperishable beauty* is a nice phrase. It won't sell a lot of cosmetics or cause a rush to health clubs, but it does sum up the Bible pretty well.

Imperishable beauty sums up the Bible's view of beauty.

Now to a Bible verse that has been the basis of countless sermons, particularly on occasions like Mother's Day: Psalm 45:13. Here is a modern, and accurate, translation: "All glorious is the princess in her chamber, with robes interwoven with gold." Hmmm. Sounds pretty *external,* doesn't it? Certainly no mention of inner beauty. And no wonder. Psalm 45 is a kind of wedding song for a royal couple.

But here is the King James Version of the verse: "The king's daughter is all glorious within." Ah, yes. Sounds much more spiritual, doesn't it? The words *all glorious within* seem to refer to inner beauty. And *the king's daughter* can be any Christian woman, since the "king is clearly God, or Christ. You can see why sermons on inner beauty have been preached on the verse "The king's daughter is all glorious within." If the King James Version had said "all glorious within the palace" (which is what it means), the verse would never have had such popularity. This is one of many cases of a verse from the King James Version being lifted out of its context completely. Certainly if you read Psalm 45 in any Bible today, you would not think, "Ah, a good passage about imperishable inner beauty."

The use of this verse as the basis for sermons on inner beauty is a "happy mistake" that readers of the King James Version have made. We have to admit that the phrase *all glorious within* has a nice ring to it, even if it is taken out of context.

42

Watching Yourself, Since You're Being Watched

"Keeping up appearances is important, because the Bible tells us to 'Avoid every appearance of evil.' "

Evangelism has gotten a bad reputation in recent years. It used to be accepted that Christians liked to convert unbelievers. Now, though, any Christian's attempt to witness to his faith is called "cultural imperialism" or "cramming your religion down someone else's throat." As people snicker at Jehovah's Witnesses or Mormons going door to door, so they also snicker at evangelical Christians trying to spread their faith. (This is an odd attitude, since people who are caught in a diet or exercise fad always "witness" to whatever kick they are on at the moment, and no one seems to mind.)

However much it may offend some people, Christianity has always been evangelistic. Jesus told his followers to "go and make disciples" around the world (Matthew 28:19–20). Christians have been following that command for two thousand years, and quite a few have been killed and persecuted for doing so. Author Mike Bryan, who is not a Christian, spent a year at a fundamentalist Bible college, trying to figure out what makes the "Bible thumpers" tick. He did not convert to the faith, but he did gain a lot of respect for the people. In his book *Chapter and Verse,* he concluded that "If you resent the Bible-toting proselytizers who go door-to-door, you don't like the Christianity of the Bible."*

The very bold apostle Paul claimed he was "not ashamed of the gospel" even though many people laughed at him (Romans 1:16). Perhaps Paul remembered Jesus' warning that if his followers were ashamed of their faith, he would be ashamed of them when he returned to earth (Luke 9:26). But it wasn't this warning that motivated the early Christians. They sincerely believed they had found the truth about life in this world and the next, and they had to share it.

You notice in the New Testament a sort of "active" evangelism (talking to people about what you believe) and "passive" evangelism (living in such a way that people will want to know more about what motivates you in life). The two go together, of course. If you live like "salt of the earth" and "light of the world" (Matthew 5:13–16), people are more likely to pay attention to your preaching and teaching. The first Christians were living in the Roman Empire, which had grown so shamelessly immoral that even non-Christians complained about the state of things. Naturally the immoral folk found the Christians laughable. But others were attracted to this new and very moral religion.

So the first Christians knew that appearances were important. Every religion, whether it is true or false, has its "public relations" aspect. You have to make a good impression to win converts. Paul told his flock, "Conduct yourselves wisely toward outsiders, making the best use of the time. Let your speech always be gracious, seasoned with salt, so that you may know how to answer each person" (Colossians 4:5–6). "Be children of God without blemish in the midst of a crooked and twisted generation, among whom you shine as lights in the world" (Philippians 2:15). Peter had similar advice: "Keep your conduct among the Gentiles honorable, so that when they speak against you as evil-doers, they may see your good deeds and glorify God on the day of salvation" (1 Peter 2:11–12). The upshot: *being* good people is the important thing, but *seeming* good is important, too.

*Mike Bryan, *Chapter and Verse: A Skeptic Revisits Christianity* (New York: Random House, 1991), p. 157.

This brings us around to another *mis*translation found in the King James Version of the Bible, a verse that has been used to mean something it was not intended to mean. In this case, the verse is: "Abstain from all appearance of evil" (1 Thessalonians 5:22). As you see, it fits right in with the verses quoted above. The verse is a perfectly acceptable bit of Christian advice. Its main idea is not wrong. It just happens to be the wrong translation of what 1 Thessalonians 5:22 actually means. And that is this: "Abstain from every form of evil." You might paraphrase it by saying, "Don't let any sort of evil show up among you."

Many wonderful and inspiring sermons have been preached on the verse "Abstain from all appearance of evil." In fact, more than three centuries' worth of sermons have been preached on it. The words are still good advice, even if they are, strictly speaking, not the best translation.

43

So Much Riding on One Little Comma

"The New Testament commands drinking all of the wine at Communion."

At the Last Supper, Jesus spoke of the cup of wine he was holding and told his disciples, "Drink ye all of it" (Matthew 26:27). So reads the King James Version. Some people have taken this to mean that when churches have Communion service, all the wine (or juice) must be consumed, with none left over. But in fact, the word *all* in the verse is connected with *ye,* not with *it* (the wine). More recent English versions more accurately reflect the Greek: "Drink from it, all of you."

44

But Where Did They Plug the Darn Thing In?

"Organs (musical instruments) existed in Bible times."

Wherever human beings exist, there are musical instruments. Sometimes these are as simple as whistles or flutes made from bones or hollow plant stems. Mankind has never tried to live without some kind of music-making device.

But *organs?* On the scale of simplicity, organs are way at the far end, among the most complex musical instruments. The archaeologists know that ancient people had some relatively complex harps and other tuned instruments. But organs?

Curiously, the organ is the first musical instrument mentioned in the Bible, way back in Genesis 4. One of the descendants of Cain, the murderous son of Adam and Eve, is Jubal, who is described as "the father of all such as handle the harp and organ" (4:21). Mercy. Within three generations of Adam, some clever person has already invented the organ? Amazing. No wonder the organ is the preferred instrument in worship services.

Naturally, the Psalms, the book of praise and worship, the book that mentions music so many times, talks about organs: "Praise him with the timbrel and dance; praise him with stringed instruments and organs" (Psalm 150:4). And poor Job, who suffered so many calamities, referred to the instrument: "My harp is turned to mourning, and my organ into the voice of them that weep" (Job 30:31). Organs in ancient Israel. Wow.

Not so fast. You will only find the word *organ* in the King James Version. Most later versions have *flute* or *pipe* or such. In the Genesis passage, the author is trying to tell us something about Jubal: he is credited with inventing musical instruments. The Hebrew original says that Jubal is the ancestor of those who play the *ugab* and the *kinnor.* We are pretty sure that *ugab* referred to some kind of wind instrument, or to wind instruments in general. And *kinnor* referred to stringed instruments. So Jubal is credited as the inventor of the two types of musical instruments used in making melody. (Ancient people also had percussion instruments like drums and tambourines, naturally.) When the Hebrew Bible was translated into Greek, the word *ugab* became the Greek word *organon.* You can see how it was an easy leap from there to our English word *organ.*

The King James Version's translators found themselves stumped by quite a few Hebrew words. They knew that *ugab* was some sort of wind instrument, but not much else. The organ, although it isn't played with the mouth like flutes and trumpets, used to be considered a wind instrument because the organ's pipes had to have air forced through them to produce the sound. This was done by someone pumping a bellows, or by foot pedals. Today, of course, this is all done via electricity.

While the King James Version is wrong about organs existing in biblical times, the main point of Genesis 4:21 still stands: Jubal is supposed to be the inventor of musical instruments for mankind. So he is, as the verse says, the "father" of all those who handle musical instruments, whether that be pipe, harp, organ, guitar, or synthesizer.

45

That Cussed Fisherman

"The disciple Peter used profanity."

In the sad story of Peter denying that he knew Jesus, Mark's Gospel notes that Peter "began to curse and swear" (Mark 14:71). Many readers assume that the overwrought, guilt-stricken Peter was using profanity. In fact, the "swearing" was literal swearing—he was swearing (though it was a lie) that he had no connection with Jesus.

PART V

FALSIFYING SATAN, DEMONS, AND HELL

SATAN
The Bible says that Satan resides in hell . . . or does he?

46

ZIP Code 66666

"Satan and the demons reside in hell."

We long ago accepted devils (usually red ones) and a fiery, smoky hell as part of "pop religion." Their locale is, of course, "down there," hell being somewhere deep underground. There they torture the human souls who somehow missed going to heaven.

All very colorful, but not having much connection with the Bible and the real Satan.

If you open the New Testament, you figure out pretty fast that the early Christians definitely believed in demons. Jesus was noted for casting out demons from people, and his disciples were able to do the same. Jesus made it clear that he had come to assault Satan's kingdom, and clearly that kingdom is not in hell (Hebrews 2:14). Satan and the demons are very active right here on earth. The Bible attributes various bodily and mental afflictions to the working of demons, but Christ and his followers are sent to release people from demonic power (Acts 10:37–38, 26:18). In Jesus' own words, "If I cast out demons by the Spirit of God, surely the kingdom of God has come upon you" (Matthew 12:28). (Does this mean Jesus was an exorcist? Not necessarily. See page 164.)

Far from being in hell (or even having their "base" there), demons are wherever people are. Satan is referred to as the "prince of this world" (John 12:31). Satan is also the "prince of the power of the air" (Ephesians 2:2). He rules over a wide kingdom, one locked in mortal combat with Christ's kingdom (Colossians 1:13).

Demons can, obviously, be "inside" a person, which is true of those who are demon-possessed. It was the chief, Satan himself, who entered Judas Iscariot, the disciple who betrayed Jesus (Luke 22:3–5).

So where did we get the idea that these fiendish beings are based in hell?

The New Testament is clear about the fate of Satan: he and his demons do a lot of mischief now, but their day is coming. "The God of peace will soon crush Satan under your feet" (Romans 16:20). Crushed, yes—but also burned. Jesus spoke about the "eternal fire prepared for the devil and his angels" (Matthew 25:41). The Letter to the Hebrews warns of "a fury of fire that will consume the adversaries" of God (10:27).

But it is the Book of Revelation that supplies us with the most vivid images of what awaits Satan. In this vision of the end of time, the devil is "thrown into the lake of fire and sulfur . . . and they will be tormented day and night forever and ever" (20:10). He is not alone in the lake, however: all human beings face the final judgment, "And if anyone's name was not found written in the book of life, he was thrown into the lake of fire" (20:15). Who might some of those people be? "As for the cowardly, the faithless, the detestable, as for murderers, the sexually immoral, sorcerers, idolaters, and all liars, their portion will be in the lake that burns with fire and sulfur" (21:8). What follows in the remainder of Revelation is the Bible's "happy ending," a mesmerizing vision of heaven (the New Jerusalem) made of pure gold. And "nothing unclean will ever enter it, nor anyone who does what is detestable or false" (21:27). End of story. Saints win, Satan and demons and bad people are tormented in a lake of fire forever.

This is all in the future. For the present, Satan and the demons are not in hell.

Yet.

47

What Kind of Footprints in the Ashes?

"The Bible depicts Satan as horned and hoofed."

One problem we have in relating to the Bible is that we live in a video age. We are a very *visual* people, and the people of the Bible were not. They were more oriented toward *hearing,* getting their information through the ear, not the eye. The stories that were written down in the Bible were stories that had been passed on by word of mouth, sometimes for centuries. Those stories did not, for the most part, provide many physical details about the characters in them.

We have no idea, for example, what Jesus looked like. We can assume that, like all Jewish men of his day, he would have had a beard, and the Gospels tell us he was about thirty years old when he began his public activity. He was thirty, Jewish, and probably bearded—and that is about all we know. Short, tall, fat, thin? We have no idea. The people who told his story did not think it was important. What he *did* was much more important than how he *looked.* In a sense, the Bible's authors had the same attitude as God: they looked on the heart, not on the outward appearance (1 Samuel 16:7). Occasionally a person is described as beautiful (Sarah, Genesis 12:14), handsome (David, 1 Samuel 16:12), or fat (King Eglon of Moab, Judges 3:17), and we get some details about freaks of nature like the Philistine giant Goliath (1 Samuel 17:4–7). But the ancient Hebrews, unlike the ancient Greeks, were not body-obsessed. It is worth remembering that God specifically prohibited Israel from making any idols. Unlike the Greeks, the Hebrews did not create divine images based on attractive human bodies.

Now consider Satan. Like God himself, Satan is a spiritual being with no body. Strictly speaking, Satan has no physical appearance at all. But that has not prevented Christian artists from having a field day in depicting Satan. While they have been reluctant to paint or sculpt God the Father, they have no qualms about artistic renderings of the great Enemy of the human race.

If an artist wants to paint a Satan, can he draw any information from the Bible? Not much. Satan is, obviously, an evil character, not only anti-God but anti-man as well. So if he had an appearance, it would be ugly. Appropriately enough, man's first encounter with Satan is in the form of a serpent. While Genesis 3 never says that the serpent that tempted Eve was Satan, later generations of Jews and Christians assumed that the serpent was simply Satan in disguise. The serpent told the woman the first lie: he claimed that, contrary to what God said, the man and woman had much to gain by eating the forbidden fruit. In fact, they would be like gods! Eve believed this, ate the fruit, then gave it to her husband to eat. Too late, they discovered the serpent had lied, and no good came of their disobedience to God's command. The couple was punished, but so was the serpent: God condemned it crawl on its belly and "eat dust" (Genesis 3:14). This suggests that, before the curse, the serpent may have walked upright or (as you will see in some paintings of Eden) lived in trees.

After Eden, there is no mention of Satan for a long time. He appears in the Book of Job as a major character. He isn't, in Job, the evil tempter of mankind. He is more of a "tester," allowed into God's heavenly court. He is a sort of court prosecutor, working to show that the saintly Job is saintly only during the good times, not the bad. Satan afflicts Job with various trials to find out whether Job will remain good under pressure. Satan does what he does only with God's approval. Even so, Satan does seem to take delight in afflicting poor Job. So it's easy to see how this prosecutor-adversary evolved into the outright enemy of mankind. (The name *Satan* means "adversary," by the way.)

As mentioned earlier, the Israelites did not make images of God. They were, however, quite aware that the nations around them made images of their various gods. Most of these images were not the beautiful naked or near-naked bodies that the Greeks created. Far from it. The nations that surrounded Israel typically made their gods look fierce. Some, like the Egyptians, gave the gods human bodies with animal heads. Other nations had gods with horns, claws, and batlike wings. The idea was this: the god we worship is fierce and will protect us.

The Israelites did not believe these pagan gods were the true God. In fact, they sometimes identified these pagan gods with demons. So the images of the pagan gods were actually images of evil spirits.

> The gods the heathen worshiped were, the Israelites believed, demonic. (See Psalm 106:36–37.)

Hold that thought for a moment, for we will return to the idea of demonic images. Now consider the New Testament. Three of the Gospels tell us that Jesus was tempted by the devil. The devil speaks to Jesus "in the wilderness," but no details are given about his appearance at all. Jesus refers many times to Satan or the devil, but makes no mention of how he looks. In Luke 10, Jesus hears a report from his followers that they are succeeding in casting out demons. He tells them that he saw Satan fall "like lightning from heaven" (10:18). It appears Jesus was telling his disciples that their ministry was having an effect on Satan and his demons. What follows is quite interesting: he tells his disciples, "Behold, I give you authority to trample on serpents and scorpions, and over all the power of the enemy" (10:18). Was he making some connection between Satan and serpents? Most likely, yes.

The apostle Paul tells the early Christians to be on their guard against false apostles, because "Satan himself transforms himself into an angel of light" (2 Corinthians 11:14). This is in keeping with the idea that Satan is a liar and deceiver, so good at guile that he can appear to be the opposite of what he is. (Shakespeare picked up on this idea in *Hamlet,* which contains the line, "The devil hath power to assume a pleasing shape.") Paul is warning people that evil does not always appear to be evil on the surface. Satan might have masqueraded as a snake in Eden, but, according to Paul, he can appear pretty at times.

Back to the serpent: the Book of Revelation gives us the most powerful visual image of Satan. He is a dragon. The Greek word is *drakon,* which can be translated "dragon," "serpent," or even "sea monster." Revelation (probably the most visual book in the entire Bible) describes him as a great fiery red dragon with seven heads and ten horns (12:3). There is no doubt that the author of Revelation intended a connection between the dragon and the serpent of Genesis. He identified both with Satan. And his visual description of the dragon is probably influenced by the various idols of other gods. The gruesome demonic idols mentioned above were often dragonlike.

The loathsome dragon of Revelation meets a dire fate. He is chained for a thousand years in a bottomless pit (20:1–3), is later released to make war for a while on God's saints, but is finally cast into a lake of fire and brimstone, where he will be tormented day and night forever (20:7–10).

So Revelation gives us the basics for an image: a red dragon with a tail (12:4), seven heads, and ten horns. This is still pretty far from the usual image of Satan: basically a man with *two* horns, a beard, and (in most artwork from the past) hoofed feet like a goat. (A lot of old paintings also add batlike wings.) In fact, our usual image of Satan isn't much like a serpent or dragon. It's more like the Greek god Pan, shown in numerous statues and paintings as horned, bearded, and possessing the shaggy legs and hooves of a goat. The early Christians would have lumped Pan with all the other false gods: not a true god, but in fact a demon, an evil being on the side of Satan.

48

My Name Is Legion

"Lucifer and Satan are the same."

The devil is a nasty but nonetheless important character in the Bible. Since he is important, he is called by a lot of different names. The Old Testament refers a few times to Satan, which is a Hebrew word meaning "adversary." The Eden story does not identify the serpent with Satan, but later generations of Jews and Christians have assumed that the snake was Satan in disguise.

By the time of Jesus, though, Satan was much more on people's minds. So in the New Testament, he is called not only Satan but also devil (which means "slanderer" or "accuser"), "the prince of this world" (John 18:36), "the god of this age" (2 Corinthians 4:4), "prince of the power of the air" (Ephesians 2:2), "the evil one" (Matthew 13:19), and several others.

In Jesus' day, people believed that the devil, or Satan, was leader of a whole horde of evil beings, called "evil spirits" or "unclean spirits" or "demons." Satan and his demons not only tempt people to do evil things, they also cause physical and mental harm. On his divine mission to mankind, Jesus is out to thwart Satan's grip on human beings. Thus Jesus casts out demons from people, which includes delivering people from demons that have afflicted them bodily. (It made sense to attribute sickness to demons. Since God's ultimate will is for people to be whole and healed, we can assume it is Satan's will for us to be in pain.)

Satan is, of course, the great tempter. Immediately after Jesus begins his public life by being baptized, he goes off alone to the wilderness, where Satan tempts him. The famous temptation story is found in Matthew 4 and Luke 4. Satan tries three different ploys: he tempts Jesus (who is fasting) to turn stones into bread, to throw himself from the temple tower so that God will save him, and to worship Satan himself to attain earthly power. Jesus refuses all three. (You might say that his resisting temptation "undoes" what happened in the garden of Eden, where Adam and Eve did *not* resist temptation.)

But Jesus is much more proactive in thwarting Satan. He doesn't just resist temptation, but also sends his disciples out to deliver people from demonic power. In Luke 10, a large group of disciples known as the Seventy gleefully report to Jesus that they have been successful in casting out demons. Jesus' reply: "I saw Satan fall like lightning from heaven." It appears that Jesus is telling the Seventy that their mission is indeed having an effect on Satan and his demons. But Jesus may have intended another meaning: don't be too proud of yourselves spiritually, because it was pride that caused Satan himself to fall. That is, as you battle spiritually against Satan's kingdom, don't commit the same sin (pride) that Satan did.

Now, finally, we're getting around to the name *Lucifer.* We know that people in New Testament times connected Satan with the sin of pride. In Jewish tradition, Satan had been an angel in the heavenly court. He began to think too highly of himself and no longer wished to serve under God. So he and some other rebel angels were expelled from heaven. In heaven, they had been beautiful, but after falling from heaven they were ugly. Once angels, they were now demons. And they believed they could hurt God by tormenting God's new creation, human beings. Taking the form of the snake in the garden of Eden, Satan managed to get Adam and Eve to commit his own sin: pride. He told them if they ate the forbidden fruit, they would be like gods. Just as Satan and his followers were cast out of heaven for their pride, so Adam and Eve were expelled from the beautiful garden of Eden for their pride.

This is Jewish tradition, but is not spelled out in the Old Testament. Still, there are a couple of places in the Old Testament that *might* refer to Satan's fall from heaven. Consider Isaiah 14:12–15. It is addressed to the king of Babylon, one of the proud and mighty ancient empires that was a thorn in Israel's side. "How art thou fallen from heaven, O Lucifer, son of the morning! How art thou cut down to the ground, which didst weaken the nations! For thou hast said in thine heart, I will ascend into heaven, I will exalt my throne above the stars of God. . . . Yet thou shalt be brought down to hell." So reads the King James Version.

If you read the verse in its context, you know it is one of the Bible's many passages condemning rulers for their egotism. That was surely what Isaiah intended. But later generations of readers believed this "Lucifer" was someone more powerful than the king of Babylon. He was the proud angel who rebelled against God and was "brought down to hell." Since Jesus claimed that he saw Satan "fall like lightning from heaven," many Christians later believed he was referring to the time when Lucifer/Satan was expelled from heaven.

There is a similar "pride" passage in the Book of Ezekiel. The prophet is speaking out against the king of the rich and corrupt city of Tyre: "Your heart was lifted up because of your beauty; you corrupted your wisdom for the sake of your splendor; I cast you to the ground, I laid you before the kings, that they might gaze at you" (Ezekiel 28:17). Ezekiel was certainly not referring to Satan, but later generations of readers believed that the verse applied anyway.

To summarize: the Lucifer named in Isaiah 14 was the king of Babylon, not Satan. And certainly *Lucifer* is a very inappropriate name for Satan, since *Lucifer* means "light bearer." This is why some readers have assumed that Lucifer was the original heavenly name of the angel that rebelled and became Satan. The good angel (Lucifer, the "light bearer") sinned and became the bad devil (Satan, the "adversary").

49

Call 'Em Whatever, They're All Nasty

"'Devils' and 'demons' are the same thing."

Demons fascinate people, don't they? While the fascination with angels continues, people have never lost their interest in the demonic. (Maybe this says something about human nature, that we find evil more interesting than good.) In the 1970s, *The Exorcist* was a hit movie, so fondly remembered that it made money when it was re-released twenty-five years later.

You might recall, if you saw the movie, that the demon that possesses poor Regan is named Pazuzu. At the beginning of the movie we see a Pazuzu statue, and it is not pretty. Claws, fangs, and wings—as vile physically as it is spiritually. This was not the filmmaker's fancy, for there really was such a demon statue found, so presumably someone in ancient Assyria did worship—or fear—or both—this hideous monster.

As stated elsewhere in this book (see pages 153–154), no one in the New Testament period doubted the reality of demons. They were blamed for all sorts of human ills, and apparently their chief pleasure was in making people miserable. Jesus, and the apostles as well, had power over them. The people rescued from demonic possession were grateful, but Jesus' enemies put their own spin on it: Jesus had power over demons because he was in league with the demons himself (Matthew 12:24)! Jesus replied, "Every kingdom divided against itself is laid waste, and no city or house divided against itself will stand. And if Satan casts out Satan, he is divided against himself. How then can his kingdom stand?" (12:25–27).

So Satan was ruler over the kingdom of devils, right? Wrong. There is only one devil, and that is Satan himself. We get our word *devil* from the Greek *diabolos* (which, you may have guessed, is also the source for *diabolical*). The Greek *diabolos* is the root of our word *diabolical.* The word *diabolos* means "accuser" or "slanderer," a related meaning to the Hebrew word *Satan,* meaning "adversary." In the story of Jesus' temptation, he goes into the wilderness to be tempted "by the devil" (Matthew 4:1). In that encounter, Jesus refers to him as Satan (4:10).

There is one *diabolos,* but many *daimonia,* demons. In one of Jesus' confrontations with a demon, he asks the demon its name, and it replies, "My name is Legion, for we are many" (Mark 5:9). Regrettably, the King James Version uses *devils* in many places instead of *demons.* Most versions of the Bible use only *demons,* which is correct.

This is not a matter to lose sleep over, but a fact worth remembering anyway: one devil, lots of demons.

50

Taking Control, the Hard (But Fast) Way

"Jesus was an exorcist."

We take our word *exorcism* from the Greek *exorkizo*—but that word is never used in connection with Jesus. The New Testament uses the Greek *ekballo,* meaning to "cast out" or "expel" a demon. To *exorkizo* a demon implied the use of conjuring and magical formulas, which is not what Jesus and the apostles did. There was no incantation or magic, just an authoritative command for the demon to leave at once. The Jews had a series of formulas for use in exorcisms, but Jesus did not need these. As the Son of God, he simply ordered the demons to go away, and they did. He pointed out that this power over demons showed that the kingdom of God had come (Matthew 12:28). Strictly speaking, Jesus did cast out demons, but he was not an exorcist, for an exorcist was one who used magical formulas to expel demons.

Regarding exorcisms today (yes, they still do take place): the various acts that accompany the command to the demon—laying hands on the person, making the sign of the cross, applying holy water—are unnecessary. The movie *The Exorcist* suggested that casting out demons is a long and involved procedure, but most often it is not. In most cases, the demon either departs quickly or not at all.

51

So What Hope Do the Rest of Us Have?

"Jesus descended into hell after he died."

Jesus in hell? Where did that idea ever come from? It might surprise you to know that millions of Christians over the centuries have stated that Jesus "descended into hell."

The Apostles' Creed, a classic summary of Christian belief, states that between Jesus' burial and resurrection "he descended into hell." This puzzles many people—why would the sinless Jesus be in hell, even if it was only temporary? The problem is one of translation: the Apostles' Creed, originally written in Greek, says Christ descended into *Hades,* the Greek word for the region of the dead, not a place of eternal punishment. Paul, in Ephesians 4:9, says that before he ascended into heaven, Christ "also descended into the lower parts of the earth." So "descended into hell" is more accurately translated "descended into Hades" or "descended into the realm of death." Many churches solve the difficulty by simply omitting "descended into hell" from the Creed. But "descended into the realm of death" is important, reminding us that Christ did indeed die a normal human death before God raised him.

By the way, the Apostles' Creed was not written by the apostles themselves. It came much later. It got its name because its beliefs reflected the teachings of the apostles. It is still widely used in churches throughout the world.

52

Antichrist, 666, and Other Puzzles

"Using the prophecies in the Bible, you can predict the events of the end times."

You'll find the phrase *the day of the Lord* many times in the Bible. The prophet used it to refer to a future time when God would intervene to punish sin and deliver his righteous ones. "The day of the LORD is great and terrible; who can endure it?" (Joel 2:11). Most of the other prophets spoke of the "great and terrible day," including Isaiah, Jeremiah, Ezekiel, Amos, Zephaniah, Zechariah, and Malachi.

The New Testament adds a new element: the return of Jesus Christ to earth, when he will judge all people. The apostle Paul referred to the "day of the Lord Jesus" (2 Corinthians 1:14). According to 2 Peter 3:10, the day will catch people by surprise and will be dramatic: "The day of the LORD will come as a thief in the night." The idea is that it will catch people unaware, thus the faithful must be alert at all times.

Now, we know that a "thief in the night" doesn't give much warning about his coming. This was exactly what Peter and the other New Testament writers meant. You have no idea when the end of time will come. But this hasn't stopped lots of people over the centuries from making some guesses.

We call this fertile—and sometimes weird—area of study eschatology, from the Greek word *eschaton,* meaning "end" or "last thing." Christians often refer to the "end times," when God brings earthly history to a close and Jesus comes back to claim his saints. People who study eschatology, the end times, try to harmonize those different parts of the Bible that refer to the end times. The inspiring but puzzling Book of Revelation at the end of the Bible is important in eschatology, and so are Paul's statements in 1 Corinthians 15, 1 Thessalonians 4, and 2 Thessalonians 2. From the Old Testament, Daniel 7–12 are studied closely.

Some people, not all of them Christians, get a kick out of this study. The idea is to match prophecies from the Bible with world events so you can see what is likely to happen next and maybe even get an idea when everything will end. (At that time, of course, no one will bother to study eschatology anymore.) Eschatology is not only interesting but profitable. The *New York Times,* no friend of Christianity or the Bible, described Hal Lindsey as the best-selling author of the 1970s. Lindsey had a string of successes, beginning with *The Late Great Planet Earth.* People were fascinated by Lindsey's prediction of the fulfillment of prophecies of the end times. As it turned out, Lindsey was, to put it politely, not always correct in his predictions. But of course, when you write a book about the future, you collect your royalty payments *before* you are proved wrong.

I'm not trying to pick on Hal Lindsey here. Using the Bible to map out a chronology of the end has been going on for centuries. Just twenty years or so after Jesus' death and resurrection, Paul had to remind Christians not to obsess about when and where the end times would come (2 Thessalonians 2). But his words have gone unheeded. There is a powerful temptation to read through Revelation and ask, "Who is this horrible 'Beast' that torments God's people? Is he someone in the future, or might he be someone now, someone like? . . ." Fill in that blank with any name you like from history: *Napoleon, Hitler, Stalin, Saddam Hussein, Emperor Nero,* whoever has caused suffering in the world. And who might be the "Antichrist" that the Bible speaks of? Someone living now, who in time will persecute God's people? In the 1500s, during the Protestant

Reformation, many Protestants said that the pope was the Antichrist. The pope, in turn, said that the Antichrist was Protestant leader Martin Luther. Pick any villain from history and we can guarantee that someone referred to him as the Antichrist. Everyone seems to have forgotten the Bible's own statement that *many* Antichrists have come into the world (1 John 2:18). People seem to take more pleasure in having one particular villain to boo and hiss.

And then there is that sinister number, 666, found in Revelation 13:11–18. This is the number of "the Beast," who is probably an evil ruler (or perhaps an entire government) persecuting the faithful, but whether past or future no one knows. People have been trying for centuries to connect 666 with some famous person's name, and probably every notable person has been accused of being "the Beast." The number gained a lot of fame from *The Omen* trilogy of movies, where the number was a kind of birthmark on the scalp of Damien, the Antichrist. Hollywood has learned from *The Omen* and its many clones that eschatology can be profitable.

Is all of this just harmless fun? Maybe not. The New Testament makes it clear that the goals in life are loving God and loving your neighbor. Eschatology can be amusing and even absorbing, but there isn't much evidence that it makes people more loving and compassionate. It is true that Jesus' return to earth is a serious concern in the New Testament. But Jesus himself emphasized something important about his return: *You have no idea when it will happen.* "Concerning that day and hour no one knows, not even the angels of heaven, nor the Son, but the Father only. . . . Therefore, you also must be ready, for the Son of Man is coming at an hour you do not expect" (Matthew 24:36, 44). Paul and Peter both referred to the return as coming like "a thief in the night."

The bottom line of what the Bible says about the end times is this: live your lives as if Jesus might return at any moment. The prophecies of the end were not made to give you an intellectual puzzle to solve, but to remind you to live the right way so you would not be ashamed if suddenly you were called to the Final Judgment.

53

Israel's Most Famous Box, and Harrison Ford

"The Old Testament ark of the covenant was guarded by protector demons."

This never crossed anyone's mind until the movie *Raiders of the Lost Ark* came out. For that matter, many people had probably never heard of the ark of the covenant until that popular movie made the ark a familiar image.

The ark seen in the movie does fit the description found in the Bible (Exodus 25:10–22). It was a gold-covered wooden chest, carried on two poles. Its solid-gold lid had images of two winged creatures (the "cherubim") facing each other. The ark signified God's presence among the Israelites. They did not actually worship the ark (since the Ten Commandments strictly forbid worshiping anything but God), but they did consider it sacred. The reason it was carried on poles was that no human hand was supposed to touch it. (More about that later on.) The ark was the centerpiece of the tabernacle, the large tent where Moses went to meet with God.

Miracles were associated with the ark: crossing the Jordan River on dry land (Joshua 3), the crumbling of the walls of Jericho (Joshua 6), and the harm the ark did when the pagan Philistines captured it and placed it in their god Dagon's temple (1 Samuel 5). After the ark brought a plague on the Philistines, they returned it to Israel.

When King David made Jerusalem his capital, he brought the ark there. During the reign of his son Solomon, the ark's resting place was the great temple that Solomon built (1 Kings 8:3–9). Inside the ark were the stone tablets with the Ten Commandments.

What became of the ark? *Raiders of the Lost Ark* was correct in claiming that it mysteriously disappeared. Most likely it was captured when the Babylonians destroyed the temple in 586 B.C. The Apocrypha contains the legend that the prophet Jeremiah hid the ark away in a cave somewhere (2 Maccabees 2:5).

If you have seen the movie (and most people have), you may recall its terrifying finale. The archaeologist Indiana Jones (Harrison Ford) has taken great pains to locate the ark, but his Nazi rivals take it from him. Rather foolishly, they open the ark, and out rush some of the worst demons (or spirits) ever seen on film. These destroy (in horrible ways) the men who have been rash enough to desecrate the sacred ark.

Anything in the Bible to indicate that such "demons" protected the ark? Not really. The Nazi capture of the ark gave the producers a chance to unleash some impressive special effects. However, the movie's writers may have been aware of one incident in the Bible where someone touched the ark and deeply regretted it. In 2 Samuel 6, we learn of the great joy when King David has the ark brought to Jerusalem. It is being transported there by oxcart, and when the oxen stumble, a man named Uzzah touches the ark to steady it. The sacred ark is *not* supposed to be touched, of course. Uzzah is struck down on the spot, "and he died there beside the ark of God." We are not told how, and we can assume that Uzzah did not die because flying demons rushed out of the ark. But the Uzzah incident emphasizes the power and sacredness that Israel attributed to the ark. The finale of the movie is a kind of high-tech Hollywood version of Uzzah's death.

PART VI

MISUNDERSTANDING ANGELS AND HEAVEN

ANGELS IN HEAVEN

There are nine orders of angels, and they reside in seven heavens . . . or do they?

54

Someone to Watch Over Me

"Each person has a guardian angel."

Ideas and beliefs go in and out of fashion, just as clothes do. While for years angels were seldom discussed (even among most Christians), they are a hot topic today. Books and magazine articles discuss guardian angels, including how to get in touch with your own. What does the Bible say about guardian angels, in the sense of one special angel guarding each person?

Not much. While angels' protection of us is mentioned many times (Psalm 91:11–12, to name one important reference), there are only two passages that hint that each of us has his own particular angel. Matthew 18:10 has Jesus saying, "See that you do not look down on one of these little ones. For I tell you that their angels in heaven always see the face of my Father in heaven" (NIV). Jesus had just spoken to his disciples about being humble like a little child, then told them the seriousness of leading a "little one" astray. While his words in 18:10 suggest that angels watch them, there is nothing said about guarding them, nor is anything said about one angel per little one.

Acts 12 tells of Peter's deliverance from prison by an angel. When free, he goes to the home of some fellow Christians, shocking the servant girl who hears his voice. His friends tell the girl, "It must be his angel." Some commentators say that the friends believed that Peter's guardian angel had appeared in Peter's place. Apparently many Jews of that time believed that a person's guardian angel could appear exactly as that person. Acts gives no indication that this is so, or that guardian angels exist.

In short, the Bible gives us no definite teaching on whether each person has a particular angel. But there are definitely angels (plural) guarding us (plural). Theologian John Calvin, who insisted on basing his theology on the Bible, said he neither affirmed nor denied if each believer has a single angel assigned to him. Calvin did affirm that angels do watch over us, and to speculate on how many there are or whether each of us has one is a waste of time.

55

Nine Angels Swarming

"There are nine categories of angels in the Bible."

Christians get (or *should* get) their beliefs about angels from the Bible, but one of the most powerful influences on belief about angels was the medieval author known as Dionysius the Areopagite. Acts 17:34 mentions that the apostle Paul converted a man named Dionysius in the city of Athens. (Paul spoke at a place called the Areopagus, so this convert came to be called Dionysius the Areopagite.) But the man who wrote theological works under the name Dionysius probably lived around the year 500, and is known to history (since we don't know his real name) as Pseudo-Dionysius. This author (whoever he, or they, may have been) had an extremely orderly mind, the type that enjoys sorting things into neat categories. In the widely read book *The Celestial Hierarchy,* Pseudo-Dionysius explained that there are nine types of angels. Moving from highest to lowest, they are these: seraphim, cherubim, thrones, dominions (or dominations), virtues (or authorities), powers, principalities, archangels, and angels. The author did not pull all these names out of thin air, for they are all mentioned in the Bible, though never in one place. Colossians 1:16 mentions thrones, dominions, principalities, and powers all together, but it is doubtful that Paul himself had any belief in the "nine orders" that Pseudo-Dionysius described.

Dionysius not only categorized the angels but also described their work, and he emphasized the importance of importance—that is, the top category (seraphim) was most important, being closest to

God, while the regular angels were the least important, but still vital, since they were the "foot soldiers" who dealt with most human beings.

Pseudo-Dionysius was widely read in the Middle Ages, even though most theologians were aware that he was not the real Dionysius of Acts 17. Probably no book (other than the Bible) has had more influence on beliefs about angels than *The Celestial Hierarchy.*

56

The Logical Number, If They Are Numbered

"The Bible says there are seven heavens."

Seven is one of the "sacred numbers" of the Bible, always a "good" number that suggests goodness, completeness. There are seven days in a week (with the seventh being the Sabbath, the holy day), and numerous other sevens. And seven is still, after all these centuries, a "lucky" number. Even someone who had never read the Bible probably knows that "seventh heaven" must mean "the best place to be." Does the Bible mention just how many heavens there are? No. But the apostle Paul mentions in 2 Corinthians 12:2 that he knew a man (he may be referring to himself) who was "caught up to the third heaven." How many heavens did Paul believe in? We have no idea. But there was a Jewish tradition that there were seven, the seventh being the highest and best.

Seven is a "holy" number in the Bible, but nine isn't bad, either. In the world's great poem about heaven, hell, and purgatory, Dante's *Divine Comedy,* there are nine (not seven) heavens, the ninth being closest to God. Somehow "ninth heaven" passed into language as "cloud nine," meaning "a wonderful place to be."

57

Taking Themselves Lightly

"The Bible says that angels have wings."

How many people predicted the angel trend that began in the 1990s? All of a sudden, bookstores were selling dozens of books about angels. Angel figurines and plaques became trendy, and there were (and probably still are) entire stores devoted to angels.

These weren't exactly the angels of the Bible or of Christian tradition. The angels popular today are mostly New Age angels, helpful spiritual guides and protectors who make no moral demands on human beings. One culture critic claimed that the angels that are so trendy today are more like "spiritual pets," providing comfort and affection but not expecting their "masters" to meet any particular standards. The angels of the angel stores are sweet, kind, and seem to have no vital connection to God or morality.

Still, the trend has led to some renewed interest in what the Bible says about angels, which is a great deal. The Bible does *not,* however, say too much about their appearance.

Before we look at what the Bible says about angels, we have to deal with a problem of translation. We use *angel* to translate the Hebrew word *malakh* and the Greek word *angelos.* Both words means simply "messenger." Neither word carries any connotation of being "heavenly" in appearance, and neither word suggests wings or white robes. An "angel" from God is simply a "messenger" from God. So an angel is a being who acts as kind of intermediary between God and man, conveying messages and carrying out God's orders on earth.

The Bible begins with God creating the world. Did angels already exist? We don't know. In Genesis 1:26, God says, "Let us make man in our image." Who is "us"? One common interpretation is that God was speaking to his angels, his heavenly court. Psalm 8:5 states that angels were present when man was created. At any rate, "our image" means that man is special. God has already created animals, but man is different, made to be like God and the angels in many ways.

The first actual mention of angels is in connection with the garden of Eden. After Adam and Eve ate the forbidden fruit, God expelled them from Eden. Genesis 3:25 says that cherubim with a flaming sword stood at the side of Eden to make sure man would not return there. What were cherubim? Definitely not the same as "cherubs," the cute cuddly winged infants that go by that name. The cherubim (that's plural—one cherub, two cherubim) in the Old Testament were the winged figures on the lid of the ark of the covenant, the gold chest made famous in the movie *Raiders of the Lost Ark*. The ark symbolized God's presence among the Israelites. It was a gold chest with, on the top, two winged figures, with the wings touching each other. Probably these figures were human in shape, but with wings. These were the cherubim, and, yes, they had wings. However, the Bible never identifies the cherubim with angels.

In fact, the angels mentioned in the Bible quite easily pass themselves off as humans. Genesis 19 tells the tale of God sending two angels to save Lot from the immoral (and doomed) city of Sodom. The two divine visitors are the object of an attempted rape by the men of Sodom.

In Genesis 22, God tells Abraham to sacrifice his beloved son Isaac. Before Abraham can do the deed, an angel stays his hand. The text tells us nothing about this angel's appearance.

Jacob, using a stone for a pillow, falls asleep and has his famous dream of a stairway with angels going up and down it. Jacob was having a vision of a "stairway to heaven" (Genesis 28). What was it about their appearance that told Jacob these were angels? We are not told.

Exodus 3 tells of Moses' fateful encounter with the burning bush. In 3:2, we are told that the "angel of the LORD" appeared to Moses from the midst of the bush. Later in Exodus, however, there is no mention of "the angel of the LORD," but only of "the LORD" himself. This happens many times in the Old Testament: a person encounters God's messenger (angel) and identifies him with God himself. Is there confusion or contradiction in this? Not at all. The person had an encounter with the divine, with the power of God. He can describe it as a meeting with God himself, or with God's angel. Either way, God's power was manifested in the meeting.

The Bible is never specific about just *how* people knew they were encountering God's messengers. Certainly it is never the messenger's appearance that gives him away. Judges 6 tells of Gideon receiving a visit from an angel, who tells Gideon that he is God's chosen one to save Israel from the feared desert raiders, the Midianites. Gideon was so skeptical of this visitor that he asked for a sign. The angel used his staff to set fire to some meat and bread. Then the visitor mysteriously disappeared.

Sometimes angels did not appear in human form. They simply did God's bidding without being seen. The death of the firstborn in Egypt is attributed to the "angel of death" (Exodus 12:23). (You might recall in the movie *The Ten Commandments* that the death angel is shown as a sort of sinister fog moving over the landscape.) Much later, the Assyrian king Sennacherib's 185,000 soldiers are struck down by the "angel of the LORD" (2 Kings 19).

The Book of Psalms says a lot about angels—but not their appearance. Several of the Psalms mention angels as being part of God's court—and as protectors of human beings. Psalm 91 claims that God's angels protect his people, that angels shall "bear you up, lest you dash your foot against a stone." No mention of wings, although it sounds as if they might be capable of flight.

The prophet Isaiah had a life-changing encounter with another type of heavenly being: the seraphim. In Isaiah's vision, the seraphim have six wings each, two for flight, two covering their faces, two covering their feet. They are caught up in praising God. Obviously these are part of God's heavenly court. But these are not the angels that are usually encountered in the Bible.

Another prophet, Ezekiel, also had a vision of heavenly beings. These were cherubim, mentioned earlier. But the cherubim Ezekiel saw were different from those atop the ark of the covenant. The beings Ezekiel saw had four wings, the feet of calves, and four faces (lion, man, ox, and eagle). They flew about and gave the impression of fire and lightning. Ezekiel 10 says that these cherubim are the guardians of the Lord's throne. Other than having wings, these look nothing like the angels we usually see in artworks.

Interestingly, the Book of Revelation speaks of four "living creatures" that sing God's praises in the heavenly court. Like the ones Ezekiel saw, these have four faces (again, lion, man, ox, eagle), but with six wings instead of four (Revelation 4:6–9). But these creatures are not referred to as angels.

To summarize: in the Bible, God's angels are always human in appearance, with no wings. The heavenly creatures known as cherubim and seraphim, however, do possess wings—two, four, or six—but are decidedly nonhuman in appearance.

58

A Gatekeeper, but No Metal Detector

"Peter stands at the gate of heaven."

You could probably fill a book—or several—with all the jokes told about someone going to heaven. Inevitably the joke includes the line, "and when he got there, St. Peter said . . ." Yes, Peter at the gate of heaven—a beloved part of "pop religion." Does it have any basis in the Bible?

Sort of—but not really.

Later in this book (see pages 269, 270) we'll look at a couple of basic Catholic beliefs: Peter was the first bishop of Rome, and Peter was "prince of the apostles" who passed on his spiritual authority to the popes. Peter was, as I've already observed, a key player in the early history of Christianity. He was the most dominant and outspoken of Jesus' twelve disciples. After Jesus' resurrection and ascension into heaven, Peter was an effective preacher and the first apostle to carry the gospel to non-Jews (see Acts 10). We can assume that this apostle, missionary, and saint would be in heaven. How did he come to be seen as its gatekeeper?

Go to Matthew 16. This is Peter's famous "confession," in which he is the first person on earth to say he believes that Jesus is the Christ, the Messiah that Israel has longed for. Jesus is extremely pleased with this: "Blessed are you . . . I tell you, you are Peter, and on this rock I will build my church, and the gates of hell shall not prevail against it. I will give you the keys of the kingdom of heaven, and whatever you bind on earth shall be bound in heaven, and whatever you loose on earth shall be loosed in heaven" (16:17–19).

As stated on page 269, these are some of the most controversial words in the whole Bible. Catholics claim that with these words, Jesus made Peter the head of the church on earth. More importantly, they believe that the popes are the inheritors of this authority. Needless to say, not all Christians have accepted this interpretation. Some Christians have been so offended by the passage that they claim it is not a genuine saying of Jesus. (It appears in Matthew's Gospel but not the others.) At no other time does Jesus use the word *church,* which to some readers looks kind of suspicious. (You do not get the impression from reading the Gospels that Jesus was out to set up any kind of institution.) I can't settle this centuries-old controversy here. It is worth repeating: the belief that Peter was invested with authority over the whole church has never been accepted by all Christians.

Aside from that, the rest of Jesus' words are puzzling. He tells Peter (or all the disciples?) he will give him the "keys of the kingdom of heaven." Ah, finally—the simple explanation of St. Peter the gatekeeper of heaven. It also explains why Peter is shown in artworks holding two very large keys. And it explains why popes have been referred to as having the "power of the keys." But frankly, no one agrees on what the "keys" mean. The idea seems to be spiritual authority, whatever that might involve. If you have the keys to a place, obviously you are a person of some authority and power in that place.

So Peter is given the "keys of the kingdom of heaven." Obviously the "keys" are meant figuratively. There is nothing in the Bible to suggest that someone who just died passes through a gateway where Peter is stationed.

Still, St. Peter at the gate of heaven is a standard part of pop religion, even if it has no real basis in the Bible. People will continue to tell and enjoy heaven jokes that feature Peter.

59

Imagine the Size of Those Oysters

"Heaven has pearly gates."

The Book of Revelation bothers a lot of people, even the most devoted Bible readers. How, people wonder, do you interpret this odd book at the end of the Bible? It's full of symbols and weird, troubling images: a dragon, a beast with several heads, a lake of fire, that puzzling number 666, and a hundred other images that leave people scratching their heads. But people are focusing on the individual trees and missing the whole forest. The basic idea of Revelation is clear enough: God's people will suffer terrible persecution, and Satan and his forces will do horrible things on the earth, but in the end God and good will triumph, and the saints will dwell forever in a heaven (the New Jerusalem) that is described splendidly.

Many of the images people connect with heaven really are found in the Bible. Streets made of gold? Yes, that's in the Bible (Revelation 21:21). "The street of the city was pure gold, transparent as glass." In fact, the whole city is pure gold (21:18). Revelation is full of images of darkness and evil, but in the book's happy ending, *light* is prominent. "The city has no need of sun or moon to shine on it, for the glory of God gives its light, and its light is the Lamb. By its light will the nations walk, and the kings of the earth will bring their glory into it, and its gates will never be shut by day—and there will be no night there" (21:23–25). A word of explanation: until the last three hundred years or so, most cities had high walls and gates in case the city was attacked. Heaven has gates, but they are never shut, meaning that there will never be anything to break the peace or threaten its people.

And speaking of gates, what about the famous "pearly gates" of heaven? This is a case in which the popular idea about heaven is almost—but not quite—in line with the Bible. Heaven's gates are not "pearly" or "made of pearl"—each gate of heaven *is* a pearl: "The twelve gates were twelve pearls, each of the gates made of a single pearl" (21:21). The passage in Revelation says that heaven's gates were never shut, so we have the image of an enormous pearl (on hinges, perhaps) attached to the walls of heaven, swung open for all eternity.

Worth mentioning: to people of the time, the pearl was the jewel above all jewels. Today we value diamonds as the finest gems, but in those days pearls were the most valuable. Among the Jews, a *pearl* could refer to a wise and valuable saying. We still use the phrase *pearls of wisdom* sometimes. Jesus told a parable of a merchant who found one extremely valuable pearl and sold all he had to obtain it (Matthew 13:45–46). Jesus was telling his listeners that the kingdom of God was a "pearl" they should desire above everything else.

Incidentally, the Greek word for "pearl" is *margarites*.

60

Announcing the End of a Fine Musical Career

"The angel Gabriel blows a trumpet."

When pop culture and the Bible cross paths, some interesting items result. Take the angel Gabriel, always connected with a trumpet. Cole Porter gave us the song "Blow, Gabriel, Blow," and a hundred other songs have Gabriel as trumpeter. In the movie *The Horn Blows at Midnight,* comic Jack Benny played a trumpeter who dreams he is the angel Gabriel. If Gabriel is remembered by most people, it is as the trumpet player whose blast on his horn signals the end of time.

Gabriel happens to be one of only two angels named in the Bible. The other one is Michael, who is described as an archangel (meaning a sort of "ruling angel"—head over other angels). The prophet Daniel referred to Michael as a "prince," a sort of heavenly protector of Israel (Daniel 10:13, 12:1). The Book of Revelation pictures a conflict at the end of time, with Michael and his angels fighting against the dragon, Satan (12:7).

Gabriel's first appearance in the Bible is in the Book of Daniel, where he is an interpreter of Daniel's mysterious visions (8:16, 9:21). But he is best known for his role in Luke's Gospel, where he announces two miraculous pregnancies: the aged Elizabeth (who gives birth to John the Baptist) and the virgin Mary (who gives birth to Jesus). Gabriel goes to Mary in Nazareth and tells her she is to bear a child, "the son of the Highest" (Luke 1:32). Mary's encounter with Gabriel is known in Christian tradition as the Annunciation (meaning "announcing," of course). The Annunciation has been a favorite subject for artists throughout the centuries.

Now back to the trumpet. In older times, trumpets were used to signal something important. Jews and Christians believed that at the Last Judgment there would be a global blast of the trumpet, with angels accompanying the appearance of God. Jesus himself said that angels would sound the trumpet and gather God's people together (Matthew 24:31). Paul spoke of the astounding event in this way: "The Lord himself will descend from heaven with a shout, with the voice of an archangel, and with the trumpet of God" (1 Thessalonians 4:16).

Alas, no mention of Gabriel and the trumpet. The Bible does not name the angel who will blow that fateful blast. So why is Gabriel connected with the trumpet? One guess: since Gabriel announced the birth of Jesus to Mary, Christians may have assumed he was the "announcing angel," so it seems logical that he would announce the end of the world.

61

The Smothers Brothers as Religious Authorities

"People become angels after death."

Remember the Smothers Brothers? Back in the 1970s, they starred in a short-lived TV sitcom. In it, brother Tommy played a deceased man who had become an angel (no wings), reporting to an unseen celestial supervisor named Ralph and intervening in the life of brother Dickie. The series reflected a popular belief that when people pass on, they become angels (or at least, *good* people do). What is the basis of this belief, other than wishful thinking?

Does the Bible anywhere suggest that a person really becomes an angel after death? The answer is "No, but . . ." Consider Acts 12, in which the apostle Peter has been freed from prison by an angel. Once free, Peter goes to the house of some fellow believers. Rhoda, the young woman who goes to answer Peter's knock at the door, is overjoyed to hear his voice and runs to tell the others. Believing Peter could not possibly have escaped prison, they insist Rhoda is mistaken. But when she persists, they say to her, "It is his angel" (Acts 12:15). How do we interpret this? Some Bible scholars claim that there was a popular belief in those days that a person's guardian angel could take on the appearance of the person himself. So the passage does not necessarily tell us that Peter's friends thought he had died and become an angel.

Heaven is the habitation of angels, and of Christians, too, so you can see why some people take and leap of the imagination and assume that Christians *become* angels when they enter heaven. (But neither they nor the angels have wings, as you can learn more about on pages 178–181.)

62

Harping on Those Golden Streets

"The Bible depicts heaven as a boring place where people do nothing but worship God forever."

Critics of the Christian view of heaven point out that it might be eternal but that it appears *eternally boring*. Who would enjoy (they ask) eternally walking on golden streets, playing a harp, and worshiping God?

I have to respond by first admitting that those particular details about heaven *are* in the Bible. All are found in the Book of Revelation, with its stunning depiction of the New Jerusalem with golden streets, gates made of pearl, and white-robed saints praising God and playing harps. Yes, all of that is in the Bible. And if that was all the Bible said about heaven, it does sound as if it could get monotonous.

I can only respond that the Bible presents us with glimpses (but not the complete picture) of heaven. In the New Testament, the authors admit that they are trying to describe the indescribable. Paul understood the difficulty: "No eye has seen, nor ear heard, nor the heart of man imagined, what God has prepared for those who love him" (1 Corinthians 2:9). Paul also claimed he knew a man who was "caught up to the third heaven . . . and he heard things that cannot be told, which man may not utter" (2 Corinthians 12:3). Paul never seems to be at a loss for words, but he becomes that way when trying to speak of heaven. Our minds and our words have limitations: "Now we see in a mirror dimly, but then face to face. Now I know in part; then I shall know fully" (1 Corinthians 13:12).

Jesus told a number of parables about the kingdom of God. In one of them, the kingdom is compared to a wedding feast, with food aplenty (Matthew 22:1–14). For its time, a wedding feast was the ultimate in a good time—food, drink, dancing, music, festive atmosphere. Keep in mind what a parable is: a comparison, a story that presents two things that are similar. When Jesus told the parable of the wedding feast, he was saying that heaven is *something like* a wedding feast. That is, heaven would generate feelings like joy, merriment, warm fellowship, security, et cetera. Even the Book of Revelation uses the image of a wedding banquet (19:9). The image of a banquet sounds appealing enough, especially when everyone would be kind to each other, with no cattiness or petty feuding as at earthly gatherings. We have to assume that a place of joy and love and fellowship would not be boring, and in such a state we might not even be conscious of the passage of time at all.

63

Celestial String Band?

"Angels in heaven play harps."

Revelation 15:2 speaks of the saints in heaven having harps to play, and harps are mentioned many times in the Bible—but not in connection with angels. Despite harps being in heaven, and despite angels portrayed as praising God, the Bible never actually mentions angels with harps. Perhaps the common image comes from John Milton, whose great epic poem *Paradise Lost* describes angel harpists.

64

Triangulation, or a Two-Party Afterlife?

"After death, a person goes to heaven, hell, or purgatory."

According to the New Testament, heaven and hell are the two final destinations for human beings. Catholics teach that there is another state after death: purgatory. There people whose final destination is heaven must first spend time "purging away" sins they committed in their earthly lives. Catholics base this teaching on a section in the Apocrypha, 2 Maccabees 12:39–45, which speaks of offering sacrifices for dead persons "that they might be delivered from their sin." Part of Catholic teaching regarding purgatory is that people still alive can do deeds to benefit people in purgatory. Catholic theologians such as the famous Augustine taught that sins that had gone unrepented at the time of the person's death would be purged by fire in purgatory—not the punishing fire of hell, but a purifying fire, readying the person for heaven.

Many people would ask the obvious question: was the belief in purgatory based on this one verse in the Apocrypha? It isn't much of a basis for belief, considering that the New Testament, which came later than the Apocrypha, never mentions purgatory but refers only to heaven and hell. In the 1500s, the leaders of the Protestant Reformation threw out the Apocrypha as a foundation for Christian belief, and they also threw out the belief in purgatory. To this day, Catholic Bibles include the books of the Apocrypha, while most other Bibles do not.

PART VII

SOME BLURRY IMAGES OF GOD

ADAM AND EVE

God imposed a mighty heavy punishment for the simple eating of one fruit . . . or was it?

65

One Strike, They're Out

"In Genesis, God is cruel because he punishes Adam and Eve for one mistake."

If you are a fan of the comic strip "Peanuts," you might recall the strip where nasty-tempered Lucy tells Snoopy to hold her balloon for a while—"And whatever you do, don't let go of it!" Snoopy, with the balloon's string in his mouth, dozes off, wakes up, yawns—and the balloon floats away. In the final panel, it is night, and Snoopy is running away, with these words over his head: "Make one mistake and you pay for it the rest of your life!" Lucy, as all "Peanuts" readers know, is not a person to trifle with.

Some pastors have used that strip as an illustration in sermons about the garden of Eden. Like Snoopy, Adam and Eve are given a command ("Don't eat from that one particular tree")—and they louse things up. In Snoopy's words, "Make one mistake and you pay for it the rest of your life!" In the case of Adam and Eve, they not only pay for it themselves but also louse things up for all of their billions of descendants.

We all know Lucy is a nasty character. But isn't God supposed to be loving and compassionate? It definitely offends our modern mentality that God's rule is "One strike and you're out." Why didn't Adam and Eve get at least a second chance? If the serpent was the real culprit, why didn't God punish it and give Adam and Eve a "slap on the wrist"? And wasn't that rule about not eating from that one tree—well, wasn't that kind of arbitrary? And if God really loved these two people, why did he allow the serpent in the garden?

Lots and lots of questions. None of them is new. Centuries ago, sensitive readers were asking the same things. There is just one problem: there are no alternate versions of Genesis. The one we have is the real article, whether we like it or not, and whether it fits our contemporary notions of fairness and responsibility. The author, or authors, of Genesis did not sit down with scrolls and ink and say, "Hmmm, what we really need to do is slant this so that in the twenty-first century people will read it and not make a fuss." In fact, we can imagine the authors saying to us, "Look, our aim is to write something eternally true. It's you who have the trendy notions about justice and responsibility." One reason many people do not read the Bible: it makes us uncomfortable, because so many of its cherished beliefs run head-on with our own cherished beliefs.

But back to Genesis 2–3 and the Fall of man. One thing you notice rather quickly about Genesis: it moves fast, especially at the beginning. By the end of the Bible's first page, the whole universe has been created. By the end of the second page, man has been given a beautiful place to live, presumably forever. By the end of the third page, everything has been seriously, and permanently, ruined. Paradise has been lost, and you will not see it again until the *last* page of the Bible, in Revelation. The story has moved so quickly that we lose all sense of time. Adam is created and put in the garden. God sees that "It is not good that the man should be alone"—but how long was this after Adam's creation? God brings Adam the animals so he can name them. Again, how long after Adam was made? Then God makes Eve from Adam's rib. How long had Adam been alive then? A day? Weeks? Years? We are not told. "The man and his wife were both naked and were not ashamed." How long were they in this innocent, and happy, condition? How long did they enjoy Eden before Chapter 3 breaks in with its "Now the serpent . . ."? The author of Genesis tells us none of these details. You almost get the impression that he had a limited supply of ink and papyrus and had to keep things very brief and to the point. Many ancient stories are told this way. You can almost picture the ancient Israelite telling the story by firelight, when his toddler interrupts: "Papa, how long were they in the garden before the serpent talked to them?" "Shh! Don't interrupt!" Details sometimes get in the way. The main point of the story was, and is, this: God made man good and innocent. Man had only to obey and be happy with his lot, and all would have been fine. But man disobeyed, and man wished to "be like God." Every one of us, in our own way, repeats the sin of Adam.

But the questions still linger: isn't God unkind? Shouldn't they have been given another chance? Or at least a lesser punishment?

Let's return to the matter of the story's brevity. If you read straight through from Genesis 1 to 4, you would think, "Boy, Paradise sure didn't last long." To repeat: we have no idea how long they were in the garden before they sinned. Perhaps many years. If it was a long period, we can easily imagine that the one restriction about that one particular tree was beginning to get to the man and woman. Genesis 3 introduces the snake so quickly that we just assume it had never crossed the humans' minds to disobey God. *But it must have.* The ancient Hebrews could not accept, any more than we could, that Adam and Eve were innocent dupes of an animal. The snake brings up the subject of the forbidden tree. But Eve betrays the fact that she has already thought about it. She says to the snake that God told them, "You shall not eat of the fruit of the tree that is in the middle of the garden, neither shall you touch it, lest you die." Eve, not the snake, is twisting God's words here, for God never mentioned *touching* the fruit. You can almost hear a pouty three-year-old: "Mommy said I couldn't open the cookie jar. She said I couldn't even *look* at it!" Eve's mind (and probably Adam's as well, though we don't know) is already primed for what the serpent tells her. How long has she been pondering that tree? A day? Perhaps, more likely, a decade?

The snake starts off playing loosely with the truth: "Did God actually say, 'You shall not eat of any tree in the garden'?" Eve adds her own distortion, the detail about not touching the fruit. In the Bible, there is usually a connection between sin and twisting the truth. Both parties have the same idea in mind: God isn't as nice as we thought, he is holding back something good from us.

There is another element in this story that most readers overlook. Before she has even eaten the fruit, "the woman saw that the tree was good for food." Hmmm. Was this an error on the author's part? Not likely. The meaning is clear enough—she already *thinks* the fruit is good, and for the basic human reason: it is off-limits. She also "saw that is was a delight to the eyes, and that the tree was to be desired to make one wise." Odd—why hadn't she noticed before that it was a "delight to the eyes"? Answer: it became a "delight" because "the tree was to be desired to make one wise."

By the time she takes a bite of the fruit, it is obvious she does not fully trust God. She has believed the serpent, not God. She does not believe God's threat that they will "surely die" if they disobey. She trusts the lowly snake more than God. Clearly the sin has already occurred before she eats the fruit.

Trust cuts both ways: God's one restriction ("Don't eat from that one tree") was a test of man. Can I trust you, Adam and Eve, to choose to obey me? Or will you "do your own thing," even if it brings you harm? Adam and Eve fail the test. God cannot trust them. (Try this analogy: God is a nice guy, overseeing the baggage scanners at an airport. He hires a man and woman whom he hopes he can trust and says, "Remember, do *not* let anyone carrying a weapon get through here!" The two fail. Can they be trusted?)

I've mentioned elsewhere in this book that a key element is missing from the story of the Fall: neither Adam nor Eve shows the slightest sign of repentance, no sign of remorse. From the Bible's point of view, that is a *major* problem. God, as seen throughout the Bible, often is wrathful, angry at sin. But a possibility is always floating around in the moral atmosphere: If you sinful people will change, turn from your wickedness, then . . . But God can't repent on man's behalf. Remember free will? Adam and Eve chose to disobey. They could have chosen to cry out, "We are truly sorry!" They didn't. Instead, they hid from God. Then Eve blamed the serpent and Adam blamed Eve. The basic juvenile tactic: hide, then when found, say, "It wasn't *my* fault." If Adam and Eve acted like adults before they sinned, they acted like children afterward.

Did they *deserve* another chance? The Genesis author doesn't deal with such questions. We can imagine his likely answer to our question about second chances: don't you think they would just mess things up again? Our honest answer: probably so. And in the theology of the Bible, *we* are all Adam and Eve. Would we have done differently than they did? Probably not.

Anyone who has ever been faced with a cheating spouse knows the main problem: something sacred has been shattered. Trust is gone, maybe forever. Once the person you loved most deceives you, do you trust again? Some do; many do not. In Snoopy's words, "Make one mistake and you pay for it the rest of your life!" It applies to adulterous spouses. It applies to the couple in Eden.

66

Fairness on a Mighty Vindictive Planet

"The 'eye for an eye' principle shows that God and the Bible are mean-spirited."

Retribution and vengeance are supposed to be "mean-spirited." Clearly we live in a mean-spirited society, then. For the first time in human history, a person spilling hot coffee in her lap can be awarded a huge sum from the corporation that happened to sell her the coffee. Fair? No one has ever said so. In these outrageous lawsuits against big corporations, "fairness" and "justice" never enter the picture. Whatever harm the so-called victim suffered, the final award can be the mountain given in place of the molehill. In addition to medical costs and the person's lost time from employment, there is that blank check called "psychological damages." People make jokes about this practice. It isn't really funny, since every corporation passes on its costs to consumers.

We have to say all this as we hark back to the *lex talionis,* the Bible's famous, or infamous, law of retaliation. "Whoever takes a human life shall surely be put to death. Whoever takes an animal's life shall make it good, life for life. If anyone injures his neighbor, as he has done it shall be done to him, fracture for fracture, eye for eye, tooth for tooth; whatever injury he has given a person shall be given to him" (Leviticus 24:17–20). Mean-spirited? Vengeful? Lacking in compassion? Perhaps. But the "eye for an eye" principle had in view not just retribution but *limits*. The custom (human nature never changes!) was (and is) to get *more* than even. (Recall our reference to lawsuits, above.) But the enlightened law of Leviticus said, "No, if you're injured you can't take two teeth because you lost one tooth." It is not a sadistic demand for vengeance, but a rule that the retribution should not exceed the actual damage done. It was actually a pretty progressive law. And you appreciate it more if you understand that in the ancient Middle East, the custom was for the family (or clan) to seek revenge if one of its members was injured or killed. Needless to say, these family feuds could escalate quickly, applying a principle like "two eyes for one eye, a whole mouth for one tooth."

Keep something else in mind: medicine wasn't too advanced in the ancient world. If you lost an eye or a limb, well, nothing much could be done. No advanced surgery, no prosthetics. You were stuck. If someone injured you severely, you could not count on your insurance company (or theirs) making the situation right through medical care or monetary compensation. But if that someone knew he would suffer the same loss as you, might that not have an effect on his behavior?

Most people are aware that in the New Testament, Jesus laid down a higher ethic: "You have heard that it was said, 'An eye or an eye and a tooth for a tooth.' But I say to you, 'Do not resist the one who is evil. But if anyone slaps you on the right cheek, turn to him the other also' " (Matthew 5:38–39). Better? Oh, definitely. We can only imagine what life would be like in a world of people who did not seek vengeance. But Jesus never said the "eye for an eye" law was bad. He was simply telling his followers that they had to aim a little higher than the law required.

The next time someone criticizes the "eye for an eye" principle, ask them if "million dollars for a burned lap" principle sounds better.

67

Good Cop, Bad Cop—Good God, Mad God?

"God is wrathful and judgmental in the Old Testament, but loving and merciful in the New Testament."

People make this accusation frequently, and the proper response to it is, "Which Bible have you been reading?"

The accusation is a very old one, though. Sometime around the year 140 a wealthy man named Marcion converted from paganism to Christianity. But within a few years he had started his own religion, a sort of "edited" Christianity. Marcion claimed that the Creator God of the Old Testament was an entirely different being from the loving and merciful Father of the New Testament. Marcion totally rejected the Old Testament as sacred scripture. He put together his own "sacred book," which consisted of Luke's Gospel and the letters of Paul. But since these quoted a lot from the Old Testament, Marcion was careful to delete these quotations; they referred to the "bad God" of the Jews.

Marcion did what hundreds of people throughout history have done: treat the Bible as if it is a cafeteria or a buffet meal, where they can walk through and select the items they like, leaving behind the items they don't like. Marcion decided he didn't like the idea of God as a wrathful judge of human sin. So he made his own religion. That religion has never died out.

Often, as people read the Bible, they see what they want to see. Does the Old Testament show God as angry and judgmental? Oh, indeed it does. Does the New Testament show God as a loving and merciful Father? Surely. But if you look at the big picture, the Old Testament speaks often about God's love and compassion, just as the New Testament speaks of God's anger at sin. A quick browse through the four Gospels will show you that Jesus spoke more often about God's wrath and judgment than about love and mercy. In fact, the proportion of "wrath verses" to "love verses" in the Gospels is almost exactly the same proportion as in the first five books of the Old Testament. Why didn't Marcion notice that? Did he ever read Numbers 14:18: "The LORD is slow to anger and abounding in steadfast love, forgiving iniquity and transgression"? This is a good summation of the whole Bible's view of God: yes, he can be angry, but he is *slow* to anger, and always willing to forgive. The same God shows up in the New Testament and the Old.

Consider Jesus himself. On one occasion, he says that "God so loved the world that he gave his only Son, that whoever believes in him should not perish but have eternal life. For God did not send his Son into the world to condemn the world, but in order that the world might be saved through him." This is the famous John 3:16, probably one of the most quoted verses from the Bible. Sounds very loving, doesn't it? It is. But look beyond the surface and notice that the verse is also a warning: those who do not believe will perish; they will not be saved. Even in the great declaration of love there is a sense of something bad happening if you reject God's love.

Look at Matthew 25:36–37: "On the day of judgment people will give account for every careless word they speak, for by your words you will be justified, and by your words you will be condemned." Strong stuff, isn't it? You can be condemned not just for horrible sins like mass murder but also for an abusive tongue. The same Jesus who said those words said these: "Come to me, all who labor and are heavy laden, and I will give you rest. Take my yoke upon you, and learn from me, for I am gentle and lowly in heart, and you will find rest for your souls" (Matthew 11:28–29). Beautiful—very soothing and compassionate. These are the type of words people like to hang on the walls as plaques or posters, or cross-stitch into a pillow.

But the whole Bible is like a marbled steak. There are words about divine wrath, anger, judgment. And there are words about divine love, mercy, forgiveness. Were the Bible's authors schizoid? Not at all. They looked at the "whole steak," the big picture. And the big picture is pretty consistent: God loves human beings, God hates sin, God punishes sin, God forgives people who repent.

Granted, the idea of God as the cosmic Judge who keeps account of our deeds is no longer popular. But the idea ought to give us comfort. It reminds us that our actions and our words matter. Would people really behave well if they thought of God as a big softy who pays no mind to human behavior?

68

Witnessing to the Divine Name

"Jehovah is the Bible's name for God."

In times past, you used to hear the name *Jehovah* fairly often. About the only reason anyone hears it anymore is because of the Jehovah's Witnesses. You won't find it in any contemporary Bible versions, and, oddly, not in the old King James Version, either.

So where did the name come from?

Open up Genesis, read for a while, and notice that God goes by two different names: God and LORD. "God" is how we translate the Hebrew word *elohim* (which means "god" or "gods"). "LORD" is how we translate *YHWH*. And *YHWH* is the Old Testament's actual name for Israel's God. Strictly speaking, *YHWH* is untranslatable. It means something like "I cause to be" or "I am who I am." When Moses has his fateful encounter with the burning bush (Exodus 3), he asks God his name and is told "I am who I am."

In the Bible, people took names very seriously. A name didn't just "sound nice." It had meaning. It revealed something about its possessor. When God told Moses that he was "I am who I am," the answer was in fact evasive. It was as if God was saying, "I am not just another god or person with a name—the important thing is, I AM!" God actually tells Moses to say to the people, "I AM has sent me to you."

Whatever its meaning, *YHWH* was the name of Israel's God. So, did it not have vowels? No, it didn't. No Hebrew words did—no vowels, just consonants. As centuries passed, Hebrew scholars went back to the sacred writings and added "vowel points," since there was a danger of later generations forgetting how words were pronounced. But vowel points were never added to YHWH. There was a fear of tampering with the divine name. Scholars guess—though they aren't sure—that YHWH would have been, roughly, Yahweh. (A trivia tidbit: the Jews refer to the word YHWH as the *tetragrammaton,* meaning "four letters.")

The Jerusalem Bible is one of the few Bible versions that actually uses the name *Yahweh.* Every other English translation uses LORD. Why? Whatever YHWH means, it does not mean "Lord." But LORD has been used for centuries. It began with the Jews themselves. When they translated the Old Testament from Hebrew into Greek, they did not try to find a Greek equivalent for YHWH. They used the Greek word *kyrios,* meaning (surprise!) "lord." Sometimes this caused problems, because the Hebrew word *Adonai* actually does mean "lord," and there are places in the Old Testament that have *Adonai* YHWH, which comes out as "lord Lord."

Well, thank goodness for SMALL CAPS. In English Bibles, you will see "Lord" and "LORD." They aren't the same. "Lord" translates *Adonai,* and "lord" translates YHWH. "Lord," by the way, is not God's name. It is a *title.* It's a way of saying that God is your master, your ruler.

Centuries ago, the Jews began to feel uncomfortable with the name YHWH. Yes, it was the name God had revealed to them. But they had become so reverent that, frankly, they ceased to use the name. It was "too holy" to even say. When they read the Hebrew scriptures aloud, they would substitute *Adonai* for YHWH. That is why, in the Greek version, they used a word meaning "lord" instead of YHWH itself.

Now, where is Jehovah in all this? Believe it or not, "Jehovah" is a very clumsy rendition of YHWH, or *Yahweh.* It goes back to the Middle Ages, a time when the letter *J* had the *Y* sound, and *V* the sound of a *W.* (In other words, if you were living in medieval Europe, you would have pronounced *Jehovah* like *Yehowah*—which isn't all that far from *Yahweh,* particularly when you consider that we aren't certain just how YHWH was pronounced.) Beginning in the 1500s, many European Bibles (though not English ones) began to use *Jehovah* in the Old Testament.

The only contemporary version of the Bible that uses the name *Jehovah* is the New World Version. It will probably not surprise you to learn that this is the version used by the Jehovah's Witnesses.

69

That Little-Known Process of Divine Adoption

"All people are God's children."

Every Christmas the song "Let There Be Peace on Earth" gets dusted off. Choirs sing it, radio stations play it constantly, and we have to admit the tune is pretty and the idea that peace should "begin with me" is worth remembering. But how about that line in the song: "With God as our Father, brothers all are we"? A nice sentiment—but not one you will find in the Bible.

Genesis tells us that God made man in the divine image. Obviously this doesn't mean physical resemblance. Human beings are somehow *like* God, but not the same as God. Some religions, like that of the ancient Greeks, had gods that actually fathered children by human women, so there were lots of "children of the gods" in mythology. But the Bible has no such god. So to be a child of God must imply some other basis of relation.

In a word, the basis is *obedience*. Spiritually speaking, in the Bible your "father" is the one you obey and imitate. We have all heard human parents say, in anger, "You are no son of mine!" They aren't denying the biological connection, they are simply saying, "If you were *really* my child, you would not behave that way." That pretty well sums up what the ancient world (not just the Israelites) thought of parenthood.

You might notice that in the Old Testament, God is rarely referred to as "Father." Occasionally the nation of Israel is referred to as a "child" that God loves. But not until the Gospels do you observe anyone calling God "Father." Jesus did it often. Of course, the early Christians believed that, in some indescribable way, Jesus was the Son of God. They assumed that Jesus fully obeyed God the Father in every way.

The first Christians believed they were all, spiritually speaking, children of the heavenly Father. They had to be *adopted,* since human beings by nature are not God's children. The idea of adoption is mentioned several times (see Ephesians 1:5). All people who accepted Christ, "he gave the right to become children of God, who were born, not of blood, nor or the will of man, but the will of God" (John 1:12–13). Paul echoed the idea: "In Christ Jesus you are all sons of God, through faith . . . heirs according to the promise" (Galatians 3:26). "And because you are sons, God has sent the Spirit of his Son into our hearts, crying, 'Abba, Father!' " (Galatians 4:5). The word *Abba* is important here. Jesus himself used the word to refer to God. It meant something like "Dear Papa," and it suggested a closeness that few people could claim with God. But Paul believed that all Christians could address God as their "Abba."

Being a child of the Father is a privilege, not a right. It is bestowed because the person has faith, not because he is a human being. Like every privilege, sonship carries responsibilities. We are back to the idea of obedience. John sets it out rather bluntly: those who do not do what is right are not children of God; in fact, they are "children of the devil" (1 John 3:10). Jesus had told his disciples that if they loved him, they would keep his commandments (John 14:15). You don't have to read far in the Bible to figure out that *love* and *obey* are always linked. God is good and loving, and his children have to imitate him (Ephesians 5:1).

In the interest of full disclosure here, I have to admit that one verse in the Bible does say that all people are God's offspring. This is found in Acts 17, where Paul is preaching to the Athenians. Looking for a point of contact with these pagan skeptics, Paul quotes from a Greek poet who had said that all people are God's "offspring." As I've already noted, Paul believed that only Christians were truly God's children. So was he being a hypocrite when he told the Athenians that all people are God's children? Not really. He was using the quotation from a Greek poet as a "hook," just as a minister today might quote the song "Let There Be Peace on Earth" at the beginning of a sermon. Worth noting: the word Paul uses is *genos,* which means "descendants" or "posterity" or, as most Bibles have it, "offspring." It is not the same word, *tekna,* that Paul uses in his letters to refer to God's children.

With all respect to that lovely sentiment, "with God as our Father, brothers all are we," those are very pretty words, but the idea is not from the Bible.

70

A "Threat" of Rain to a Desert People?

" 'Rain on the just and the unjust' means God sends bad things to all people."

In his famous Sermon on the Mount, Jesus observed that God "sends rain on the just and on the unjust" (Matthew 5:45). So many people miss the meaning: they take it to mean that all people, good and bad, receive their share of woes in life. In fact, in the dry land of Israel, always on the verge of a drought, rain was a good thing, the water of life, necessary for crops and for human existence. In the modern world, we think of rain as what causes us to cancel picnics and sporting events, but Jesus' words on rain would have had a purely positive meaning for his first hearers.

71

JFK, Ben Franklin, and Which Part of the Bible?

"The Bible says that 'God helps those who helps themselves.'"

Our everyday language is sprinkled with words and phrases from the Bible. More often than not, the people using those phrases have no idea they are from the Bible. But sometimes the reverse is true: a quote that is supposed to be from the Bible really isn't.

Take this one made famous by a man named John F. Kennedy: "God helps those who help themselves." An interesting quote—but not from the Bible. It didn't originate with Kennedy (or his speechwriter), either. We know it was said sometime in the 1700s by Benjamin Franklin. And it's possible Franklin was quoting some other source—but definitely not the Bible.

It is a kind of wise quote for the president of a country to use. It reminds people not to depend on others (such as the federal government) to do things for them. Help yourself first—as much as you can, anyway. The old American tradition of self-reliance is pretty admirable. You have to wonder what would happen to government budgets if everyone took to heart the saying "God helps those who help themselves."

What about those who cannot help themselves? The Bible has a lot to say about those people: help them. God, according to the Bible, has a special concern for the weakest members of society—

widows, orphans, the lame, the blind. The Lord hears the cries of his needy ones (Psalm 69:33). He helps the oppressed, those who have no one else to defend them (Psalm 72:12). He does not reject the pleas of the destitute (Psalm 102:17). The Lord is the poor's defender, and he will do harm to those who harm the poor (Proverbs 22:22–23). Jesus told his followers that when they spread out a banquet, instead of inviting their rich acquaintances they should invite the poor, the crippled, and the blind (Luke 14:12–14).

What about ourselves? Are we supposed to rely on ourselves or on God? Both. From the very beginning, human beings are expected to trust God. (Eve foolishly believed the serpent instead of trusting what God had said about the forbidden fruit.) "Trust in the LORD with all your heart, and do not lean on your own understanding. . . . Be not wise in your own eyes" (Proverbs 3:5–7). "The steps of a man are established by the LORD, when he delights in his way. Though he fall, he shall not be cast headlong, the LORD upholds his hand" (Psalm 37:23–24).

Does all this mean people can simply lie back and let God do everything? "Let go and let God"? Definitely not. The Bible isn't opposed to self-reliance. It is opposed to relying on yourself *alone*. The Bible is thoroughly anti-pride and anti-arrogance. The person who has too high an opinion of his own mind and strength and talents is sure to fall eventually. "Everyone who is arrogant in heart is an abomination to the LORD" (Proverbs 16:5). God rescues the humble but humiliates the proud (Psalm 18:27). In the Bible's view, people who worship themselves are worshiping the wrong god. People who pride themselves on their independence and self-reliance are forgetting they are mortal and forgetting that it is God who controls everything (see James 4:13–15).

Back to Kennedy's famous quote: it is not from the Bible. While it isn't in direct conflict with what the Bible teaches, it doesn't really reflect the Bible's view of human beings' dependence on God.

PART VIII

MISREADING THE DIVINE COMMANDMENTS

THE DESCENT OF THE SPIRIT AT PENTECOST
The Bible says all believers should have the Spirit's gift of speaking in unknown tongues . . . or does it?

72

Taking the Pledge (But Why?)

"The Bible requires Christians to abstain from alcohol."

The obvious response to this lie, or misconception, is, "It doesn't." Neither the Old Testament nor the New preaches abstinence. In fact, it is so obvious to us that we find it hard to believe that in 1919 the U.S. Congress, under great pressure from Christian churches, passed the Eighteenth Amendment, bringing in the Prohibition era.

To give these people credit, their hearts were in the right place. Alcohol abuse was (and is, obviously) a serious social problem. Beginning in the 1800s, many revival preachers in America included abstinence in their program for moral reform. They saw the harm that excessive alcohol could do, and they understood that there are plenty of weak souls who cannot take "just one drink" but inevitably go overboard. The most sensible course, many Christians believed, was to avoid alcohol altogether. Individuals and the nation at large would, they said, be better for it. Such prominent Christians as evangelist Billy Sunday and statesman William Jennings Bryan lent their powerful voices to the abstinence movement.

Granted, not all Christians who were teetotalers believed that this was *the* Christian view as taught in the Bible. Quite a few of them understood that the Bible does not command abstinence. But there were some who came up with the "two-wine theory"—that is, they claimed that some of the biblical words for "wine" actually were referring to nonalcoholic grape juice. Still, most people did not think that the two-wine theory could hold water. The movement for Prohibition was based not on the Bible but on the multitude of alcohol-related social problems. They were visible for all to see, and condemning such ills did not require support from the Bible.

While the Bible does not prohibit alcohol consumption, it has strong words to say about drunkenness. The wisdom-saturated Book of Proverbs refers to wine as a "mocker" (20:1), warns that wine lovers will end up poor (21:17), and advises against socializing with drunkards (23:20). Proverbs 23:29–35 is probably the Bible's most famous passage, condemning those who "tarry long at the wine." Yet the same Book of Proverbs tells us to "Give strong drink to him that is ready to perish, and wine to those that are of heavy hearts" (Proverbs 31:6–7). This is a reminder that in the age before pain relievers and anesthetics, alcohol did have real medicinal value.

The New Testament likewise condemns drunkenness, but not drinking. Paul told Christians to be drunk with the Spirit, not with wine (Ephesians 5:18). Jesus had warned against people letting their hearts be occupied with drunkenness (Luke 23:34). But of course, according to John's Gospel, Jesus' very first miracle was turning water into wine (John 2:1–11), a pretty fair indication that he did not condemn drinking it.

In fact, the New Testament has a pretty stern warning to teetotalers: don't try to make your own personal preference into a universal law. Paul the apostle made it clear that freedom from legalism was a part of the Christian life. You can see this in Colossians 2:16–23, in which he makes it clear that no one should pass judgment on the Christian "in questions of food and drink." He goes on to condemn "self-made religion and asceticism and severity to the body." Christianity, in Paul's view, is not a list of strict rules but a matter of dedicating your whole life to God, doing everything for God's glory.

One more interesting point from the Bible: the invention of wine making is attributed to one of the most saintly men in the Bible, Noah (Genesis 9:20).

73

"That Ten Percent Thing" of Mrs. Lennon

"Christians are required to tithe."

Yoko Ono, widow of John Lennon, once stated that one thing she did find to admire in Christianity was "that ten percent thing." She was referring to tithing, the centuries-old practice of giving 10 percent of your income to the church. Yoko assumed, as do many Christians, that the church will put it to good use, preferably in some form of charity. Is this based on the Bible, and is it required?

The Bible says a lot about tithing—not all of it good. When the tribes of Israel asked for a king to help them band together, their leader Samuel warned them that a king would force them to give up a tithe (tenth) of their grain and flocks (1 Samuel 8:10–18). Even in the ancient world, people were aware that government likes to tax and spend.

Still, tithing was built into the law given by God to Moses. The Israelites were required to give a tenth of their crops, fruits, and livestock (Leviticus 27:30–32). An owner of livestock would count his beasts as they passed by him, and every tenth one was given "to God." (The reason for doing it this way was to prevent owners from searching through their herds for the most inferior animals to give as tithe.)

How do you give grain and fruit and sheep to God? Well, you don't. In practice, you can only give these things to human beings. In the case of Israel, the tithes went to the Levites, the tribe that took care of the temple and also the tribe from which the priests came. You might say that the tithes were paid to the "clergy." The Levites, unlike the other eleven tribes of Israel, did not possess a certain territory. They had no income, livelihood, or inheritance to support them, so they depended on the tithes to live (Numbers 18:21–24). The Levites themselves had to present a "tithe of the tithe" to the priests.

The proper place to offer the tithe was Jerusalem. Those who lived far off faced a transportation problem, so instead of hauling their tithe so far, they could sell it and send the money to Jerusalem.

The tithe was not just to maintain the Levites. Every third year, a local tithe was imposed. It was to benefit not the Jerusalem temple but "the sojourner, the fatherless, and the widow who are within your towns." These people "shall come and eat and be filled, that the LORD your God may bless you in all the work of your hands that you do" (Deuteronomy 14:29).

So the tithes had a commendable charitable aim. But like any religious duty, tithing was often considered a pain. Even so, some people got caught up in it and took pride in tithing everything. Jesus criticized self-righteous people who patted themselves on the back for even tithing the herbs they grew for seasoning (Matthew 23:23).

In the New Testament period, Israel was under the thumb of the Roman Empire, which loved to tax the people it conquered. This put Jews in the unhappy position of having to pay taxes to Rome while also paying the tithe to maintain the Jerusalem temple.

Since the first Christians were Jews, they continued for a while in the practice of tithing. But as the faith spread to non-Jews, there was obviously no point in asking them to tithe to support the Jewish religious establishment in Jerusalem. Still, the early Christians were extremely generous in getting up voluntary contributions to help each other. The apostle Paul was zealous about helping poor Christians in Jerusalem (see Acts 11:29–30, Romans 15:26–28). Paul instructed the Christians in Corinth to set aside each Sunday something for this collection (1 Corinthians 16:1). He gave no instructions about tithes or percentages, but told each person to give what he could afford.

This is the New Testament principle of giving: give what you can. The old expression "Give till it hurts" seems to fit. It fits in well with the New Testament's emphasis on Christian freedom. Instead of imposing a legalistic rule (a certain percentage), Christians are urged to give what they can, out of love for their spiritual brothers. *The New Testament does not require Christians to tithe. It does instruct them to be generous in giving, and to always remember the poor.*

The Old Testament tithing laws really did not fit the Christians. The first Christians had no church buildings, no paid clergy, no religious establishment—no "overhead." So long as the church was composed of groups of like-minded people meeting in homes or outdoors, tithing really was not necessary. Christians could, and did, give aid to their poorer brethren.

In time, of course, Christianity changed. It acquired all the things that Judaism had had: buildings, paid clergy, et cetera. Church officials began to urge Christians to tithe. Roughly about the time of Emperor Charlemagne (A.D. 800), most Christians in Europe were required to tithe. The church had moved a long way from the voluntary generosity of the first Christians. Many sensitive Christians resented paying to support lavish church buildings and clergy who were often immoral.

America established in its Constitution that there is no state church, so, happily, no one in the United States is required to tithe. Many Christians choose to do so, and some give way beyond 10 percent. Some churches are more aggressive than others in urging (sometimes pressuring) their members to tithe. As we already noted, they cannot appeal to the New Testament, because tithing is not mandated there. They cannot appeal to the Old Testament Law, either, since most Christians don't feel that the laws of Leviticus and Deuteronomy apply to them. But quite often, a verse from the prophet Malachi gets quoted: "Will man rob God? Yet you are robbing me. . . . Bring the full tithes into the storehouse, that there may be food in my house. And thereby put me to the test, says the LORD of hosts, if I will not open the windows of heaven for you and pour down for you a blessing until there is no more need" (Malachi 3:8–10).

You could probably paper over the Great Wall of China with

solicitation letters from churches that quote this "windows of heaven" verse from Malachi. And thousands of sermons have been preached on that verse.

And if people wish to tithe, fine. But the command of the New Testament is not "Tithe" but "Give generously, especially to aid the poor."

74

Sweatin' to the Scriptures

"Paul's words about our bodies being 'God's temple' mean that Christians should be concerned about diet and health."

Sometimes a whole culture can appear to be schizoid. Take the present attitude toward the body. Physical beauty and youth are the goal, muscles are in, fat is out, and the only concept of "sin" that many people have is taking in too many calories and too much fat. Health clubs are a booming business, as are the many tummy-reducing machines and workout videos.

The flip side: every few months, some "university study" concludes that people are overweight, that kids are fatter than they have ever been, that people need to exercise more, eat less, and so on, and so forth.

In short, diet and exercise are *in*, but not everyone seems to care. Even so, most people agree on the basic idea: you should live as long as you can, stay as thin as you can, look as young as you can. Even the couch potato with his chips in one hand and beer in the other knows that *he* is not the ideal that people are striving for. (It is, of course, possible that he may be *happier* than the person obsessed with cholesterol count and abdominal muscles.)

Two thousand years separate us from the first Christians, but things are not as different as you might think. When the apostles lived, the Greeks and Romans they encountered were obsessed with physical beauty. The statues of their exquisitely beautiful gods still impress us. They are well muscled, well proportioned, and unwrinkled. Even more mature gods like Zeus and Hera show no signs of middle-aged spread. Of course, the average Greek or Roman did not necessarily look like the statues. But they were the ideal, and we know that those who worshiped such gods were concerned about appearance. There was no tradition among the Jews of "working out," but the Greeks and Romans were as fanatical about it as Americans are today.

The Book of Acts tells us that the apostle Paul visited Athens, the chief city of Greece. "His spirit was provoked within him as he saw that the city was full of idols" (Acts 17:16). The "idols" were the statues of the various gods. Paul reacted to these for two reasons: as a faithful Jew, he could not stomach the idea of honoring any kind of image. And he would have been offended at the nakedness or near nakedness of the statues. (We can safely assume that contemporary advertising would have offended him deeply.)

For Paul, creation was good. God made all things, including the human body. But, good Jew that he was, Paul believed it was wrong to *worship* anything but God. Paul surely understood that not only did the people of Athens worship their human-shaped gods, but they also worshiped the images of youth and beauty.

> It isn't that physical things don't matter, but that eternal things matter more.
>
> 

Paul and all the early Christians had their minds on eternity. "Though our outward man perish, yet the inward man is renewed day by day" (2 Corinthians 4:16). "Bodily exercise profits some, but godliness is profitable to all things, having the promise of the life that now is, and of the life which is to come" (1 Timothy 4:8). "All that is in the world, the cravings of the sinful nature, and the lust of the eyes, and the pride of life, is not of the Father, but is of the world" (1 John 2:16).

Jesus understood the human tendency to fret over bodily concerns. "Do not be anxious about your life, what you will eat, nor about your body, what you will put on. . . . Which of you by being anxious can add a single hour to his span of life? If then you are not able to do as small a thing as that, why are you anxious about the rest?" (Luke 12:22, 26).

This is the basic thrust of the New Testament: do not obsess over things the rest of the world worries about. Eternity is more important than this world anyway.

Historically, Christians have taken that approach. There have always been exceptions, fanatics who took pleasure in starving themselves, never changing their clothes, never bathing. But these are the exceptions.

Until recently, that is. If you browse a Christian bookstore or watch Christian television, you might wonder if Christians have conformed to the world after all. There are Christian workout videos (Pat Boone has one), and dozens (probably hundreds) of books on diet and exercise. Weight loss, it appears, is one of the great concerns of Christians today. So is longevity. There are plenty of books claiming to present the Bible's pathway to nutrition, lower cholesterol, a flatter stomach, what have you. Churches have jumped on the bandwagon, with many of them hosting weight loss groups, aerobics classes, nutrition seminars. Some Christian-run companies have offered programs in which they paid bonuses to employees who lost weight and kept it off.

Some churches even sponsor "Temple" programs. Why "Temple"? Here's why: "Do you not know that your body is a temple of the Holy Spirit within you, whom you have from God? . . . So glorify God in your body" (1 Corinthians 6:19–20). Fine words, and perfectly in keeping with what I said earlier about Paul. Paul definitely did *not* intend his words to be the foundation for Christian Body Mania. In fact, a few verses earlier, Paul said, "Food is meant for the stomach and the stomach for food—and God will destroy both one and the other." The message got repeated again: don't obsess over these things. When he told the people that their bodies were "temples of the Spirit," he was reminding them to avoid sexual immorality. You cannot link your body (which belongs to God) with the body of a prostitute.

Yet this "Temple" verse, taken out of its context, is today one of the most quoted verses from the whole Bible. You can almost imagine Paul's reaction: *"I told you to glorify God with your body, not to glorify the body. I told you your body was the temple of the Spirit, but you have turned it into an idol."* He might even quote his own words to the Romans: "Do not be conformed to this world, but be transformed by the renewal of your mind" (Romans 12:2).

We can say, respectfully, to Christians who produce and market the hundreds of diet and exercise books, videos, and programs: you are misguided, and you are using the body-as-temple verse to promote your products. Good capitalism, but bad Christianity.

75

Meating the Animals for Lunch

"God intended us to be vegetarians."

Old diet fads never die, they just pop up again and again in history. One that is alive and well at present is vegetarianism. Your local yellow pages probably lists several vegetarian restaurants and markets. This isn't surprising, at a time when a favorite topic of conversation is cholesterol, and when groups like People for the Ethical Treatment of Animals make everyone more aware of some of the nastier aspects of meat processing.

Interestingly enough, vegetarianism did and does have a connection with belief in reincarnation. Some ancient philosophers, such as the Greek thinker Pythagoras, denounced flesh eating because it involved the murder of humans, humans who were (temporarily) in animal bodies. The same thought certainly occurred to the people of India. These were also motivated by another thought: the concept of *ahimsa,* doing no harm to any living being. Obviously vegetables are living beings, too, but it is all right to eat them, since they are not aware they are being eaten. Because every animal resists being killed, however, it is—so they say—clearly wrong to deprive it of its life just to feed humans.

What about Christians? They don't believe animals are reincarnated souls. But fairly early in Christian history, some Christians associated meat eating with the life of luxury. Sounds silly to us, but not so silly in a time and place where meat really was a luxury for most people. The devout Christians who withdrew to monasteries and convents often gave up meat altogether, or ate it only sparingly. Many monks lived to a ripe old age on a diet of water, grains, fruits, and vegetables. (Did the monks believe the rumor that a meatless diet made people less lustful?)

The biggest motivation behind vegetarianism today is health. People wish to live longer, to stay younger looking longer, and vegetarianism seems to be a means to delaying the inevitable (old age and death, that is). If red meat raises your cholesterol, then red meat is an obstacle to living longer—so eliminate red meat. Better yet, eliminate meat altogether. Then who knows how long you might live?

Christians today have definitely jumped on the diet-and-exercise bandwagon (see page 227). The Christian "spin" on the obsession with diet is that our bodies are the temple of God, and that we must maintain them. In fact, this "spin" brings us to an important point: most vegetarians throughout history had *ethical* concerns, not *physical* ones. Today, for example, animal rights groups complain repeatedly about some of the horrors of slaughtering animals for food. No doubt a lot of people who once worked in slaughterhouses became vegetarians later on. Whether or not animals have "souls," people are rightly concerned about animals being raised for food then killed just because some human beings desired that particular food. Chickens, turkeys, and calves that spend their entire brief lives in tiny cages are, many would say, something no sensitive person could enjoy watching. People have grown more sensitive to animal suffering, and that in itself is a good thing.

But there is more to vegetarianism today than just concern for animals. In a vague kind of New Age way of viewing the world, vegetarianism is a way of proving you are a "progressive thinker." Your parents were churchgoers and had meat at every meal? You can prove you are different (and better) by forsaking not only their religion but also their dietary habits. (So instead of conforming to your parents' habits, you can be a nonconformist—and conform to the dietary trends of today.)

You may have discovered that vegetarians can be extremely "evangelistic." People who believe they have found The Truth like to share it, whether it is The Truth about proper diet, The Truth about morality, or both. And some vegetarians are Christians, who like to incorporate The Truth about diet with the gospel of Christ (which, in the Christian view, really is The Truth). As mentioned earlier, Christians in monasteries and convents often lived without meat. Most other Christians have not done so—in fact, most Christians have done what human beings throughout history have done: eat as much meat as they can, whenever they can get it. But in the 1800s, vegetarianism became trendy among some Christians. A group called the Bible Christians published a vegetarian magazine in England and the United States. The Seventh-Day Adventists pushed for a strict diet, and many of them are vegetarians.

This brings us around to the main topic here: does the Bible address this issue at all?

Well, it definitely talks about diet. The kosher laws in Leviticus have a long list of prohibited "unclean" animals. But it leaves lots of "clean" animals for human consumption, including cattle, sheep, deer, chicken, and most types of fish. The New Testament, however, pretty much does away with any restrictions. The Gospels say that Jesus himself "pronounced all foods clean" (Mark 7:18–20). One of Jesus' disciples, Peter, had an amazing vision that confirmed what Jesus said: the old distinction between "clean" and "unclean" animals no longer applied (Acts 10:9–16). Christians who were Jews did not immediately start eating nonkosher, of course. (Old habits die hard.) But one of the earliest controversies among Christians centered on food. The big question: did Christians from non-Jewish backgrounds have to abide by the Old Testament food laws? A few Christians said yes, but most, including the influential apostle Paul, said no.

Paul was aware of a basic human trait: making yourself feel important by observing a lot of fussy rules. He didn't think this was what the Christian life was all about. And he found some rules, especially those about food, to be pointless. "The kingdom of God is not food and drink, but righteousness and peace, and joy in the Holy Spirit" (Romans 14:17). "Let no man judge you in food, or in drink, or in observing of a holy day. . . . Since with Christ you died to the principles of the world, why, as though living in the world, do you submit to regulations—'Touch not, taste not, handle not'? All these refer to things that perish with use. They are the commandments and teachings of men" (Colossians 2:16–23). "To the pure, all things are pure" (Titus 1:15).

Paul rather nicely summarized the truly spiritual life in this way: "Whether you eat or drink, or whatever you do, do all to the glory of God" (1 Corinthians 10:31). But it would not have surprised Paul that Christians throughout the centuries went on fussing about meaningless rules, including rules about food. We can imagine him speaking to vegetarians today and saying, "Look, if you choose this, fine. Just don't try to impose it on other Christians and say it's the only way to be spiritual, because that isn't true."

Putting it bluntly: the Bible does not command people to be vegetarians.

The Bible does, however, dangle a curious fact before us: there is no mention of meat eating before the story of Noah. When Noah and his family exit the ark, Noah sacrifices animals to God. God tells Noah, "The fear of you and the dread of you shall be upon every beast of the earth, and upon every bird of the heavens, upon everything that creeps upon the ground and all the fish of the sea. Every moving thing that lives shall be food for you. And as I gave you green plants, I give you everything" (Genesis 9:2–4). This doesn't absolutely prove that this is where meat eating began, but that is the most likely interpretation. Given that God himself puts his approval on it, what do the vegetarians say? They point back to Eden: clearly, the original plan was for human beings to live on fruits and vegetables. And to this, many would reply: maybe so, but we are no longer in Eden.

76

A Tasteless Place to Shoot Dice

"The Bible condemns gambling because the Roman soldiers gambled to get Jesus' robe."

"Playing cards is sinful." Have you ever heard anyone say that? Probably not, but a generation ago it was sometimes heard. I can personally recall an older lady telling me that the deck of cards I was playing with were "gambling cards." Her facial expression told me that she did not approve. In fact, my family played cards frequently and got lots of innocent pleasure from it. But we never gambled and, as churchgoers, we believed that our fellow church members neither gambled nor approved of gambling. My grandmother's generation can recall that the card game Rook was popular with people who would not allow a standard deck of cards into the house because they were "gambling cards." (Rook has its own deck and thus did not have the stigma of regular cards. Human nature being what it is, however, I am sure that people have played Rook for money.)

What does the Bible say about gambling? Not a great deal, actually. One thing that archaeologists have discovered, though, is that gambling certainly went on in biblical times. In fact, gambling appears to be universal. There were games of chance in ancient Egypt, and we know that the Greeks and Romans loved to bet on the outcomes of athletic contests and chariot races. You might say that "to gamble is human." Even so, the Bible says practically nothing about it—not directly, anyway.

The Bible does have a lot to say about financial responsibility. The word Christian authors like to use is *stewardship*. The idea is that Christians are stewards of whatever possessions, money, and talents that God has given them. In the Bible's view, everything a person has is from God and belongs to God. If this is so, then people ought to use whatever they have in ways that God would approve of. People are told to honor the Lord with their wealth (Proverbs 3:9). In fact, whatever people do is to be done for the glory of God (1 Corinthians 10:31).

The Bible also has a lot to say about covetousness. In fact, coveting what someone else has is prohibited by the last of the Ten Commandments (Exodus 20:17). While the word *covet* isn't used much anymore, we are all familiar with envy and greed—wanting what someone else has, and wanting more than we ourselves need. All these are heartily condemned in the Bible. Paul wrote that the love of money is the root of all kinds of evil (1 Timothy 6:8–10). In fact, Jesus and the apostles spoke out frequently against worship of material wealth. Does any of what they said apply to gambling? Of course it does. Gambling is, most often, "just for fun"—true enough. But behind it is one of humankind's less attractive qualities: wanting something for nothing. It is unlikely the Bible would approve of someone throwing money away on lottery tickets or racetrack bets in the hope of getting rich. The Bible does approve of hard, honest work—but not the love of money.

> Couldn't people take the money they fritter away on gambling and use it to help the poor?

Of course, rich people can afford to gamble—and to lose huge sums. Is that their own business? Maybe. But the Bible has harsh words to say about the "idle rich" who have no concern for the poor.

What about the poor who gamble? People in dire financial straits are often willing to risk what they have in the hope of a sudden change in fortune. This desire is, in fact, what lies beyond the old fundamentalist view of gambling. The stricter Christians could see that plenty of lower-class families had fallen into ruin because of gambling. Taking money needed to buy food for your family and using it to gamble is, obviously, a bad thing. The best thing, the fundamentalists said, was never to gamble at all.

But as we already have seen, there is no particular passage in the Bible to back up this strict view of gambling. So one was found: the passage in John's Gospel reporting that the Roman soldiers at Jesus' crucifixion cast lots to see who would get Jesus' robe (see John 19:23–24). Strictly speaking, this wasn't even gambling. They were simply casting lots (something like rolling the dice) to see which soldier would get the robe. Quite a few Christians over the years have pointed this out as a condemnation of any form of gambling.

Actually, John's Gospel says nothing disapproving about what happened. It is simply reporting what the soldiers did. Certainly Roman soldiers were, on the whole, a pretty crude bunch. It strikes us as somewhat callous, doing what they did while the owner of the robe was in agony on the cross. But it hardly qualifies as grounds for saying "Christians should never gamble, period." As noted above, the Bible's view of money and greed is a much better foundation for not gambling.

77

Shear Controversy

"The Bible teaches that women should not cut their hair."

One of the first laws you learn in science class is that "For every action there is an equal and opposite reaction." This is true in physics. In some ways, it's true in culture also. Our own culture has, without any doubt, grown steadily more liberal in regard to sexual habits, man–woman relations, and child rearing. Whether you applaud this, lament it, or don't really care, you know it has happened. What you might not know is that while society in general has gotten more liberal about these things, churches that teach a more traditional morality are growing. Yes, really. While the more liberal churches are declining, conservative ones are on the upswing. The very conservative Pentecostal denomination known as the Assemblies of God is one of the great success stories in American religion in recent years.

Smart culture-watchers would say, "We aren't a bit surprised." In times of rapid (some might say *frightening*) social change, many people like to stick with the tried-and-true. For many conservative Christians, their churches are like anchored ships in the middle of a moral storm.

Of course, *conservative* is a relative term. It can vary with geography, also. Conservative Christian women from Germany visit the United States and are puzzled that their American sisters in the faith *do* wear makeup but *do not* drink wine. The American sisters might be just as puzzled by the German women doing the opposite. Is there a practice that is *the* Christian way to do things? Or is there, in fact, a lot of leeway?

The answer is "a lot of leeway." You find a lot of attention devoted to this issue in the New Testament. There was a lot of tension in the early church between very lenient believers and very strict ones. Some said they could pretty much do whatever they pleased. Some took the position of "the more rules, the better." Paul and the other New Testament authors had to mediate between these two extremes. Paul always came down on the side of Christian freedom. That didn't mean you could lie, steal, sleep around, or do other things that were clearly wrong—but in the "nickel-and-dime" stuff, Christians could be free. (See Galatians 5 for a basic statement about freedom.)

Now, back to those conservative churches in America today. In some of those churches, women do not wear makeup or cut their hair or wear pants. In the United States, these practices have been standard in the Church of God, headquartered in Cleveland, Tennessee. Several other small denominations also followed these practices. They are by no means all "boondocks" churches now. Every town and city has such churches, and it sometimes surprises passersby to see a parking lot full of shiny new SUVs and cosmeticless women that seem rather plainly attired.

> We were told this as kids: real beauty is on the inside, not the outside.
>
> 

One of the Bible's statements on women's appearance is in 1 Peter 3:3–4: "Do not let your adorning be external—the braiding of hair, the wearing of gold, or the putting on of clothing—but let your adorning be the imperishable beauty of a gentle and quiet spirit, which in God's eyes is very precious." Even someone with no religious convictions at all might find this appealing. It strikes a chord.

Of course, Peter doesn't supply specifics about what "external adorning" is. We can assume that going to church "dressed to kill" is a bit much. What about makeup? None? Maybe just a bit? Is touching up the gray okay? (Some other amusing questions come to mind: what would Peter have said to Tammy Faye Bakker?)

Peter said nothing about cutting hair, but Paul did. Paul stated that long hair was wrong for men, but "if a woman has long hair, it is her glory." This is found in 1 Corinthians 11, where Paul goes into great detail about how women should wear head coverings at worship while men must not. This passage is the reason that many women still insist on wearing a hat to church. (Some hats are so extravagant that we can assume the women must have forgotten what Peter said about "external adorning.") Frankly, this chapter either bores or puzzles most modern readers. Paul was talking about modes of dress and hairstyle two thousand years ago. Does any of this matter now?

Some of these conservative church women would reply, yes, it does matter. Yet one of the ironies of these women is that while their hair is in fact long, they do not wear it that way. They wear it pulled up in a "bun" atop the head. When Paul approved long hair on women, he was no doubt talking about it being loose about the shoulders.

In fact, if Christian women wished to follow Paul's principle, they would do this: dress differently from men. That is Paul's main point in 1 Corinthians 11: God made the sexes different, and they ought not try to blur those differences. Hairstyles are not the same as they were in Corinth two thousand years ago, but men and women are still different, and this should be made clear, especially in Christian worship. This is not a principle that many churchgoers today would find hard to follow.

78

Organ, Piano, Kazoo, or Just Humming?

"The Bible teaches that we should not use musical instruments in worship."

Christians are human, and humans do fuss and fight, often over very petty things. This is true of church music, as every pastor and every church choir member knows. People fret and fuss over who is the "star" of the worship service. Is it the pastor, or the music director, or the choir soloist? Is one solo singer hogging all the limelight? Every pastor has wished at some point that the church music program would just suddenly disappear.

And some churches choose that route. They have no musical instruments, only a cappella singing by the congregation. Very simple, very basic. No choir fights, no church money spent on instruments or choir robes, a lot of headaches eliminated. Does the Bible *require* this?

Let's begin with the first Christians. They had no church buildings. They met in homes, sometimes outdoors, sometimes (literally) underground (remember the Roman catacombs?). We know that they sang, usually Psalms from the Old Testament. We don't know if they used musical instruments, but if they did, nothing fancy.

Then Christianity changed from a small fringe minority religion to the official religion of the Roman Empire. Church buildings were constructed, some of them huge and lavishly decorated inside and out. These beautiful buildings had to have beautiful music. Early forms of the organ were used, and so were huge choirs, which were trained to sing complicated music. What had been the "congregation" became an "audience." The great mass of people were nothing more than spectators. In time, singing by the congregation pretty much ceased. The emphasis was on spectacle—mosaics, stained glass, incense, luxurious robes, huge choirs, an organ blasting away. Impressive—but a long way removed from the more cozy Christianity of the New Testament.

A major change came in the 1500s with the Protestant Reformation. Martin Luther and other Protestant leaders wanted to "clean up" worship, so they toned down the spectacle and, more importantly, restored congregational singing. Luther himself loved to sing and play the lute, and he wrote hymns, including "A Mighty Fortress Is Our God." Christians in the pews found themselves participating again.

But the urge for spectacle never went away. Even Protestant churches, when they had enough money, spent huge sums on organs, full-time musicians, robes, even paid soloists for the choir. Most churchgoers accepted this, and it was (and still is) common to hear someone say, "Oh, you must visit our church sometime, we have such a good music program."

So what does the Bible say about music in worship?

If you do a word search through the Bible's Book of Psalms, you will find literally dozens of references to the harp, lyre, trumpet, tambourine, and other musical instruments—all used in the praise of God. Solomon's beautiful temple in Jerusalem did not have a cappella worship. There were choirs, there were musical instruments, and it was all very impressive, as it was intended to be.

In the New Testament period, we know that Jesus, his disciples, Paul, and probably every other New Testament character visited the temple in Jerusalem. Not one of them is recorded as speaking out against the style of worship there.

However, Paul did make one very important mention of music: "Be filled with the Spirit, addressing one another in psalms and hymns and spiritual songs, singing and making melody to the LORD with all your heart" (Ephesians 5:18–19; similar words at Colossians 3:16). Much has been made of "with all your heart." It is the basis for the "noninstrumental" churches. The best known of these are the Churches of Christ. These had their beginnings on the American frontier (where, for obvious reasons, the use of musical instruments in church was usually a moot point). The founders of the Churches of Christ claimed to be "Restorationists," wishing to restore Christianity to its New Testament purity. Not finding any references to musical instruments in Christian worship, and remembering Paul's words about making melody with your heart, they did not use musical instruments in worship.

There is a lot to be said for this. Churches without lavish music programs can budget for other items—say, charity, maybe? They can, as we noted earlier, avoid a lot petty of quarrels. And a cappella singing, though it strikes some people as too stark, can be very pretty, especially among people accustomed to it. Granted, members of such churches don't often issue the invitation, "Come visit us, we have a great music program." But then, is that really the best reason to attend a church?

Still, using the New Testament as the basis for noninstrumental worship is questionable. It does *not* specifically forbid the use of instruments. And I can't close this chapter without mentioning the Bible's last book, Revelation. In both 14:2 and 15:2, we learn that there are harps in heaven, and the saints use them to make music to God.

79

Speaking, Nonspeaking, Anti-Speaking, Et Cetera

"True Christians should speak in tongues."

"Christians should no longer speak in tongues."

According to an old hymn, "God Moves in a Mysterious Way." That seems to be true of Christianity in the past century. Who would have predicted, one hundred years ago, that middle-class and upper-middle-class people in American suburbs would freely admit that they "spoke in tongues"? Who would have thought that an activity connected with (horrors!) the poorer sort of Christians would become not only *respectable* but even *admired?*

But one thing might have been predicted: if tongues speaking ever became widely practiced, it would definitely be controversial. It still is. It is a fascinating topic, one that can't really be considered unless you look at the source of speaking in tongues: the Holy Spirit.

Where is the proper place to begin? Probably at Genesis 1. There we encounter the first mention of the Spirit of God, when the world is being created: "The Spirit of God was hovering over the face of the waters" (1:2). The Hebrew word that we translate as "Spirit" (or sometimes uncapitalized, "spirit") was *ruach,* which could mean "spirit" or "wind" or "breath." It could even mean "power." Genesis 1 gives us the image of God breathing out his power on his new creation. Throughout the rest of the Bible, God's Spirit is seen as a source of power—sometimes in selected individuals, sometimes in a whole community.

Exodus 31 tells us that the craftsman Bezalel was "filled with the Spirit of God," which showed itself in "all manner of workmanship, to design artistic works." So the first person in the Bible mentioned as "having the Spirit" is not a prophet or king or a military leader but a craftsman. Bezalel was given a high task, however: constructing the tabernacle, the center of Israel's worship.

We later learn that the great leader, Moses, is empowered by God's Spirit, which is not surprising. Moses witnesses God himself coming down in a cloud and placing the Spirit upon Israel's seventy elders. Moses exclaims, "Oh, that all the LORD's people were prophets and that the LORD would put his Spirit upon them" (Numbers 11:29). This verse has been quoted quite often in recent years, as some Christians believe that Moses' wish has been fulfilled.

After Moses, many of Israel's leaders were said to have God's Spirit. One was Moses' successor, Joshua (Numbers 27:18). Later, some of the Bible's toughest tough guys had the Spirit of God. That includes several of the "judges" (really military leaders) in the Book of Judges. Gideon and Jephthah were empowered by the Spirit, but the most famous of all was strongman Samson. More than once "the Spirit of the LORD came mightily upon him" (Judges 14:6, 15:14). The power enabled him to tear a lion apart with his bare hands and (on more than one occasion) to slay Israel's enemies, the Philistines.

Then there was Israel's first king, Saul. Tall, handsome, and brave, Saul was also a failure as king. For reasons the Bible does not make clear to us, Saul was under the good influence of the Spirit, but later the Spirit was withdrawn from him. At one time, however, Saul came under the Spirit's influence and "prophesied" (1 Samuel 19:23–24). Apparently it was common in those days for certain persons to "get possessed" by their god. They might go into trances, dance, or shout ecstatically. Such behavior was not "normal," but it wasn't frowned on, either. There is something in us that wants to "cut loose," to overflow with enthusiasm. We see it at sports events, at concerts, at many other public activities. We don't usually associate it with religion, but it is an element of almost all religions. It can't be avoided, really. Human beings love to clap, shout, dance, sing loudly. They like to cheer something, applaud something big or impressive. If that is so, wouldn't deeply religious people be wildly enthusiastic for God? Don't quite a few of the Psalms sound kind of madly ecstatic in their praise of God? A good question, and one that relates to the subject of tongues. Read on, but hold on to that key idea: *religious enthusiasm*.

The Hebrew prophets had a lot to say about the Spirit. Isaiah referred to the Spirit more than any other book in the Old Testament. He mentioned the Spirit in connection with the promised Messiah (called the "Servant"), upon whom the Spirit would rest (11:2, 42:1). He also predicted that a descendant of Jesse (King David's father) would have the Spirit (11:1–2). These prophecies were, Christians believe, fulfilled in the life of Jesus. Isaiah looked forward to a time when more than a few select individuals would have God's Spirit (32:15, 34:16). Consider 44:3: "I will pour water on him who is thirsty, and floods on the dry ground; I will pour my Spirit on your descendants and my blessing on your offspring."

Another prophet, Joel, also looked forward to a time when the Spirit would be poured out on many people: "It shall come to pass afterward that I will pour out my Spirit on all flesh; your sons and your daughters will prophesy, your old men shall dream dreams, and your young men shall see visions. Even on the male and female servants in those days I will pour out my Spirit" (2:28–29). You will hear this passage quoted often—*very* often—by Christians today who claim to be "Spirit-filled." And with good reason: centuries after Joel, in the Book of Acts, the apostle Peter quoted Joel's prophecy in a stirring sermon on the day of Pentecost. The early Christians saw the Spirit empowering all people who put their faith in Christ, fulfilling Joel's prophecy.

In the New Testament, we shift from Hebrew to Greek. Instead of the Hebrew word *ruach* for the Spirit, we have the Greek *pneuma*, but the same richness of meanings: "spirit," "breath," "wind," "power." (It made its way into our language in words like *pneumonia* and *pneumatic*, by the way.) Here, as in the Old Testament, certain special individuals are said to "have the Spirit." One of these is John the Baptist, who is "filled with the Holy Spirit, even from his mother's womb" (Luke 1:15). All four Gospels report John's ministry of baptizing repentant people in the Jordan River. John told his listeners that he baptized with water, but soon there would be one mightier than him, who would baptize people "with the Holy Spirit and with fire" (Luke 3:16). He was referring to Jesus, who came to him for baptism. In one of the Bible's most famous scenes, John baptizes Jesus, and when Jesus comes up out of the water, the Spirit, in the form of a dove, descends upon him, and a voice from heaven says, "This is my beloved Son, with whom I am well pleased" (Matthew 3:17). This famous incident is the reason that the dove is, for Christians, a symbol of the Holy Spirit.

Following this, the Spirit led Jesus to the wilderness, where he successfully resisted Satan's temptations. Afterward, Jesus "returned in the power of the Spirit" (Luke 4:14). Luke, like the other authors of the Bible, connected the Spirit with *power,* which Jesus revealed in his healings, casting out of demons, and other miracles.

Witnessing his power over demons, some of his enemies claimed he could do so because he was in league with the devil himself. Jesus replied that "If I cast out demons by the Spirit of God, surely the kingdom of God has come upon you" (Matthew 12:28). He was claiming that his casting out of demons was a sign that the kingdom of God and the kingdom of Satan were in obvious and open conflict.

So far, we know that John the Baptist and Jesus had the power of the Spirit. Did Jesus' followers? John's Gospel reports that on the first Easter, the newly risen Jesus breathed on his disciples and told them, "Receive the Holy Spirit" (20:22). This reminds some people of the creation of Adam in Genesis 2:7, where God "breathed into his nostrils the breath of life, and man became a living being." Jesus "breathes" the power of the Spirit into his disciples. They now are empowered to do the things he has done.

Finally we arrive at the New Testament's key passage dealing with the Spirit—and with tongues. In Acts 2, the disciples were gathered in Jerusalem for the Jewish festival of Pentecost. In the house where the disciples were gathered, they experienced "a mighty rushing wind" that "filled the entire house." Then, "they were all filled with the Holy Spirit and began to speak in other tongues, as the Spirit gave them utterance" (2:2–4).

What were these "other tongues"? Acts is very clear on this: the Jews who had gathered for Pentecost spoke many different languages. Yet they marveled that somehow the disciples were able to speak to them in their native tongues. "We hear them telling in our own tongues the mighty works of God" (2:12).

The religion scholars have a name for this phenomenon: *xenolalia,* meaning "foreign speech." The idea is that somehow, miraculously, a person can speak a language he does not know. Sheer nonsense? If you don't allow for the possibility of miracle, yes, it is nonsense. Oddly enough, it has been reported occasionally throughout history. Francis Xavier, the renowned Catholic missionary to Asia, was reported to have had the gift.

When Christians refer to "speaking in tongues," however, this is not usually what they mean. But before we turn to that, one more word about Pentecost.

After the Jews in Jerusalem heard the disciples speaking their own language, they marveled. Some apparently were skeptical, for they said of the disciples, "They are filled with new wine." Peter had to answer this charge, and he did so with one of the best-known sermons in the Bible. In it, he referred back to Joel's prophecy of the Spirit being poured on all mankind. Peter then related Jesus' life, death, and resurrection. Jesus was, Peter declared, the fulfillment of the Jewish prophecies. Then the climax: "Repent and be baptized, everyone one of you in the name of Jesus Christ for the forgiveness of sins, and you will receive the gift of the Holy Spirit" (2:38). And suddenly three thousand people were added to the Christian fellowship.

This happened at Pentecost, and this is why to this day Christians connect "Pentecost" and "Holy Spirit." Prior to this, only select individuals were "filled with the Spirit." Now all who put their faith in Jesus are filled. Pentecost became a key holy day in the church's life, a remembrance of the "descent of the Spirit." Denominations that call themselves "Pentecostal" are those that emphasize the Spirit and its role in Christian life.

And they emphasize the "gifts of the Spirit," which brings us, finally, to speaking in tongues. I've already talked about *xenolalia,* the gift of speaking in languages you don't know. But when the New Testament refers to tongues, it usually means *glossolalia,* "tongue speech." This refers to a special prayer language or praise language. The person, under the influence of the Spirit, makes words or sounds that do not belong to any known language.

If you have ever heard someone speaking in tongues, you may have been shocked, puzzled, disturbed, amazed, enchanted—any or all of the above. It is, to a first-time hearer, unusual, to put it mildly. People who attend churches or groups where it occurs often take it in stride. Even those who do not do it themselves accept and approve of the practice. To them, it is just what the Bible says it is: a gift from the Holy Spirit. People who practice it claim it enriches their spiritual life.

The Book of Acts says that some of the early Christians spoke in tongues (10:46, 19:6). But the Bible's main passage on tongues is 1 Corinthians 12 and 14. In Chapter 12, Paul talked about the various gifts of the Spirit: healing, miracles, prophecy, utterance of wisdom, and others. Tongues is on the list—as is interpretation of tongues. Paul reminded the Christians that not everyone had the same gift, but they all had the same Spirit. In Chapter 14, he got down to brass tacks: Speaking in tongues was disrupting worship, plus there was a danger of people getting so wrapped up in their own spiritual ecstasy that they were neglecting the community. Paul made it clear that he himself spoke in tongues—"more than all of you," in fact (14:18). And it is fine for people to speak in tongues for their own spiritual life, but "the one who speaks in a tongue builds up himself, but the one who prophesies builds up the church. Now I want you all to speak in tongues, but even more to prophesy" (14:4–5). Prophesying does not mean, by the way, predicting the future. It means something more like "speaking the word of the Lord." *Proclaiming* might be a good synonym. Paul knows this is more important for the fellowship than tongues is. For those who do speak in tongues in church, there should be an interpreter, one who "translates" the Spirit language for the other members (14:28).

All of this would seem to punch a hole in one of the lies about the Bible: *Christians should no longer speak in tongues.* However, those who oppose the practice point to Paul's own words in 1 Corinthians 13:8: "Love never ends. As for prophecies, they will pass away. As for tongues, they will cease." Clearly, in the New Testament, that time had not yet arrived. But later generations of Christians believed that the Spirit's gifts had passed away when the first Christians died off. Both Catholic and Protestant theologians explained it this way: the dramatic gifts of the Spirit described in the New Testament were necessary to "jump-start" the church. Once

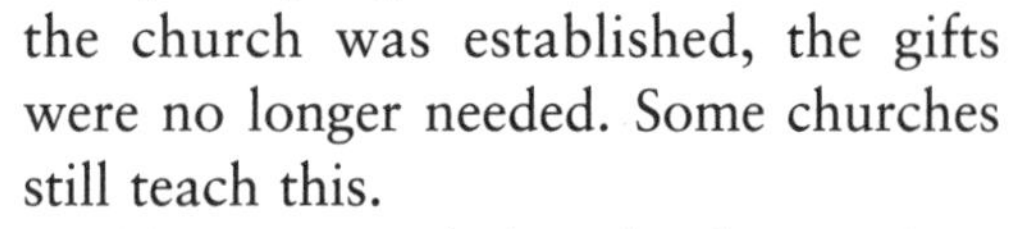

the church was established, the gifts were no longer needed. Some churches still teach this.

> Many of the Spirit's gifts, especially tongues, went "underground" for long periods.

Tongues tended to be frowned on by the church authorities, who feared it might lead to heresy. The truth is, authorities dislike activities they cannot control, and the Spirit's gifts are, obviously, not under human control. When, for many centuries, laymen were forbidden to read the Bible, the clergy seldom preached on spiritual gifts, so most laymen had no knowledge of them. But tongues never entirely vanished. The famous Francis of Assisi claimed to have been "drunk in the Spirit," caught up in a trancelike state. Some believe he may have spoken in tongues. His spiritual sister, Clare, definitely spoke in tongues. Various fringe groups, often those persecuted by the official church, encouraged speaking in tongues.

But the "new Pentecost" really dates from the twentieth century. In January 1901, at a Bible school in Kansas, several people began speaking in tongues. The group's leader, Charles Parham, spread the news of this. One of his associates, a black pastor named William Seymour, watched as a similar "outpouring of the Spirit" occurred in Los Angeles in 1906, in what is known as the Azusa Street Revival. These and similar occurrences provoked a lot of laughter and criticism—not just from unbelievers, but also from many Christians. Some Christians said tongues speaking had it source in Satan, who wished to make Christianity appear silly. This was understandable. Christian worship in general had become, frankly, pretty dull. Church involved singing hymns (without much enthusiasm), praying, taking up a collection, and hearing a sermon. If you were lucky, your preacher was dynamic. Most were not. But people had become used to this unexciting form of worship. And because some of these early outpourings of the Spirit happened among lower- or lower-middle-class folk, some snobbery came into play. Affluent Christians felt themselves to be above such lowbrow activity as tongues speaking. And for much of the twentieth century, so it was: Christians who called themselves Pentecostals were not far up on the social ladder.

This changed very dramatically in 1960. An Episcopal minister, Dennis Bennett, shocked his church when he announced that he and some church members had spoken in tongues. What a jolt: tongues speaking in the denomination known for its extremely dignified (and upper-class) worship. Bennett's bishop announced a ban on tongues in churches under his authority. But a movement was under way. *Time* and *Newsweek* ran articles on what is still known as the charismatic movement. (It is from the Greek *charismata,* "gifts," because the movement emphasizes all the Spirit's gifts, not just tongues.)

The movement is transdenominational. All the older denominations—Episcopalian, Lutheran, Methodist, Presbyterian, even Catholics—eventually made a place at the table for their members who called themselves charismatics or Spirit-filled Christians. Pope John Paul II told Catholic priests to adopt a "welcoming attitude" toward the charismatic movement.

As the movement has become respectable, some of that respectability rubbed off on the older Pentecostal denominations. Many of these are growing tremendously, and not all Pentecostals today are on the lower part of the economic ladder.

Whether you are a believer or not, you would observe, if you attended a charismatic or Pentecostal church, that the worship is livelier than in most churches. As stated several paragraphs ago, something in human nature desires *enthusiasm,* something you sense in the Book of Psalms but not in a lot of Christian worship services. In a charismatic or Pentecostal service, people may dance, clap, sway, speak in tongues (so long as it is not disruptive) and generally "have a good time."

Now, back to the lie at the beginning of this chapter: True Christians should speak in tongues. Well, should they? Paul did tell the

Charismatic churches are growing, while many of the older (and duller) churches are losing members.

Corinthians he wished they all spoke in tongues (1 Corinthians 14:5). But obviously all Christians do not. There are some very saintly Christians who, for various reasons, still frown on the practice. Are they not *true* Christians, then?

Back to human nature: people love to be part of an elite. If you spoke in tongues, it might mean so much to you that you encouraged everyone to do it (meaning, pray that the Spirit will affect people as it has affected you). But then, you might also begin to look down on people who have not spoken in tongues, right? This happens quite often, and is the reason many pastors regard charismatics as troublemakers. For people who have the gift, it is evidence the Spirit has come upon them. It is only natural to conclude that other Christians might be . . . well, not quite as spiritual.

Go back to Paul and 1 Corinthians 12: there are several gifts of the Spirit. Speaking in tongues is just one of those. Not all Christians have it. Those who have it should thank God for it, but also be thankful for gifts that others possess. Bottom line: *You can be a Christian, be filled with the Spirit, and do not have to speak in tongues.*

And anyway, Paul assures us that what really counts is "faith, hope, and love," and there is no doubt that "the greatest of these is love" (1 Corinthians 13:13).

80

A Perfectly Perplexing Command

"The Bible says Christians are to be perfect, which means Christians can live without sin."

A few years ago, a movie starring John Travolta and Jamie Leigh Curtis was titled *Perfect.* The title referred to being perfect *physically,* which is never the kind of perfection that is important in the Bible. The Bible sets a high *spiritual* standard, with not much interest in the externals.

"You therefore must be perfect, as your heavenly Father is perfect" (Matthew 5:48). "Be perfect," you say? Impossible, you say? Most people would agree. But strangely enough, the quest for Christian perfection has been going on for two thousand years. In the early years of Christianity, some people withdrew to the wilderness, believing that living among other people made them more likely to sin. (Probably true.) Influential church leaders like Augustine taught that while we lived on earth, true perfection was not possible. Augustine's opponent was Pelagius, who taught that sin was a bad habit that could be broken if people really tried. Most theologians sided with Augustine, but there were always those who believed that Christians could achieve perfection. One of these was George Fox, the Englishman who started the Quaker movement in the 1600s.

Fox believed that if people truly relied on Christ, they could give up sinning altogether.

But the big name in Christian perfection is John Wesley, the founder of Methodism. Wesley believed that God's grace could fill the heart and exclude all sin. He wrote a very influential book, *A Plain Account of Christian Perfection.* In it, he taught that the Bible holds up a standard of perfection, a standard we can meet by living without deliberate sin. (The key word is *deliberate,* obviously.) Wesley's book came to be honored not by the Methodists but by what is called the Holiness movement, which has emphasized continually growing in grace. The Holiness movement, like Wesley, has assumed that the command "Be perfect" means just what it says, with no loopholes.

Whatever "Be perfect" means, it does not mean "Be sinless." The New Testament has way too many references to Christians sinning for it to mean that. For example, 1 John 1:8–10: "If we say we have no sin, we deceive ourselves, and the truth is not in us. If we confess our sins, he is faithful and just to forgive us from al unrighteousness. If we say we have not sinned, we make him a liar, and his word is not in us."

But the classic statement on the saint who still sins is from Paul: "I do not do the good I want, but the evil I do not want is what I keep on doing. . . . Wretched man that I am! Who will deliver me from this body of death? Thanks be to God through Jesus Christ our Lord! So then, I myself serve the law of God with my mind, but with my flesh I serve the law of sin" (Romans 7:19, 24–25). Most Christians would raise the obvious question here: if Paul admitted he had trouble with sin, can us ordinary Christians hope to do any better? The spirit is willing, as Jesus himself said, but the flesh is weak (Mark 14:38).

Back to the command "Be perfect." To us, this means "flawless." But the Greek word *teleios* in Matthew 5:48 means something like "whole" or "complete" or "undivided." Paul uses the word at times to mean "mature." It really does not mean "perfect" in the usual sense. Jesus' command to be *teleios* occurs when he is telling his followers not just to love their friends but their enemies as well, because that is what God does. God loves all people, and Christians must do the same. This is how we show we are *teleios*. Real love, the kind God has, encompasses even our enemies.

Does all this shed some light on that awesome command "Be perfect"? It is remarkable that with all the dozens of good Bible translations available today, none of them has figured out a good alternative to the familiar words "Be perfect, as your heavenly Father is perfect."

81

Hiding Out From the Wild World

"The warning about being 'unequally yoked' means Christians should avoid dealings with unbelievers."

The question "Should Christians withdraw from the world?" has one obvious answer: "They can't." You can't withdraw from human nature, and you can't withdraw from sin. Christians are human. Christians can be petty, deceitful, hypocritical, and, in short, can be guilty of every sin that non-Christians are guilty of.

That hasn't stopped people from trying. From the earliest times, Christians withdrew from "the world" to live in monasteries and convents. Some even went and lived as hermits in the wilderness. The goal: to live a pure life that is (to use a phrase from the Bible) "unspotted from the world" (James 1:27). But that is not easy, even among people who believe the same things. The Amish in America live in their communities and have little contact with "the English," but they, too, have to cope with pettiness and sin, as all humans do.

Aside from not being easy, avoiding "the world" is not right. Jesus and his disciples were "in the world," definitely. Jesus' enemies criticized him for hobnobbing with prostitutes, tax collectors (who were notoriously corrupt), and other undesirables. Jesus replied that he had not come to the world to call the righteous, but to call sinners to repentance (Matthew 9:10–13). Note that he did not condone what the prostitutes and tax collectors did. But he did not shun them, either. He knew it is not easy to convert people unless you have contact with them.

Ditto for Paul. The great missionary-apostle was willing to debate the snobbish philosophers of Greece in the public arena. He risked being ridiculed—and got ridiculed. Instead of withdrawing to nurse his own faith with a group of like-minded believers, he trekked around the Roman Empire, meeting all sorts of people from all kinds of backgrounds. The early Christians were not monks and were not Amish. They took seriously Jesus' words about letting their "light" shine for all to see (Matthew 5:14–16).

But there is a flip side to this: the early Christians knew they needed each other. There is no concept of "solitary religion" in the Bible. There is plenty of emphasis on fellowship, what the first Christians called *koinonia.* Trying to live out a new faith in a world where people mocked and scorned them, they needed and gave peer support. While sharing their faith with "the world," they knew that many people in that world detested them. But in their own warm fellowship, they could build each other up. This is why one author reminded them to "forsake not the assembling of yourselves together" (Hebrews 10:25). Paul often referred to them as "one body," made up of many members but very much one living unit.

Inevitably there is some tension in this idea of being "*in* the world, but not *of* the world." How does the Christian live among unbelievers without lowering his own standards? A difficult question that has been hotly discussed for two thousand years. One Bible passage that has kept the discussion interesting is this item from Paul: "Do not be unequally yoked with unbelievers. For what partnership has righteousness with lawlessness? Or what fellowship has light with darkness?" (2 Corinthians 6:14). Pretty strong stuff, isn't it? Paul was quite blunt here: the good guys versus the bad guys. The image of being "yoked" is from farming, where, for obvious reasons, you don't hitch two different kinds of animals to a plow together. It is as if the Christian and the non-Christian are two different species.

Was Paul contradicting himself? In 1 Corinthians 5:10 Paul said that we have to go "out of the world" avoid immoral people, and that is neither possible nor desirable. Such people cannot see that you are the "salt of the earth" if they cannot see you. So what had happened in 2 Corinthians 6? Was he correcting what he said in 1 Corinthians 5?

No. Because the key word here is *yoked.* That implies a common purpose, an association that is not casual. Not all associations are "yokes." Marriage obviously is a yoke, which is why Paul had to give advice to Christians who were already married to unbelievers. (The upshot of his counsel: stay in the marriage if you choose, but you don't have to.) Paul doesn't give any specifics here about just what other "yoke" relationships Christians should avoid. Perhaps he expected people to use some common sense. Would he have approved letting a non-Christian put a roof on a Christian's house? Probably. A Christian patronizing a non-Christian hairstylist? Probably. A Christian working at an adult bookstore? Probably not.

Whatever the full meaning of "Do not be unequally yoked with unbelievers," it does *not* mean "avoid them as much as possible."

82

Paul's Marital Loophole

"The only grounds for divorce is adultery."

The Old and New Testaments have radically different teachings on this subject. Christians believe that the New, because it reflects Jesus' teaching, is binding. Essentially the Old Testament left divorce at the husband's discretion—if she "finds no favor in his eyes because he has found some uncleanness in her" (Deuteronomy 24:1), he wrote a "certificate of divorce," put it in her hand, and announced publicly, "She is not my wife, and I am not her husband." In the case of divorce, neither husband nor wife could remarry (thus you could not divorce in order to marry your mistress).

Still, divorce was not common in Israel, and most people took their marriages very, very seriously. In fact, marriage was so serious that the prophet Malachi proclaimed that God himself had said, "I hate divorce" (Malachi 2:16).

Jesus set a strict standard: no divorce at all (Mark 10:11–12, Luke 16:18) or (according to Matthew's version, 5:32) divorce only because of the other spouse's adultery. This obviously gave women a boost in status, since divorce was no longer a husband's prerogative.

In the past, very strict Christians chose to follow Jesus' standard in Mark (no divorce, no matter what) or in Matthew (divorce only when the spouse commits adultery). But in fact, the New Testament itself has another option.

This is what is sometimes called the "Pauline privilege." (*Pauline* means "relating to the apostle Paul.") Paul told the early Christians that a marriage between a believer and an unbeliever could be dissolved with no guilt on the believer's part (1 Corinthians 7:12–16). However, it can only be dissolved if the unbeliever chooses to get out. If the unbelieving spouse is willing to stay in the marriage, the Christian is bound to stay also. Paul held out the hope that an unsaved spouse might eventually be won to the faith by the believing spouse.

Paul was in accord with Jesus on a very important point: the divorced Christian must not remarry. Think of what this meant: you could not bail out of your marriage in order to marry someone else who is "waiting in the wings."

Worth noting: most Christians in America today, even very conservative ones, have not let the New Testament's statements on divorce hinder them from divorcing.

83

That Old Seventh/ Sabbath Issue

"Christians should worship on Saturday, not Sunday, since Saturday is the true Sabbath."

Most Christians worship on Sunday, a notable exception being the Seventh-Day Adventists, who are correct in their belief that Saturday, not Sunday, is the Sabbath day. Considering that the Sabbath was taken so seriously in the Old Testament, how did we get into the habit of having Sunday as the day of worship?

In the first place, all the first Christians were Jews, as Jesus himself was. While Jesus argued with some of the Jews about the purpose of the Sabbath (Mark 2:23–28), he still held to the Sabbath as a day of rest and worship. After Jesus' resurrection (on the first day of the week), Jewish Christians stuck with their old habit: the Sabbath was a sacred day. But as the new faith spread to non-Jews, the apostles had to deal with that ticklish question: how much of the Jewish religion did these non-Jewish Christians have to practice? The answer was, "Not much," and they were definitely not required to observe the Sabbath. Naturally as the faith spread, there were more Christians from non-Jewish backgrounds than from Jewish. So there was no particular reason to stick with the rule about the seventh day.

Paul, the dutiful Jew who grew up observing the Sabbath faithfully, never told Christians to do so. Paul, the "apostle to the Gentiles," felt no obligation to impose the old Jewish Sabbath on non-Jews. Christians who insist on observing Saturday as the Sabbath are faced with this fact: Paul, considered a great authority among the first Christians, did not require Sabbath observance.

Still, the Christians did not throw out the baby with the bathwater. There was something good in the Sabbath: the idea of dedicating one day of the week to rest and worship of God. It made sense for Jewish Christians to continue using the Sabbath for that purpose. But for other Christians, it made sense to observe Sunday, the day of Jesus' resurrection, as the holy day.

Keep in mind that Christianity was being spread throughout the Roman Empire. Most of the empire's residents had no concept of a "day of rest and worship" every week. Since most people had to work every day during daylight hours, many Christians formed the habit of assembling together on Saturday evenings. (This was already true in Paul's time. See Acts 20:7.) At some point, probably under the Roman emperor Trajan, these Saturday-evening assemblies were outlawed, so Christians began to gather together early on Sunday, the day of resurrection. Some Christian authors claimed that the first day of the week was "the new Sabbath," and that the Sabbath principle was still the same, since one day out of seven was reserved for God.

It was Constantine, the first Christian emperor of Rome, who made Sunday a weekly day of rest. In 321, he decreed that people should "rest on the venerable day of the sun." People throughout Europe and the Americas can thank Constantine for this, even if they associate Sunday more with fun than with rest and worship.

84

Is Damp Enough, or Do We Need a River?

"Baptism should be by immersion."

It isn't nearly as common as it once was, but in times past many churches insisted on performing baptisms in flowing rivers or streams. Does the Bible command this? No, but the great role model for baptisms was John the Baptist, who baptized people (including Jesus) in the Jordan River. Many rural churches in the South liked to continue this tradition—weather permitting, of course—as a kind of baptism "New Testament style." As the country has grown more urbanized, river baptisms are fewer and fewer, although some churches settle for second best: a painting of a river on the wall behind the church's baptismal pool. The painting is supposed to represent the Jordan River. If you have traveled in Israel, you may have noticed that a lot of tourists there choose to be baptized (or rebaptized) in the Jordan.

The wilderness prophet-preacher John the Baptist baptized repentant people in the river. Did John merely sprinkle them with water, or were they totally immersed? Tradition says that they were totally immersed. More important: the Greek word *baptizo* in the New Testament does mean "to dip" or "to immerse."

The apostle Paul supplied a good reason for immersion: baptism is a reminder of Jesus' death (going under the water) and resurrection (coming back out again). So besides being a symbol of being washed of one's sins, immersion is a way of identifying with Jesus (Romans 6:3–5).

We do not know if *all* baptisms in the early church were done by immersion. Obviously the climate had to be considered. Fairly early, baptism came to be done by pouring or by having the pastor place his hand in a bowl of water and then place his wet hand on the person's head (called "sprinkling," oddly enough). It is probably safe to say that most Christian baptisms over the centuries have been done by pouring or sprinkling. Many Christian groups, notably the Baptists (obviously), insist on baptism by complete immersion. (In most Baptist churches, they would require you to be immersed before joining their church—even if you had been baptized already by sprinkling.)

In the 1800s, some American churches felt so strongly about immersion that they insisted that John be referred to in new Bible translations as "John the Immerser" instead of "John the Baptist." Spencer Cone, an official with the American Bible Society, urged that group to publish an "immersion version" of the Bible. The society refused, so Cone left to form his own American Bible Union. With William Wyckoff, he hastily prepared an "immersion version" of the King James Version. The upshot was this: Cone and others who believed strongly in baptism by immersion wanted the Bible to make it clear that *baptism was by immersion only.* So in Cone's immersion version (and there were many others), the words *immerse* and *immersion* were substituted for the King James Version's words *baptize* and *baptism.*

Does this sound like much ado about nothing? Perhaps it was. The point was, the pro-immersion people did (and still do) believe that immersion is the only proper way to do baptism, the way commanded by the New Testament. The logic of having an "immersion version" was pretty obvious: if you said you believed in the Bible and you read the "immersion version," you would have to say you believed in baptism by immersion. If you read the regular Bible, which used the word *baptism,* you could interpret that to mean "baptism by whatever method."

With all due respect to Christians who insist on immersion, the New Testament does not lay down an iron law that it be done by immersion. The key idea is that the person undergoes a public ritual (involving water, of course) in which words are said to indicate that the person is willing to be identified as a Christian.

PART IX

WHAT THE CHURCHES FUSS OVER

PETER DENYING CHRIST
Though Peter denied the arrested Jesus, the Bible says he became chief apostle with authority over all Christians . . . or does it?

85

The Leap From Fisherman to "His Holiness"

"Peter was the first bishop of Rome."

Even if you are not a Catholic, you probably know that the grandest church in Rome is St. Peter's Basilica. According to tradition, the actual body of the apostle Peter is buried there. And to this day, the popes have been referred to as the "successors" of Peter. He was, so Catholics believe, the first bishop of Rome—that is, the first pope.

Was he?

Let's jump back to the 1500s. An Englishman named William Tyndale is doing something illegal, something that eventually leads to his execution: he is translating the New Testament into English. This has been expressly prohibited by England's king, Henry VIII. But Tyndale perseveres in the name of the faith. He encounters a problem: the Greek word *episkopos*. How to translate that? It means, literally, "overseer" or "superintendent." In one of Paul's epistles (1 Timothy 3), the word is used, and it refers to a man or men "overseeing" a group of Christians. It roughly corresponds to what we would call a "pastor" or "minister." Tyndale is aware that *episkopos* is usually translated "bishop." But "bishop" doesn't seem right to him. In his day, bishops were church officials who supervised the work of a large group of pastors, spread out over a fairly large territory. And there was another problem: bishops lived well—sometimes lavishly—were paid by the state, had political power, and in many cases were shamelessly immoral. This, Tyndale knew, was not the meaning of the word *episkopos* used by Paul.

In fact, at the time the New Testament was written, there were no "bishops" such as later generations knew. A local group of Christians was lucky to have one *episkopos* and a number of deacons to assist. Several years were to pass before the church was large enough and organized enough to have an "organizational chart."

Tyndale knew this, and translators know it today. If you pick up several different Bible versions, you will see that some use *bishop* and some use *overseer*. Whichever word they use, the translators know that an *episkopos* was, basically, a local pastor, not a bishop in the later sense. The local *episkopos* had no authority outside his own local group.

Now, back to Peter and Rome. At the time Peter lived, a fairly large group of Christians was in Rome. Considering how far Rome is from Israel, this fast growth is amazing. Of course, Rome was the largest city in the empire, and it drew people from everywhere. It was inevitable that some of Jesus' apostles would visit the city's Christians, not necessarily to dominate them, but to provide them with eyewitness testimony of the Lord's doings.

The Bible itself does not say that Peter visited Rome. There is a pretty sound tradition that he did go there. The epistle known as 1 Peter claims to be written from "Babylon," which in those days was kind of code name for Rome, and that is probably what the epistle meant. Several very early Christian authors claim that Peter was martyred during the persecution of Christians by the loathsome emperor Nero. According to one very old tradition (or legend?), Peter was about to be crucified and stated that he was not worthy do die as Jesus had died. The Romans obliged him by crucifying him upside down. Paul, tradition says, died about the same time as Peter.

The Christians at Rome were, naturally, pleased to have been visited by two great apostles. Rome also had their "trophies"—meaning, probably, their tombs. By about the year 300, Rome celebrated a festival day in honor of both Peter and Paul. As time passed, "trophies" of Christian martyrs became very important in the church, and Rome became extremely proud of its martyrs' graves, particularly those of Peter and Paul. In time, the bishop of Rome came to have such prestige that he felt obliged to give spiritual advice to churches elsewhere. Eventually the bishop of Rome came to see himself as *head* bishop of the whole church. This claim never went undisputed, of course. There were cities—notably Jerusalem—that had had Christian fellowships longer than Rome had. But of course, the name of Rome itself had a lot of clout. To be the bishop of the church in the chief city carried a great deal of prestige. One of his claims to be *the* bishop was the belief that Peter was "prince of the apostles," appointed to that post by Jesus himself. Also, Peter was (tradition said) Rome's very first bishop. This meant that later bishops inherited his authority.

By the time the bishop of Rome could make such extravagant claims for his authority, things had (obviously) changed a lot since Peter's day. By the year, say, 500, a bishop was much more powerful, better paid, and (alas) probably less spiritual than the *episkopos* of the New Testament.

This brings us back to the basic question: Was Peter actually the bishop of Rome? Ever its *episkopos?* One early Christian writer claimed that Peter was martyred after "shepherding the flock at Rome for a few months." This may be correct. We can't be certain. There is no real reason to doubt that Peter went to Rome and was martyred there. Certainly he would have been spiritually qualified to shepherd a flock of Christians. The New Testament gives us no help here. It is worth noting that the Book of Acts, which mentions Paul being in Rome, does not mention Peter being there at the time.

Summing up: Peter may possibly have been a leader in the Christian group in Rome. If he was, he definitely did not wield the power that later bishops of Rome claimed they inherited from him. So in the later sense of the word *bishop,* Peter was not the bishop of Rome.

86

A Bold Jewish Boy Named "Rocky"

"Jesus made Peter the chief of the apostles, with spiritual authority over all Christians."

If you want to meet a very appealing, and very human, character in the Bible, you can't do any better than Peter. The fisherman of Galilee, chosen to be one of Jesus' twelve disciples, is at times impulsive, brave, cowardly, meek, temperamental—and always interesting.

Peter was from the small town of Bethsaida and was named Simon before Jesus bestowed on him his other name. He worked with his father and his brother Andrew in their fishing business on the Sea of Galilee, where he first met Jesus. At the beginning of his ministry, Jesus called Peter and Andrew from their work, telling them he would make them "fishers of men."

Peter occupied an important place among the twelve disciples. In all the New Testament's list of the twelve, he is always named first. With the apostles James and John (who were brothers, and also fishermen), Peter formed a kind of "inner circle" of the twelve. These three alone witnessed the Transfiguration (Jesus appeared in a sort of vision with the long-dead Moses and Elijah). The three were with him in the garden of Gethsemane, where he agonized over his inevitable death on the cross.

But despite being one of the people closest to Jesus, Peter could be rash and foolish. When Jesus predicted that his disciples would run away when he was arrested, Peter was quick to announce that *he* would not. Jesus then predicted that before cock's crow in the morning, Peter would deny him three times. The prophecy came to pass, and when Peter remembered it, "he broke down and wept" (Mark 14:72). According to John's Gospel, at the time of Jesus' arrest, Peter became violent. He took his sword and cut off the ear of the high priest's servant. Far from praising this, Jesus scolded Peter: "Shall I not drink the cup that the Father has given me?" (John 18:11).

Sometimes Peter's rashness could be amusing. John 13 records that Jesus washed his disciples' feet, showing them that humility and service to others was his standard. Peter would not have it: "You shall never wash my feet." Jesus answered, "If I do not wash you, you have no share with me." Peter then typically went overboard: "Lord, not my feet only but also my hands and my head!" (13:8).

But the most famous event in the Gospels concerning Peter is his famous "confession," found in Matthew 16. Jesus asked the disciples who people thought he was. Then he asked them who *they* thought he was. Peter's famous reply: "You are the Christ, the Son of the living God." Jesus' equally famous reply: "Blessed are you Simon Bar-Jonah! For flesh and blood has not revealed this to you, but my Father who is in heaven. And I tell you, you are Peter, and on this rock I will build my church, and the gates of hell shall not prevail against it" (Matthew 16:13–19).

Pause for some brief explanations: Peter's real name was Simon. Jesus nicknamed him Peter (it's the Greek word *petros*, "rock"—*petros* as in *petroleum*). Jesus was clearly pleased that Peter had realized the truth: Jesus was the Christ, the Messiah (the two words mean the same thing, "Anointed One").

Now, here is where we find one of the great controversies in religious history: what did Jesus mean when he said "on this rock I will build my church"? Did he mean, build it on Peter? Or build it on what Peter had said, that Jesus was the Christ? Catholics go with the first option: Peter himself is the foundation of the church. Most Protestants go with the second option. And even Protestants who believe that Peter himself is "the rock" believed that he was called this *because of* the confession he had just made that Jesus is Messiah. More ink has been spilled over the interpretation of this passage than any in the New Testament.

According to Catholic tradition, this famous passage shows that Jesus made Peter the "prince of the apostles" and the foundation stone of the church. There might be some truth in the "prince of the apostles" claim, even though Jesus himself made it clear that such lofty titles had no place among his followers. Peter was, in the Gospels, clearly the dominant one. This was true after Jesus' resurrection, when Peter was the first to enter Jesus' empty tomb. Later, we learn from John 21, Jesus commanded Peter to "feed my sheep." As the Book of Acts opened, Peter was definitely at center stage. In Acts 2, he preached his famous Pentecost sermon, which was so effective that three thousand people joined the fellowship. Of the twelve disciples, he was clearly the most prominent in Acts. Later in Acts, it was Paul (who was not one of the twelve) who took center stage. This doesn't mean Peter ceased to be important. It most likely means that the author of Acts had a lot more detailed information about Paul's activities.

But despite the attention devoted to Peter, Acts does not give the impression he was "in charge." At the "Jerusalem council" in Acts 15, it was not Peter who presided, but James, the brother of Jesus. In his Letter to the Galatians, Paul referred several times to Peter. For him, Peter was apostle to the Jews, as Paul was apostle to the Gentiles. Paul referred to "James and Peter and John," who were "reputed to be pillars" of the Jerusalem church (2:9). If Paul knew that Peter was the "prince of the apostles," he certainly never let on. In fact, in 2:12, he hinted that Peter was under the dominance of James.

Also worth noting: two letters in the New Testament are supposed to be from Peter. In both he referred to himself simply as "an apostle of Jesus Christ," the same words Paul used. This does not sound as if Peter believed himself as somehow above the other apostles.

But in Catholic tradition, Peter is still "prince of the apostles" and also, supposedly, the first bishop of Rome. This means that he was the first pope. (See pages 265–267.) Popes down to the present day claim they have inherited the authority of the first pope, the authority that Jesus conferred on him when he said "on this rock I will build my church." As I already noted, not all Christians accept that interpretation. And also, there is nothing in the Gospels to suggest that any of the first Christians thought there should be a "head bishop" or any kind of centralized authority in the church. There is no hint in Acts that Peter was that person or wished to be. Another item worth remembering: the Catholic Church uses the incident of Matthew 16 to support its belief in Peter as head of the church. But no one ever quoted Matthew 16 in this way until about the year 200.

Summing up: Peter is one of the most fascinating and most important people in early Christianity. But he was not the head of the Christians and did not "pass on" his authority to the popes.

87

Getting Right About Rites

"The Bible teaches that there are seven sacraments."

Millions of Christians across the globe take great spiritual comfort from the sacraments. And millions of Christians have no idea what a sacrament is.

What does the Bible say—if anything—about this?

In the first place, you won't find the word in the Bible. You will find a Greek word, *mysterion,* which in Latin is *sacramentum.* The word *mysterion* means (no surprise here) "mystery" or "secret." In the New Testament, it sometimes refers to the hidden plan of God to save mankind through Jesus Christ. In Christ, Paul says, God's hidden plan breaks into the world. God reveals his *mysterion* to the people he saves (see Romans 16:25, Ephesians 3:3).

When the new faith spread, people translated the Greek *mysterion* into the Latin *sacramentum.* The Latin word had a shade of meaning that the Greek word lacked. A *sacramentum* could be the oath a person took on being initiated into the military or a secret society. The idea is that you were joining something, committing yourself to it, and that it was very solemn.

It was only natural that Christians would apply *sacramentum* to the Lord's Supper and to baptism. Both these rituals were taken very, very seriously. Baptism, of course, was a onetime event, one that said to the world, "I am a changed person, I have owned up to my sin, I want to lead a new and better life, I want to walk with God from now on. I am a Christian." It was usually done publicly (you could not be a "secret" Christian), and by full immersion. It had several meanings. One, your past sins were symbolically washed away. It was a kind of "spiritual bath." Two, going under the water and coming back up again identified the person with Jesus himself—dead and buried, then resurrected (Romans 6:3–5). The baptized person is, like the resurrected Jesus, born to "newness of life." The person is "dead to sin but alive to God" (Romans 6:11).

The early Christians took this very seriously. It was, to them, much more than just being dunked in water. It symbolized a change in the person's eternal destiny. They did not, apparently, believe the ritual itself had any power. But over time, that idea crept in. In the New Testament, we know only of adults being baptized. They make a conscious choice to be baptized and to identify with Christ. By the time the practice of infant baptism is common, a major change has occurred: people have begun to believe that the ritual itself has some kind of power.

Let's look at the other ritual of the New Testament, Holy Communion, or the Lord's Supper. As you might guess from its name, this was begun by Jesus himself. On the night he was betrayed and arrested, Jesus shared a meal (the "Last Supper") with his twelve disciples. Distributing bread and wine to them, he spoke the immortal words: "This is my body" (the bread) and "This is my blood" (the wine). It is clear that at the time the disciples did not understand what he meant. (See Luke 22:14–23.)

Only later was the meaning understood: Jesus was the Ultimate Sacrifice for human sin. In the old Jewish system, animals were sacrificed to God to make amends for sin. (This is fairly common throughout human history, by the way.) Jesus' sacrifice of himself does away with the old system. He is a once-for-all sacrifice. He is the sinless human who gives up his life on behalf of sinners. The blood he sheds is the "blood of the new covenant," a new arrangement between God and man.

After Jesus' death and resurrection, the apostles reenacted this Last Supper. It became, and still is, a standard feature of Christianity around the world. The impression you get from Acts and from Paul's letters is that originally it was an actual meal, a sort of fellowship supper that climaxed with someone repeating the words Jesus spoke about his body and blood being the bread and wine. According to Paul, "This cup of blessing that we bless, is it not a participation in the blood of Christ? The bread that we break, is it not a participation in the body of Christ?" (1 Corinthians 11:16).

Unlike baptism, which occurred once in a person's life, the Lord's Supper was repeated often. In time, Christians celebrated it every time they gathered together. It was not to be done flippantly. Paul ordered each Christian to "examine himself" before participating. He seems to suggest that people have become sick from participating "unworthily" in the Lord's Supper (1 Corinthians 11:27–30).

Pretty early, baptism and the Lord's Supper each came to be seen as a *mysterion* or *sacramentum*. It was believed that Jesus himself had established them as binding on Christians. They were, so people began to believe, absolutely necessary for salvation.

Augustine, a prominent theologian in north Africa, came up with a definition of *sacrament:* "an outward sign of an inward grace." In other words, in baptism and the Lord's Supper, something happens in the material world (immersion in water, eating bread and drinking wine) and in the spiritual world. Augustine used the term *grace,* and this led to the belief that the rituals had a kind of magic power of their own. Christian ministers who presided at baptism and the Lord's Supper were, you might say, turned into wonder workers, since their performance of the rituals conferred God's grace. Catholics believe that in the Lord's Supper, the bread and wine actually *become* (in some mysterious way) the body and blood of Christ. Critics have claimed that this makes the priest into a sort of magician.

We can, definitely, doubt whether the New Testament supports this concept of sacraments. But most Christians around the world do believe that baptism and the Lord's Supper are very important and (maybe) necessary rituals—whether they are called sacraments or not.

But *seven* sacraments? What are they, anyway? For Roman Catholics, the seven are: marriage, holy orders (ordination), penance, confirmation, extreme unction (the "last rites" before dying), plus baptism and the Lord's Supper. In the Catholic view, all seven sacraments were "instituted" by Christ himself or his apostles. There is, frankly, not much evidence for this. It was fairly late (about the year 1200) that the Catholic Church decided that there were seven sacraments. Protestant Christians accept only two sacraments, baptism and the Lord's Supper, since the Bible is clear that these are a vital part of the faith.

In fairness to Roman Catholics, there is nothing particularly wrong with having seven sacred rituals. Many people find them comforting, and many people have been drawn to Christianity because of the solemnity of Christian rituals. But we can safely say that Jesus and the apostles did not institute seven sacraments.

88

Do Only Good Things Come in Sevens?

"The Bible lists seven deadly sins."

Just seven? Actually, the Bible names *lots* of sins. But in fact, the biggest concern of the Bible is not *sins*. The real problem is *sin*.

Sin is an unpopular, old-fashioned-sounding word today, but it occurs so often in the Bible that you can hardly read a page without coming upon the concept of sin. We think of it as a "killjoy" word—that is, a sin is something we enjoy that God doesn't want us to enjoy, maybe drinking, drugs, sex, even dancing and card playing. But in the Bible, sin is the broad concept of doing something that offends God and that harms others and ourselves. God wants what is best for man, makes his intentions clear, then men consciously disobey him.

The word *sin* seems dated, but the concept remains: most people today have the general feeling that we aren't all we're supposed to be. This explains why self-help books, psychologists, diets, exercise programs, and the like, are so popular. There is the feeling that *something is wrong with each of us*. We believe we ought to improve, become better. All the world's religions have this idea: whatever I am, I'm not quite what I was meant to be. According to the people who wrote the Bible, our failure is that we don't honor and love the God who made us. As a result, we do harm to others and to ourselves. Until we "get right with God" (as the old highway signs said), we can't be the people we were meant to be.

The first few chapters of the Bible tell the story of Adam and Eve, the first human beings, who are given a beautiful place to live but who choose to disobey the one rule God imposes on them. According to the Bible, each human being repeats the mistake of Adam and Eve. (For shorthand, we call this beginning of sin the Fall.) Each person chooses to disobey God's orders. Sin is universal—every human being sins, even good people. The New Testament says, "All have sinned and fall short of the glory of God" (Romans 3:23). Sin is not confined to another nation, race, class, gender, or political group. Each of us is in the same boat.

Sin is not just deeds but an attitude—worshiping ourselves instead of giving first honor to God. Sin is connected with the idea of *idolatry*—worshiping something or someone other than God. God wishes to be not only worshiped but also loved—freely, of our own will. We have the freedom not to—that is, we have the freedom to sin, to say no to God. Sin is bad, but it is a sign that God made us capable of choosing. We can choose to love God or snub him. If we were not capable of sinning, we would be like robots, without free will.

In the Old Testament, when people knew they had offended God by disobeying him, they had a system of sacrifices—offering up an animal as a sign that they were sorry for what they'd done and wanted to make amends. In the New Testament, a new idea was introduced: instead of repeatedly sacrificing animals to show we wanted a right relationship with God, there was a final sacrifice: Jesus, who was executed by crucifixion. Jesus was the Ultimate Sacrifice, who restores us to a right relationship with God. Jesus is often called Savior because he saves people from their sin.

Yes, the Bible is indisputably "anti-sin." But looked at in a more positive way, it is "pro-happiness." In the Bible's view, people cannot find true happiness or joy in life unless they put God first. The purpose of avoiding sin is to have the most important relationship of all, peace with the Maker and Sustainer of everything.

Now, back to those Seven Deadly Sins. Catholic tradition naming the seven goes back to as early as A.D. 600. The Bible never actually lists the seven together, but the New Testament does name, and condemn, all seven. They are: pride, avarice (greed), lust, anger (wrath), gluttony, envy, and sloth.

Why seven? You don't have to read too far in the Bible to figure out that seven is a special number. At the very beginning, God creates the world in six days, then rests on the seventh. In the Ten Commandments, man is ordered to observe the seventh day (the Sabbath) as a sacred day. I can't list all the many "sevens" in the Bible, but suffice it to say, seven is a "good" number.

Now, what about "deadly"? This doesn't refer to "lethal to the body," but, more importantly, "lethal to the soul." None of these sins is unforgivable, for God is infinite in mercy. The key idea is that these sins, if the person persists in them and never repents, will put one in danger of missing heaven. (Putting it bluntly, you will go to hell.)

As I've already said, the Bible does *not* list these sins together. It does condemn them all. More importantly, it dwells on the opposite of each, a positive virtue. The opposite of pride is humility, which time and time again in the New Testament is held up as a great Christian virtue. It doesn't mean hating yourself or having low self-esteem. It means seeing yourself objectively and not constantly comparing yourself to others. The opposite of avarice (or greed) is generosity—not just with money, but with time, praise, and so on. The opposite of lust is (believe it or not) self-control. The idea is not "no pleasure" but "not letting the desire for pleasure control us." The opposite of gluttony is temperance, moderation. (Like lust, gluttony means letting our enjoyment of things get out of hand.) The opposite of sloth is zeal, enthusiasm—for the right things, of course. The opposite of anger (or wrath) is kindness and mercy. And the opposite of envy is love—seeking the good of others instead of fretting over our own condition.

In case you didn't notice, all of the seven deadly sins are just aspects of *selfishness*. That brings us back to the basic concept of *sin* at the beginning of this chapter. Sin, in the Bible's view, is the selfish soul crying out, "I! Me! Mine!" The various sins are just different ways of proving that selfishness. And the reason the Catholic Church put together the list of Seven Deadlies long ago was it was a useful way of "taking our spiritual temperature"—of thinking through the various ways we might be manifesting our selfishness.

89

Among the Preachers' Favorite Topics . . .

"Stewardship *refers to tithing.*"

If you enter a church that is having "Stewardship Sunday," you can bet that the pastor's sermon will be on the subject of tithing. I discuss tithing elsewhere in this book (see pages 221–224) and conclude that tithing is: (1) a good thing, but (2) not required by the Bible. Pastors preach on the subject for the obvious reason: they need people to contribute money to the church. Churches are voluntary organizations, and they require voluntary contributions. It strikes some unbelievers as crude and materialistic, but pastors, like all people, have to eat, church buildings must be maintained, utility bills must be paid, and the like. And many churches run charity programs. All this requires money.

> If it's crude for churches to ask for money, it's just as crude for PBS television stations to do so.
>
> 

Having said that, it is also true that "Stewardship Sunday" gives a pretty distorted view of what stewardship is all about. In the Bible's view, it certainly involves much more than giving 10 percent of your income to the church.

You might say that stewardship started in Eden. "The LORD God took the man and put him in the garden of Eden to work it and keep it" (Genesis 2:15). Adam wasn't just a tourist soaking up the scenery. He had a task. God had planted the garden and God continued to give it life. But Adam had a role, too. The task was not burdensome, as we see in 3:37–19: not until after Adam and Eve disobeyed God was Adam cursed with *hard* labor in the world.

Adam in Eden was a kind of steward—not the owner of the place, but a kind of overseer or guardian, one who looked after things on behalf of the owner (who was God, of course). The words *steward* and *stewardship* entered the Christian vocabulary because of Luke 16:1–8, Jesus' parable about a dishonest (but shrewd) steward. Jesus concluded his parable with these words: "One who is faithful in a very little is also faithful in much, and one who is dishonest in a very little is also dishonest in much." The idea: prove you can be trusted with small tasks, then you can be trusted with grander tasks.

Jesus told another parable to illustrate what stewardship meant. This is the well-known parable of the talents in Matthew 25:14–30. In the parable, a *talent* is a unit of money. (It was only later that the word came to refer to a person's abilities. In fact, our use of the word *talent* is due to this parable.) In the parable, a man going on a journey calls his servants to him and gives each one some money, "to each according to his ability." The servant who is given five talents manages to turn it into ten. The servant given two talents also doubles it. But the servant given only one talent buries it in the ground. To the two who doubled what they had, the master says, "Well done, good and faithful servant. You have been faithful over a little. I will set you over much. Enter into the joy of your master." But the master is harsh with the "wicked and slothful servant," the one who buried his one talent in the ground. "Cast the worthless servant into the outer darkness. In that place there will be weeping and gnashing of teeth." If the master (God) entrusts you with something, you do not bury it. You invest it wisely.

Jesus' parable is, of course, referring not just to money. Whatever gift people have, they are expected to use wisely in God's service. This idea is found again and again in the Bible. Consider 1 Peter 4:10: "As each one has received a gift, use it to serve one another, as good stewards of God's varied grace." You find the same idea in Proverbs 3:9: "Honor the LORD with your wealth and with the first-fruits of your produce." Paul told the early Christians that their bodies (meaning their lives, of course) were to be offered as "living sacrifices" to God (Romans 12:1) Whatever we do is to be done "all for the glory of God" (1 Corinthians 10:30–31).

Summing up: stewardship is more than putting money into God's service. And it is certainly more than tithing.

But having said that, here is a tidbit worth remembering: the word we translate as "steward" in the English Bible is the Greek word *oikonomos*—the root of the word *economy*.

90

Is God Fussy About Posture?

"Bowing your head and closing your eyes is the correct posture for prayer."

Kneeling is the common position for prayer, along with bowing the head. Is this the "Bible-approved" position? Yes and no. Some people did pray while kneeling. But some people prayed while standing (Jeremiah 18:20), sitting (2 Samuel 7:18), and even lying facedown (Matthew 26:39). Some people prayed with hands lifted up, which is now becoming common again, especially among charismatic Christians (1 Kings 8:22, 1 Timothy 2:8). People prayed both silently (1 Samuel 1:13) and out loud (Ezekiel 11:13). They prayed alone (Matthew 6:6) and in groups (Acts 4:31). They prayed in an open field (Genesis 24:11–12), in the temple (2 Kings 19:14), by a riverside (Acts 16:13), on a seashore (Acts 21:5), in bed (Psalm 63:6), and on a battlefield (1 Samuel 7:5). At the time of Jesus, devout Jews would pray, while standing, at several set times per day.

In short, the Bible depicts people praying in many locations and in many positions. Over the centuries, praying with the head bowed and eyes closed has become the most common posture. But it is definitely not commanded in the Bible.

Only one verse in the Bible hints that people bowed their heads while praying. King Hezekiah and his officials "bowed their heads and worshiped" (2 Chronicles 29:30). Even in this verse, we aren't sure that bowing the head was actually connected with praying.

And what about closing the eyes while praying? The Bible never mentions it. It doesn't mention placing your hands together, either.

Praying silently is a standard procedure today. But in the Bible, most people prayed aloud, even when they were alone. Among the Israelites, the spoken word was somehow believed to be more "real" than just thinking the words in your head. Hannah, the woman who gave birth to the great leader Samuel, was accused of being drunk by the priest Eli when he saw her praying silently. Hannah was "praying in her heart," and her lips were moving but her voice was not heard. Eli thought she was drunk and scolded her. Hannah replied that she was not drunk but merely pouring out her soul to the Lord (1 Samuel 1:9–15).

Summing up: you can pray in any position, silently or aloud, eyes open or shut.

91

What Every Good Pray-er Ends a Prayer With

"The Bible instructs us to say the words in Jesus' name *when we pray."*

Custom is a powerful force. In any social situation, we say and do things we don't really analyze. We do them out of habit. There is nothing wrong with this, except that habits have a way of becoming meaningless and empty. Things that were once done with purpose and meaning turn into motions that we go through.

You will find this in churches and Christian fellowship groups, as in any other meeting of human beings. Take the word *amen.* Does it have a meaning? Well, it *did* at one time. The Hebrew *amen* can be translated as "So be it!" or "Yes, indeed!" or "Truly!" Used in both the Old and New Testaments, it came to be used in Christian worship, and in particularly at the end of prayers. Jesus himself used it often in his teaching, and it is sometimes translated "truly," as in "Truly, truly, I say to you . . ." It was a way of getting people's attention, like "Get ready, important message coming up . . ." Some later Bible translations have him saying, "I tell you the truth." In the Greek originals, he actually said, *Amen, amen.* Revelation 3:14 calls Christ "the Amen, the Faithful and True Witness." (This is why one contemporary hymn refers to Jesus as "God's Yes.") The Book of Revelation (and thus the whole Bible) ends in this way: "The grace of our Lord Jesus Christ be with you all. Amen" (22:21).

Are most people aware of all this? Probably not. It might be worthwhile for pastors to take the time occasionally to explain to people just what *amen* is all about. This might not be necessary in those churches where people still feel free to shout "Amen!" when the pastor makes a point they agree with. Those people are probably well aware that their "Amen!" means "I agree, preacher!" or "Yes, indeed, preacher!"

Consider another much-used but not-much-thought-about habit: tacking on the words *we pray in Jesus' name* to a prayer. (These would be spoken just before the *amen,* of course.) Most pastors do this, as do most Christians in prayer groups and fellowship groups. The phrase *in Jesus' name* is full of meaning. To pray in someone's name means "on his behalf." You are praying as if you represented that person. So to pray "in Jesus' name" is like saying "in the character of Jesus." The practice is rooted in the words of Jesus himself: "Truly, truly, I say to you, whatever you ask of the Father in my name, he will give it to you" (John 16:23). This must have been an important point, for Jesus repeated those same words several times in John's Gospel.

Spiritually speaking, it is a wonderful idea: keeping your prayers in focus with the thought "Would Jesus approve of this? If I'm praying on his behalf, I guess it seems kind of wrong to pray for that new Lexus and a bigger bonus and . . ." See how it works? If you are praying "in Jesus' name"—on Jesus' behalf—you are less likely to pray just to satisfy your own selfishness (or pray for someone else's harm).

But in the realm of habit, the words *in Jesus' name* are "those words you say at the end of the prayer because that's what Christians are supposed to do." Note that the Bible does not command people to say those words. (It doesn't command *amen,* either.) There is nothing wrong with using the words, but as with *amen,* it would be smart to go beyond the habit and find out the richer meaning of the words.

PART X

AND THINGS LEFT OVER

SAMSON AND DELILAH
The longhaired Hebrew strongman and his infamous barber . . . or was she?

92

Be Born Again—and Again?

"The story of Jesus and the man born blind shows that Christians believed in reincarnation."

A century ago, hardly any people outside Asia believed in reincarnation. Now, as religious polls show, lots of people do. As a general rule, people who claim to be Christians do not believe in reincarnation. However, some people have tried to make a case for reincarnation being taught in the Bible.

Let's do a quick review of just what the Bible says about the afterlife. To begin with, the Old Testament says very little about it. The ancient Hebrews shared a belief with the ancient Greeks, the belief that the afterlife was a kind of gloomy half existence, probably somewhere underground. If you ever read the Greek epic *The Odyssey,* you might recall that the hero Odysseus visits Hades, the land of the dead. There he is touched to see dead friends and relatives locked forever in this sunless, joyless place. While it isn't really hell, it certainly is not heaven, and life on earth is clearly preferable to life in Hades.

This is how the Hebrews pictured Sheol, the land of the dead. Everyone, good or bad, goes to Sheol. The faithful Hebrew hopes for a long life in this world, producing many children, worshiping God, and dying at a ripe old age. Sheol is nothing to look forward to. The ancient Egyptians had a rich mythology about a happy afterlife, but this was certainly not true of the Hebrews.

But there are hints in the later parts of the Old Testament that this was changing. Daniel, one of the last Old Testament books to be written down, speaks of people being raised to eternal life, while others are raised up for everlasting shame and contempt (12:2–3).

In the period between the Old and New Testaments, belief in the afterlife took hold. Devout Jews found in the Old Testament that some holy men, such as Enoch and the prophet Elijah, never died but were taken into heaven (see 2 Kings 2). The Jews began to believe that saintly people might all be in heaven, while for the wicked there might be annihilation or, worse, eternal punishment. By the time of Jesus, most Jews did believe in heaven and hell.

Jesus certainly did. He had a lot to say about the "kingdom of heaven," and a lot to say about God's compassion and forgiveness of sinners. But there was a flip side to this: the Teacher of God's mercy also warned that a dire fate awaited those who rejected God's kindness. In fact, Jesus apparently believed that there would be more people in hell than in heaven, for he warned that the way to destruction was broad, while the way to eternal life is narrow "and there are few who find it" (Matthew 7:14). Jesus, the man who called God "Father" and spoke of his love and kindness, also spoke often about God's wrath. He spoke of the wicked being cast into "outer darkness" where there would be "weeping and gnashing of teeth" (Matthew 8:12).

These are the options that the New Testament presents for human beings: heaven or hell. If you love God and your neighbor and follow Christ, you get heaven. If not, you get hell. The apostle Paul claimed that even people who had never heard Jesus' message would be judged, since all people possess some instinctive knowledge of God and the truth (Romans 1:18–20).

This traditional Christian belief strikes a lot of modern people as, well, judgmental. It also strikes people as *final.* One life on earth, and your fate is decided for all eternity. In our day, not many things are final. Any commitment, including marriage, can be broken. Heavily tattooed people show up on talk shows and claim that they like the idea that *something* (their tattoos) lasts forever. The belief in reincarnation fits in well with the contemporary mind. You live one lifetime, mess it up, so you keep coming back again. For the modern mind, nothing is, strictly speaking, final. Your soul just keeps on and on through centuries. Hinduism and Buddhism have taught this for centuries. Obviously it doesn't fit at all with the New Testament's view of death and eternity.

But some people like to fit square pegs into round holes. Take the American psychic Edgar Cayce, the "sleeping prophet." Cayce, who died in 1945, claimed to be a Christian but also believed in reincarnation. He established the Association for Research and Enlightenment, which is today a noted New Age center. Cayce was one of the first people to claim that the Bible itself taught reincarnation. Which part of the Bible? John 9 relates the story of Jesus healing a man who was born blind. Jesus' disciples asked him, "Rabbi, who sinned, this man or his parents, that he was born blind?" According to Cayce, the disciples must have believed in reincarnation—that is, they believed that the soul of the man born blind had existed previously. In other words, they were speculating that his blindness was a punishment for sins of a past life.

This is definitely not the correct interpretation. In the first place, it does not fit with what the rest of the Bible teaches about the afterlife. In the second place, the Jews seemed to have believed in "prenatal sin." Some of the rabbis had taught that if a pregnant woman worshiped in a pagan temple, her sin would "pass on" to her unborn child. Some others taught that God had foreknowledge of everything, and thus the blindness could be a "prepunishment" for sins he would commit in his life. Yes, both these alternatives seem silly to us, but it's likely that they are what the disciples meant, for they certainly did not believe the man had lived a previous life.

Of course, there is one familiar New Testament expression that some say teaches reincarnation: *born again.* Jesus told the teacher Nicodemus that a man must be "born again" (John 3:3), although the Greek words here can also mean "born from above." The key idea is of a *spiritual* birth, not a physical one. Jesus makes this clear when he tells Nicodemus that what is born of the flesh is flesh, while what is born of the spirit is spirit (3:6). The "rebirth" Jesus is talking about is clearly not the same as reincarnation.

93

Was It Shear Malice?

"Delilah gave Samson his fateful haircut."

You can go to a Christian bookstore and buy a Samson doll. (Oops. Boys don't play with dolls. You can buy a Samson *action figure.*) There is probably no harm in this, and it does give parents an excuse to tell Bible stories to the kids. But Samson is hardly the Bible's best role model. On the other hand, he is certainly one of the most colorful characters in the Bible.

Samson's story is told in the Book of Judges, which is one of the most badly named books in the whole Bible. If you read the book, you see that these men were not "judges" in our sense of the word—far from it. They were tough guys, strongmen, military leaders. God raised them up to help deliver Israel from the oppressive nations around it. They were "judges" only in the sense that they fought the injustice of oppressors. The Hebrew title of the book is *Shophetim,* which means something like "liberators."

If you ever read Greek mythology, you might notice some resemblances between that world and the world of Israel's judges. This was not a world of soft-spoken Sunday school teachers. It was a violent world, a world that prized bravery and physical daring. Passions ran high, and romantic (or erotic) love was a key theme. The man who was admired was the man who fought and loved. Later in the Bible, people would value men who were more civilized. But in the time of the judges, tough guys ran over weak ones. What Israel needed was guys who were tougher than their enemies. These included the Midianites, the world's original "camel jockeys," famous for their fast and furious raids. Perhaps most famous of Israel's enemies were the Philistines, those notoriously *un*circumcised men of the coastal plain, fierce warriors and worshipers of a peculiar fish-shaped god named Dagon. It was against the Philistines that Israel sent its strongman, Samson.

Before going any farther, we have to deal with religion. The Book of Judges is not just a tale of war and lust. There is a formula that gets repeated throughout the book: the Israelites repeatedly did "what was evil in the sight of the LORD and served the Baals." That is, they caved in to local custom and started worshiping false gods (which included engaging in ritual orgies and child sacrifice). The book makes a connection: you sin, you suffer. You follow false gods, you fall prey to these oppressive nations around you. God is the major character in the book, not the various tough guys he uses to help rescue Israel.

Back to Samson. At the time of his birth, Israel had done "what was evil in the sight of the LORD" again, so for forty years the Philistines had oppressed them. A man named Manoah had a wife who couldn't bear children—considered the ultimate tragedy for women in those times. An angel appeared to tell her she would bear a son—but must dedicate him to the Lord. He was to be a Nazirite—a group whose regulations are spelled out in Numbers 6. (The name has no connection with Nazareth, Jesus' hometown, by the way.) As a Nazirite, he could never touch wine, never cut his hair, and never touch anything "unclean." The Nazirites were not monks. They did not live apart from society, and they were not celibate (as we shall soon see in Samson's case). Most men took the Nazirite vow for only a few weeks, but some, like Samson, were bound for life. It was not unusual for barren women like Samson's mother to make the vow on behalf of their unborn child. There is a lot of speculation about just what the vows "meant." Why not cut the hair? Why not drink wine? No one is sure. At any rate, those were the restrictions Samson lived with.

"And the young man grew, and the LORD blessed him. And the Spirit of the LORD began to stir in him" (Judges 13:24–25). But oddly, the first thing told of him is that he sought out a wife from the enemies—the Philistines. As it turned out, she was Samson's way of getting at the Philistines. He did marry her, which turned out to be a disaster, giving Samson an excuse to kill and plunder some of the Philistines. One of his stunts was to catch foxes (or jackals?), tie torches to their tails, and set them loose in the Philistines' fields. On another occasion, "the Spirit of the LORD rushed upon him," giving him the strength to kill a thousand Philistines with the jawbone of a donkey. On still another occasion, he visited a Philistine prostitute. The men of her town plotted to ambush him when he slept. Samson slipped out at midnight and skipped town—carrying the city gates on his back (16:1–3).

Now, Delilah. "He loved a woman in the Valley of Sorek, whose name was Delilah." The Philistine rulers offered her a huge reward in silver if she could wheedle from him the secret of his strength. She asked Samson, and he told her—a lie, that is. He told her if he was bound with seven bowstrings, he would be "like any other man." She bound him up, then called out, "The Philistines are upon you, Samson!" Naturally he roused up and snapped the bowstrings like threads. He used a couple of similar lies on her, and of course she pouted. Samson was, she whined, making sport of her and did not really love her. Her wiles worked: he told her that if his head was sheared, he would lose his strength (16:17).

She called the Philistine rulers to claim her reward. Then "she made him sleep on her knees. And she called a man and had him shave off the seven locks of his head. Then she began to torment him, and his strength left him." Thus ends one of the more disastrous romances in the Bible.

Note: Delilah did *not* give Samson his haircut. He was slumbering "on her knees" when one of the Philistine men did the dirty deed.

"And the Philistines seized him and gouged out his eyes and brought him down to Gaza and bound him with bronze shackles. And he ground at the mill in the prison." End of story? Not yet. "The hair of his head began to grow again after it had been shaved." More to come? Definitely.

The Philistines were pleased to have captured the Hebrew muscleman. They staged a grand celebration in the temple of their god

Dagon. The highlight was, of course, bringing in the blinded Samson himself. "Call Samson, that he may entertain us." But a man like Samson does not end up "entertaining" the enemy. Samson prayed his final prayer: "O LORD God, please remember me and strengthen me only this once, O God." Standing between the two main pillars of the temple, Samson pushed them apart, saying, "Let me die with the Philistines." He literally brought the house down. Three thousand Philistines died, as did Samson. And "the dead whom he killed at his death were more than those whom he killed during his life" (16:30).

Colorful, yes? No wonder the movie director Cecil B. DeMille made a grand epic out of it, starring Victor Mature as Samson. DeMille, praised for the movie, claimed that "Credit is due to the Book of Judges, not to me."

94

A Million Paintings, All Wrong?

"Jesus was crucified nude."

Probably the most controversial movie of 1988 was *The Last Temptation of Christ.* Directed by Martin Scorsese and starring Willem Dafoe as Jesus, the movie got a lot of free publicity due to the many Christians who protested it. The movie was not very popular anyway, and viewers wondered what all the fuss was about. People who saw it might recall that Jesus is shown naked on the cross. Was this historically true, or was it one of the many liberties the scriptwriters took with the facts? It certainly was a dramatic change from all the thousands of pictures we have seen of Jesus in agony, wearing only the loincloth that was the standard underwear for a Jewish man of his day.

Well, to begin with, crucifixion was an extremely humiliating punishment, clothed or naked. It was intended to be. It had been used for centuries throughout the Middle East, long before the Romans adopted it. The Roman Empire used various forms of capital punishment. For those who were full "citizens" of the empire, the fairly quick and merciful method of execution was beheading by ax or sword. (The apostle Paul, who was a Roman citizen, is supposed to have been martyred by beheading.) For common criminals, more painful methods were used. Crucifixion was generally considered the worst form of execution. It was used for slaves and rebels. Spartacus, the ex-gladiator who led a famous slave revolt against Rome, was crucified.

Plenty of sermons have been preached about crucifixion, but a few points bear repeating: the criminal, who had usually been whipped severely, had to carry his own crossbeam to the place of execution. (Since his back was usually bleeding from the whipping, this was an agonizing task.) Once there, he was stripped bare and laid flat on the ground, with his wrists (not hands) nailed to the crossbeam. The beam was raised by ropes to the vertical beam that had already been fixed in the ground. Normally the victim's feet, which were either nailed or tied, were not that far above the ground. The distance above the ground did not matter, for what killed the person was long, slow suffocation and heart failure.

Jesus himself died fairly quickly on the cross, as mentioned in John 19:32–34. The Roman soldiers used an iron club to break the legs of the victims to hasten their deaths, but they found Jesus already dead. Since the usual victim of crucifixion was the nastier sort of criminal, we can assume they were more "muscled up" than Jesus and harder to kill. In some cases, the victims took several days to die. Sometimes the Roman authorities left the bodies to rot where they were.

One key word to remember about crucifixion is that it was *public*. Almost all executions in the ancient world were. The governing power wanted to communicate a clear message: this is what we do to bad guys. Crucifixions usually took place along well-traveled roads or other very public places, so that people could see what fate awaited rebels against Rome. Over the head of the crucified person was a wooden plaque that had his name and his crime. Passersby had no qualms about heaping words of abuse on the criminals. The Roman soldiers also hurled abuse at Jesus: "If you are the king of the Jews, save yourself!" (Luke 23:37). And of course, the priests and scribes who had clamored for Jesus' death also mocked him. Most of his followers were (for obvious reasons) either absent or watching from a distance. It was a truly horrible way for anyone to die, particularly one who had committed no crime. No wonder Jesus cried out, "My God, my God, why have you forsaken me?"

Was he totally naked when he said those words? No, he wasn't. The people who produced *The Last Temptation of Christ* may have shown Jesus nude just to generate controversy. But they may also have been aware of a historical fact: Romans did crucify people nude. There was no sexual element to this at all. Being stripped naked was intended to add to the humiliation of being killed slowly in a public place. It was total degradation: we kill you legally, hang you up for all to see, and do not even allow you the small dignity of having your private parts covered.

Except in the case of Jews. Yes, strange as it seems, the Romans sometimes altered their customs to fit the people they conquered. They had reason to: the Jews were not an easy people to rule. Small in numbers, they were full of fight, especially where their religion was concerned. When the Roman governor Pilate tried to set up the imperial standards (flags, that is) in the Jerusalem temple area, the priests there staged a "sit-in," baring their necks for the Roman swords. Pilate backed off and withdrew the standards.

The ancient Jews were much more offended by nudity than the Romans or Greeks were. In between the Old and New Testaments, Alexander the Great conquered Israel and introduced Greek customs into the region. Devout Jews were horrified to learn that Greeks actually exercised naked. Years later, they were horrified to learn that the Romans not only crucified rebels, but crucified them stark naked. The Jewish leaders managed a concession from the Romans: if you must crucify Jewish rebels against Rome, please allow them a bare minimum of clothing. The Romans, being a practical people, probably didn't mind giving in to this. A dead Jewish rebel is dead, nude or not.

As Jesus predicted, some of his followers suffered the same fate as he did. Christianity somehow managed to take the cross, a symbol of crime and humiliation, and turn it into a symbol of salvation and divine mercy.

Crucifixion ended in the Roman Empire when the emperor Constantine became a Christian.

95

Plain Truth About the Landscape

"Jesus was crucified on a hill called Calvary."

"On a hill far away stood an old rugged cross, the emblem of suffering and shame." Those are the opening words of "The Old Rugged Cross," written by George Bennard in 1913. It is probably one of the best-loved and most sung hymns ever written. And it's a pretty good summary of the Bible's teaching about what Jesus' crucifixion meant.

However, one minor detail: the *hill* part is doubtful. The four Gospels in the Bible give us several details about the site of Jesus' crucifixion. *But it is never once referred to as a hill.*

In fact, the site is not even called Calvary in most versions of the Bible. Here is one contemporary version: "And when they came to the place that is called The Skull, there they crucified him, and the criminals, one on his right and one on his left" (Luke 23:33). "The Skull" is the English translation of the Greek word Luke uses, *kranion* (which is the root of our word *cranium,* obviously).

However, Luke 23:33 in the beloved King James Version of 1611 has *Calvary.* The King James Version borrowed it from the long-used Latin version of the Bible, the Vulgate, which uses the Latin word *calvaria*—meaning "skull." The other three Gospels use the name that the locals themselves would have used: *Golgotha,* which is the Aramaic word for (you guessed it) "skull."

Whatever the modern translations say, the King James Version had more than three hundred years to influence the Christian vocabulary. And let's be honest and admit that *Calvary* does have a nice ring to it. Hundreds of churches across the world bear the name, as do numerous schools, colleges, and Christian ministries. The name crops up in hundreds of hymns and poems. Certainly it sounds much more pleasant than The Skull or Golgotha or *kranion*. We can thank the King James Version for lending a fine word to the Christian tradition.

But back to the issue of the hill: might the site—Calvary, Golgotha, The Skull—have been a hill? Frankly, we have no idea. One possibility is that the site might have been a hill that somehow resembled a skull. One creepier possibility is that it was a site connected with skulls—that is, a place where executions took place. The Romans liked to crucify criminals in the most public of locales, so a hill would have the advantage of visibility.

> Worth noting: The Holy Land was the world's first tourist attraction.

As Christianity spread across the Roman Empire, believers felt drawn to visit the places connected with Jesus' life and work. (*Pilgrimage* is the word used to mean "visiting sacred places.") A rather awkward historical fact is that in the year 70, the Romans very ruthlessly put down a Jewish revolt. They not only destroyed the temple in Jerusalem but also managed to, well, rearrange the landscape around the city. So by the time Christian pilgrims began to journey to Jerusalem, there was already some doubt about just where Jesus had been crucified, buried, and so on.

When the Roman emperor Constantine became a Christian in 312, he quickly took an interest in New Testament sites. His mother, Helena, might well be called the world's first archaeologist. She journeyed to Jerusalem and the surrounding area and picked people's brains for what they knew about places connected with Jesus. As a result of her sleuthing, Constantine built the Church of the Holy Sepulchre on the place that (according to his mother) was Golgotha.

They were not absolutely sure then, and we are even less sure now. Visitors still flock to the church, which is beautiful and rich in history even if it is not on the precise place of Jesus' crucifixion. One alternative site is called Gordon's Calvary, which is a low hill that (some way) resembles a skull. Most Christians would probably agree that identifying the spot is not a major concern.

In summary: we do not know exactly where Jesus was crucified, and the Bible does not tell us it occurred on a hill. As for the name *Calvary,* even though the Gospels do not use it, it has a nice ring to it, and we can assume that Christians will continue to use it.

96

As If Monogamy Wasn't Enough Trouble

"The Bible condones polygamy."

If you know anything about the Latter-Day Saints (the Mormons, that is), you know they met with a lot of violence in their early days. Though the Mormons consider themselves Christians, many people in the 1800s couldn't stomach some of the Mormon beliefs. What was probably more offensive than their beliefs was their revival of polygamy, having more than one wife. Christians in America had grown up reading the Bible and being aware that polygamy was practiced in the Old Testament, but they could not accept a renewal of the practice. Even after trekking to Utah so they could live as they pleased, the Mormons met resistance from the U.S. government, mostly because of polygamy. Utah applied for statehood as early as 1849, but Washington would not consider it. In 1882 and 1887, the United States passed anti-polygamy laws, which everyone knew were directed at the Mormons in Utah. Finally, in 1890, the Mormons' president announced he would submit to U.S. law and persuade all Mormons to do so. Utah finally achieved statehood, and the feature of Mormonism that had offended most Americans was abolished.

Many people find the polygamy of the Old Testament offensive. Men who are held up as models of godliness were polygamists—Abraham, Jacob, David, and, most notoriously, Solomon, with his seven hundred wives and three hundred concubines. Even allowing for some exaggeration, it is safe to say that Solomon had what later generations would call a harem, and obviously most of these women were there primarily for his physical pleasure.

But fortunately, Solomon is not the norm for the Bible. At the very beginning, God created for Adam "a helper fit for him." He gave him one woman, not several. Adam referred to her as "bone of my bones and flesh of my flesh." Genesis tells us that a man and his wife become "one flesh." We get the impression that polygamy was not the original plan.

The Bible attributes the origin of polygamy to descendants of the first villain, Cain. Recall that Cain was the first murderer, the slayer of his brother Abel, and Cain's grandson Lamech (also a murderer) was the first man to take more than one wife (Genesis 4:19). It appears that even while the people of Israel tolerated polygamy, they felt uncomfortable with it, since they connected it with such rogues as Lamech. Several passages in the Old Testament show the harmful effects of multiple wives and "blended families," as in the families of Jacob (Genesis 35:22, 37:18–28), David (2 Samuel 13:1–29), and especially Solomon (1 Kings 11:1–12). Certainly the soap opera antics of David's wives and children are a stern warning: "Don't try this—it only leads to trouble!" By the time of Jesus, polygamy had ceased among the Jews. Jesus himself made it clear that monogamy was what God intended (Matthew 19:3–6).

Strictly speaking, the Bible never condoned polygamy. The practice was tolerated (which is not the same as *approved*) in the Old Testament, but not even tolerated in the New Testament.

97

Did They Know You Would Read This?

"Prophets were those who predicted the future."

A large chunk of the Old Testament is known as the Prophets. Some of what is contained in those books is predictions of the future—some, but not much. That wasn't their purpose, frankly.

The Greek word *prophetes* referred to "interpreter," meaning "one who speaks the mind of another." This was the same idea behind the Hebrew word *nabi*—a "spokesman." The prophet himself isn't that important. He is a spokesman for someone more important than himself. In the Bible, that someone is God, of course. When the prophet speaks on God's behalf, it is God's word, not his own. This is why the phrase *Thus says the Lord* is so important in the Bible. The prophet isn't just acting pompous. He believes he is genuinely telling people a message that God wants them to hear.

The first important prophet in the Bible is Moses. He not only led the people out of their captivity in Egypt, but was also God's spokesman, both to Israel and to the Egyptian pharaoh.

Following the death of Moses, we don't hear much of prophecy until 1 Samuel. There Samuel himself was a prophet, and one badly needed, for "the word of the LORD was rare in those days" (1 Samuel 3:1). Samuel was obviously a major authority figure, but he was pressured to give Israel another type of authority figure: a king. So he anointed Saul as the first king. Saul turned out to be a major disappointment as king (which was true of most of Israel's monarchs, actually). Samuel was present as a reminder that Israel may have fared better under prophets than under kings.

The kings had their own court prophets—some of them sincere, some of them "false prophets" who spoke whatever message they thought would please the king. One of the great scenes in the whole Bible involves the prophet Nathan, who told his master, King David, a story about a poor man who had his pet lamb taken away by a rich man who had many sheep of his own. David was furious at such horrible behavior. Nathan had caught David in a trap: he knew David had committed adultery with Bathsheba, the wife of one of David's military men. David had many wives and concubines; the military man only one. The parallel with David and the rich man in Nathan's story was clear to Nathan, but it did not immediately sink in with David. When Nathan told the story of the rich man taking the poor man's lamb, David said, "The man who has done this deserves to die." Nathan's famous reply: "You are the man!" (2 Samuel 12:1–7). Nathan went further to reveal God's will: David's sin had brought a curse on his household. The first sign of this was that David's child by Bathsheba would die. Clearly, in some cases, prophets did predict the future.

But you can see here the main function of prophets: delivering God's word to people who were straying. The same function was fulfilled by the great Elijah, who confronted Israel's vilest royal couple, King Ahab and his idol-worshiping wife, Jezebel. She was such a devoted worshiper of the god Baal that she did her utmost to stamp our worship of the true God. Elijah had a famous confrontation with the Baal prophets (1 Kings 18). This passage is interesting for various reasons, one being that it shows the bizarre behavior that pagan prophets sometimes engaged in (slashing themselves with swords, for example). Elijah was, 2 Kings says, taken into heaven in a fiery chariot. He was succeeded by his protégé, Elisha, a noted miracle worker as well as prophet.

The people of Israel had a great love for Elijah. To this day, Jews reserve an empty chair for Elijah at their Passover meal. In the Jewish tradition, he symbolizes all the prophets. You see this in the New Testament event known as the Transfiguration, in which Jesus is seen conversing with both Moses and Elijah (Matthew 17:1–13). Moses symbolizes Israel's law, Elijah symbolizes the prophets. At the end of the Old Testament, the prophet Malachi predicted that Elijah the prophet would return to "turn the hearts of fathers to their children and the hearts of children to their fathers" (Malachi 4:5).

Prophets like Elijah did not write down their own books. Several "writing prophets" did, those being the ones found in the last part of the Old Testament. These include Isaiah and Jeremiah, two of the most read and best-loved books in the Bible. You will find in Isaiah 6 the "commissioning" of Isaiah: he had a vision of God in the temple and heard God saying, "Whom shall I send, and who will go for us?" And Isaiah replied, "Here am I! Send me!"

Something important to remember about these books: these prophets' words (or, rather, the Lord's word spoken through them) were directed to the people of their own day. They were trying to correct the moral and spiritual lapses of their contemporaries. But the books are still read, centuries later. Why? Because the issues have not changed. When the prophet Amos attacked religious hypocrisy in ancient Israel, his words applied then, but they still apply. When Jeremiah proclaimed that "The heart is deceitful above all things, and desperately sick. Who can understand it?" he was speaking to people he knew, but also to millions of readers across the centuries.

> The prophets are read for their spiritual value, not because they predicted future events.
>
> 

You will notice that most of the prophets' books begin with "The word of the LORD that came to [name of prophet]." Again, the prophet was God's spokesman. He was not a fortune-teller, though many of the prophets did predict future events that came to pass. But between the Old Testament and the New, "the word of the Lord" was not heard. The Jews in this period were guided by their Law and by their "wise men" (who were responsible for the types of sayings you find in Proverbs). Certain priests and military men arose as leaders, but, strictly speaking, there were no prophets. The wise men, priests, and fighting men may have acted on God's behalf, but there were no prophets speaking for God.

Not until Elijah came back, that is. And he came back "in disguise," in the form of the wilderness prophet John the Baptist (Matthew 11:14, Luke 1:17). John was the Elijah the Jews had been expecting, but not all of them accepted it. Some thought that Jesus himself might be Elijah (Luke 9:18–20). Others thought that he was definitely a prophet of God. Jesus accepted the title of prophet (Matthew 13:57, Luke 13:33). People accepted him as a prophet long before they realized he was the Messiah the Jews had hoped for. But this is worth noting: *Jesus never used the prophets' phrase "Thus says the Lord."* He spoke on this own authority (Matthew 7:28). John's Gospel states that Jesus himself is the Word of God (1:1–5).

Jesus did predict many things that came to pass, such as his death and resurrection and the eventual destruction of the temple in Jerusalem. But anyone familiar with Jesus' story knows that predicting the future was only a minor part of his work. Like the prophets of the Old Testament, his work as a prophet involved making God's will known to the people.

98

The Only Verse the Gourmet Ever Memorized

"Wine is recommended in Paul's words 'a little wine for the stomach.' "

Must Christians be teetotalers? No. That error is discussed on pages 219–220 of this book. Just to reiterate that chapter: Christians can drink alcohol. Drinking itself is not a sin.

Paul, the great apostle, told Christians to be "filled with the Spirit" instead of being drunk with wine (Ephesians 5:18). The "high" of a life with God is better (and less destructive) than the temporary high of being drunk.

But Paul is more famous for another statement about wine: "a little wine for the stomach." Those words have been quoted, requoted, but definitely *misquoted* countless times. Rare is the dinner or party where someone doesn't ask, "A little wine for the stomach?" It is a slightly arty, slightly off-center way of asking, "Want some wine?" Perhaps one out of ten people who ask the question know they are quoting the Bible. The 10 percent who know probably only know that the source is the Bible, but not why Paul even spoke of "a little wine for the stomach." It certainly was not Paul's way of saying, "Drink up!"

Paul's words were addressed to a young man named Timothy. The novelist Gore Vidal ruffled some feathers a few years ago in one of his novels, depicting Paul and Timothy in a homosexual relationship. That situation is, to put it mildly, very unlikely. But in the two letters in the New Testament addressed to Timothy, it is clear that Paul and Timothy were very close. Timothy is addressed as Paul's "true son in the faith" and "my beloved son." The childless Paul, the great missionary and pastor, was not just a Christian friend but also a spiritual mentor to Timothy, who was the spiritual head of the Christian fellowship in Ephesus. That group had its problems, such as false teachers and useless bickering over minor theological issues. Another problem was that Timothy was young, which led Paul to suspect that his friend wasn't being respected enough. Paul advised Timothy on how to deal with people of different ages, and he emphasized that the best way to gain respect was to live a life without reproach. He also laid down some rules for people in leadership positions in the church. These rules have, over the centuries, continued to apply in many churches.

Paul's two letters to Timothy (and a letter to Titus, another protégé) are known as the Pastoral Epistles. Paul was giving advice to the two young pastors on how to be faithful in their tasks. He was a compassionate man, so the two letters are not just "shop talk." In a few places, Paul's advice was extremely personal, such as this: "No longer drink only water, but use a little wine for the sake of your stomach and your frequent ailments" (1 Timothy 5:23). We have no other details about what prompted this piece of advice. If Timothy drank only water, he was departing from the norm of those times. Paul was probably giving advice that anyone of the time might have given: drink wine sometimes, son, because you have all these ailments, and they may be connected to your drinking only water. (Microorganisms in water can still wreak havoc in people's bellies.) In effect, Paul was saying that wine might be good for what ails you. But he certainly wasn't telling Timothy to "cut loose and let the good times roll."

So the next time you hear someone say "A little wine for the stomach?" feel free to amuse (or bore) them with these tidbits about two people who lived two thousand years ago. It might surprise them that the words are those of the apostle Paul.

99

Those Amazing Globe-Trotting Israelites

"The ten 'lost tribes' of Israel settled in Britain and America."

How do you "lose" something as big as a tribe? You don't. They have to be *somewhere.* But they can be "lost" in the sense of "no trace," like the famous "Lost Colony" that the English planted off the Carolina coast in the 1500s. No one knows what became of those settlers, and no one knows what became of the ten tribes of Israel that were conquered by the Assyrians. But that hasn't kept people from coming up with some clever theories.

A quickie on the history of ancient Israel: the patriarch Jacob, also called Israel, had twelve sons. His story, and theirs, is related in the last chapters of Genesis. The twelve became the ancestors of the twelve "tribes" (or clans) that made up the nation. They were a loose confederation, each occupying its own territory. They were constantly preyed upon by marauding nations such as the Philistines and Midianites. The military deliverers from these predatory nations were known as the "judges" (oddly enough), and their story is told in the Book of (surprise!) Judges. Eventually the twelve tribes felt they needed a stronger organization to fend off their foes, so they asked for, and got, a king. The first one was Saul, a handsome man and brave warrior, but with feet of clay. He was succeeded by the much more charismatic David, Israel's most famous king. After

David came the wise and wealthy Solomon, who built the famous temple in Jerusalem. But Solomon was a notorious taxer-and-spender, and after his death, ten of the twelve tribes broke away and became their own nation. They kept the name *Israel;* the two other tribes (which included the city of Jerusalem in their territory) were known as Judah.

The two nations sometimes fought each other, but more often they were busy fighting off their neighbor nations. This is all told with a lot of color and surprising brevity in 1 and 2 Kings. Chapter 17 of 2 Kings tells of how Israel (the ten northern tribes that broke away) was conquered in 722 B.C. by the powerful nation of Assyria (roughly the same territory as Iraq today). The Assyrians not only conquered Israel but also brought foreigners in to settle in the towns. They also had a policy, when they conquered a nation, of deporting its leading citizens and leaving only the common folk behind. The assumption was that with the "cream" removed, rebellions were less likely. Probably a tenth of Israel's population was deported, with the rest of the people remaining where they were, and under the thumb of Assyrians. The descendants of the ones who remained in the land eventually became known as Samaritans. You might remember from Jesus' parable of the Good Samaritan that Jews and Samaritans despised each other.

The deported one-tenth of the population became known as the "lost tribes" of Israel. In all likelihood, these people gradually merged into Assyrian society and may (or may not) have maintained their worship of the God of Israel. The "lost tribes" have fascinated people because they were, after all, descendants of Jacob and of Jacob's famous grandfather, Abraham, the "father of the faithful." That makes them "children of the covenant," and it has stimulated the imagination of many people, who speculate that these descendants of Abraham might have ended up as far afield as England or America.

In the Middle Ages, a Jewish author named Eldad ha-Dani claimed to be a descendant of one of the lost tribes (Dan) and said that they still existed "beyond the rivers of Abyssinia" (Abyssinia being Ethiopia, in Africa). Somehow his story caught the imagination of both Jews and Christians. People began to wonder just how far away the "lost tribes" might be. Some Christians believed that if the lost tribes were ever found and converted to Christianity, Christ might return to earth again.

Fast-forward a few centuries to Christopher Columbus, who eventually accepted that he had not reached Asia but discovered a New World. Columbus speculated that the natives of America might be descendants of the lost tribes of Israel. That idea was floated around often in the 1800s, a fertile time for the religious imagination in America. Interestingly, the Latter-Day Saints (the Mormons, that is) have been accused of teaching that the ten lost tribes immigrated to America and were the ancestors of the Indians. This isn't so. The Book of Mormon has a fairly detailed history of refugees from Jerusalem, who settle in America after fleeing the conquest of Jerusalem by the Babylonians in 587 B.C. These "tribes" are not, however, the ten lost tribes of Israel. (Regrettably, in the Internet age, a lot of false information gets spread. There are probably a thousand Web sites that claim, erroneously, that the Book of Mormon says that the lost tribes settled in America.) Still, the lost tribes are of interest to Mormons. Article 10 of their Articles of Faith predicts the future restoration of the "Ten Tribes" under Mormon auspices. This will occur in America, of course.

While many Americans speculated that the lost tribes had come to America, some ideas about the lost tribes were spreading in England also. Known as British Israelism, the movement caught the fancy of many Christians, who rather liked the idea that the descendants of the great faith hero Abraham were (you guessed it) the British people themselves.

All of this is, of course, harmless speculation. It is also scientifically and historically pretty silly. There is not one shred of evidence to prove the "lost tribes" ended up in America, England, or any place very far from Assyria, the nation that had conquered Israel. You are free to believe that people several centuries before Christ somehow managed to sail to America and became the ancestors of the Indians, just as you are free to believe in the mythical continent of Atlantis.

100

The Department of Redundancy Department

"The Bible tells us to walk the 'straight and narrow path.' "

Ah, the wonderful King James Version of the Bible. Published in 1611, it has been one of the glories of the English language. Even atheists and agnostics have praised its timeless beauty. In the twenty-first century, it still sells.

And it is also a monument to how much language changes. Few people can now read it without pausing every few paragraphs and puzzling over an odd word or phrase. Of course, the words weren't odd in 1611. The English people in those days knew exactly what they meant. But words change, and whole patterns of thought change. If the King James Version was, as many people believe, a gift from God, so are the more up-to-date translations that followed it.

In the King James Version, Matthew 7:13–14 reads thus: "Enter ye in at the strait gate, for wide is the gate and broad is the way that leadeth to destruction, and many there be which go in therat. Because strait is the gate, and narrow is the way, which leadeth unto life, and few there be that find it."

"Strait is the gate, and narrow is the way" somehow passed into the language as such phrases as "walking the straight and narrow" and "the straight and narrow path."

Things like these pop up all the time on *Jeopardy!* They are called homophones—words that sound alike but are spelled differently. *Straight* hasn't changed its meaning at all since 1611, and for that matter neither has *strait.* But you don't hear *strait* much any more, except perhaps in the phrase *dire straits.* In fact, *strait* means "narrow" or "tight." A straitjacket is so named because it's a tight fit (tight enough to restrain a psychotic person, in fact). A narrow passageway in the sea is a strait. In Matthew 7, *strait* and *narrow* pretty much mean the same thing.

The King James Version has an even quainter word than *strait:* several times it uses *straitly,* which means "strictly" or "severely."

The New Testament does, in fact, make one reference to straight paths: "Strengthen your weak knees and make straight paths for your feet" (Hebrews 12:13).

Of course, no person was ever (pardon the expression) led astray by being told to "walk the straight and narrow path."

INDEX